Howard knew that he was looking dead ahead at the perfect kill zone. He sensed that there were VC in the ravine looking at him through the sights of their AK-47s at that very moment. . . . Slowly he dropped to one knee, trying to give the impression that he didn't suspect anything. But he was desperately trying to buy some time to think of a way to extricate himself from the life-threatening predicament. . . .

His only chance to survive the next few minutes was to somehow make it to that low spot and hope that the Good Lord had made it deep enough.

By Gary A. Linderer
Published by The Ballantine Publishing Group

THE EYES OF THE EAGLE: *F Company LRPs in
    Vietnam, 1968*
EYES BEHIND THE LINES: *L Company Rangers in
    Vietnam, 1969*
SIX SILENT MEN: *101st LRP/Rangers:* Book Three
PHANTOM WARRIORS: Book I: *LLRPs, LRPs, and
    Rangers in Vietnam*
PHANTOM WARRIORS: Book II

PHANTOM WARRIORS

BOOK II

Gary A. Linderer

BALLANTINE BOOKS • NEW YORK

A Ballantine Book
Published by The Ballantine Publishing Group

www.randomhouse.com/BB/

Library of Congress Catalog Card Number: 00-109371

ISBN 0-804-11940-6

Manufactured in the United States of America

First Edition: April 2001

10 9 8 7 6 5 4 3 2

This book is dedicated to Specialist Four Terry Clifton, Company F, 58th Infantry (LRP), 101st Airborne Division, KIA 20 November 1968. You know why, my friend.

And to all the men who served in the LRRP, LRP, and Ranger companies of the Vietnam War. You were and still are America's finest. Carry yourselves proudly until the final bugle call.

Acknowledgments

The author wishes to thank the following people:

Owen Lock for his faith in us.

The veterans honored in these stories for sharing their experiences, private thoughts, and pain with me.

My wife, Barbara, and sons, Kirk, Josh, and Sean, for supporting and loving me.

Foreword

I can think of no one better qualified or more aptly suited to write about LRRP/Ranger operations during the Vietnam War than Gary Linderer. His credentials are impressive.

He is a highly decorated combat veteran who in 1968 served with the 101st Airborne Division's F Company, 58th Infantry Long Range Patrol unit, earning three awards for valor, including the Silver Star, and two Purple Hearts.

He has written four excellent, well-received, and successful books on the subject and has authored numerous articles on U.S. military special warfare operations for a wide variety of publications. As founder and executive editor of *Behind the Lines* magazine, he was instrumental in inspiring many new writers and introduced literally dozens of books on military science into the marketplace. With the advent of btlworld.com online, he continues to serve as one of the few notable authorities in the field.

Linderer makes the past come alive, a rare ability among historical writers, and in *Phantom Warriors Book Two,* he deftly demonstrates once again that, fueled by the pulse and power of memory, time machines do exist.

In the following pages Linderer quickly and carefully

takes us back into the Vietnam War, back into the steamy jungles, the swampy delta, and the rugged highlands of Southeast Asia on combat patrols with some of the best of the U.S. Army's LRRP/Ranger teams.

Linderer succeeds in bridging the gap between then and now with a host of true-life accounts of daring that will startle, amaze, and sometimes frighten. His uncanny ability to thrust the reader into the very middle of the heart-pounding action along with those who were there is his trademark. Linderer not only makes history come alive again, he makes it gasp. That's talent, and more than that, it is a significant achievement, because story after story reminds us of the human consequences of a failed foreign policy that sent courageous young soldiers in harm's way in a misbegotten attempt to achieve it. The cost of history, in particular the LRRP/Ranger history, is infinitely more than a book's cover price, and Gary Linderer knows this. In *Phantom Warriors Book Two,* he helps us to better understand and appreciate their value.

You're in good hands. So read on. The past is waiting.

—Kregg P. J. Jorgenson
H Company, 75th Infantry (Ranger),
1st Cavalry Division

Introduction

As a matter of historical importance, the 1982 Veterans Day dedication of the Vietnam Memorial was a time of realization, of opening wounds that had scabbed over in time, but now were bleeding profusely. It was also a time intermixed with extreme joy and pride. I distantly recall now a gathering in Washington, D.C., during the dedication of the memorial in November 1982, when a handful of LRRP, LRP, and Rangers, along with author Lee Lanning and publisher Owen Lock, gathered in a hotel hospitality suite to comfort ourselves with men who had common experiences and to seek refuge from the scores of news reporters lurking about looking for stories.

In the course of our impromptu meeting we recalled fallen teammates, both American and Vietnamese, and courage and moral resolve under tremendously trying circumstances. We also spoke of the courage and ability of the North Vietnamese Army, Viet Cong, and Warsaw Pact counterparts who faced us, serving as the measure of the danger, daring, and resolve we contested as members of LRRP/Ranger units, lest we be delusional in our chest beating and paint a fantasy picture of extremes that would for the most part be untrue to what really took place. I was grateful for this, for, as a Sicangu

Lakota Kit Fox soldier, it had been a long-standing tradition in the Tokala Society to recognize your enemy and his courage as a measure of your own ability and courage. A long-dead Sicangu Tokala elder once said, "If you cannot respect your enemy as your equal, how can you respect yourself?" However, over Jack Daniels, copious rum and Cokes, and sundry drinks, a consensus was reached among us former LRRPs, LRPs and Rangers: we needed a formal organization, an organization capable of representing and substantiating our combined historical experiences. In relation to this organization, a conduit would be needed to give our folks the opportunity to tell their stories, not in the manner of the clinical, official, military unit histories and after-action reports, but more in the form of individual and team oral histories based on accurate recollection of their missions.

One of the chief drivers behind all of this was 101st Airborne Division LRRP/Ranger veteran Kenn Miller, whose influence among us grew out of his LRRP experience and his extremely well-received novel based on it, *Tiger the LRRP Dog*. Inspired by Miller's book and the advice of Owen Lock, Lee Lanning, and some of the boys who were lawyers, we were reminded by those gathered in that hospitality suite that organization and media are and were important in telling our story. Armed with this knowledge, the task was then to "operationalize" an organization and to allow a conduit to develop to debrief our guys and formulate individual and team experiences into accurate stories.

• • •

Most of us felt an urgent need to organize in order to counter the tales of the wanna-bes, for lack of a better word, and those who are prone to rewrite fact so as to build their social standing within and without the LRRP/Ranger community. We had all watched the Special Forces and SEAL veterans experience the "Rambo phenomenon" as the Vietnam Memorial festivities unfolded around us in 1982; it appeared that every "ragbag" in the world was drawn to the Wall and to the reunions. All of course were the "only survivors" of outrageously improbable missions, and in most cases their descriptions of their exploits outdid the authentic veterans of real missions. Granted, time and the individual's perception of combat often affect the description of actual events but, clearly many of those claiming special warfare experience in Vietnam—as LRRPs/LRPs/Rangers, SEALs, Force Recon and Battalion Recon, Special Forces, Air Commandos, etc.—had penetrated no closer to actual combat than the local surplus store. That said, we must discuss the importance of the evolution of the code of honor that had been passed to us by the early rangers and raiders, the Indian Scout service, Darby's Rangers, Merrill's Marauders, the Alamo Scouts, and the Korean Rangers, to name a few similar units. In almost ten years of combat operations in Vietnam, and by happenstance, we refashioned the code by our resolve and our courage so well that later that code of honor was summarized by Command Sgt. Maj. Neal Gentry in the form of the Ranger Creed. This code and creed still works its magic and influences moral responsibility of most of us on a daily basis. If one becomes quiet and mindful enough, the words can still be heard through time itself:

If one goes, we all go; an LRRP never leaves an
LRRP behind; once an LRRP, always an LRRP;
Rangers lead the way.

Mind you, there are those who are unconscious of
this simple code, but those who are not in such an al-
tered state of consciousness are indeed mindful of it. It
echoes still, in our modern day LRSUs and the Ranger
Regiment, where the Ranger Creed is the moral founda-
tion of the unit.

Besides having the honor of being asked to write this
introduction to Gary Linderer's *Phantom Warriors
Book Two,* make no question that this book and the series of books he has produced are the stories of the
courage and resolve of outstanding team leaders and
heroic team members. Often, time shades the events of
the past. In combat, in those brief firefights or prolonged battles, or in the sheer trauma of no-quarter
combat, the truth is often misplaced by the war story.
This results from the many perceptions of individuals
experiencing the trauma of combat and the passage of
time. Gary Linderer has developed not only a conduit
for recording history, but a method of debriefing team
members in a way G-2 and S-2 could never accomplish.
He has in the process of writing these books allowed the
team members to reconstruct and substantiate the
events of the day among themselves, and even though it
has been acknowledged that a story may have forgotten
something or overlooked someone, the interesting thing
is that every effort to provide a clear and accurate account of the patrol's activities and teammates' thoughts
has been made. These books are the accounts of the

combined experiences of these teams, and not war stories. There is no chest beating or a "there I was . . ." tale, only a story of six good and very brave men who never wavered in duty or in the light of the Ranger Creed, and that's as good as it gets.

—Tom Roubideaux
  1st Brigade LRRP, 101st Airborne Division;
  Brigade LRRP, 173d Airborne Brigade;
  74th Inf. (LRP), 173d Airborne Brigade;
  Co. N, 75th Inf. (Ranger), 173d Airborne Brigade;
  81st Ranger Co., South Vietnamese Army

Prologue

This is the final installment of a project that gradually came about after I completed my first two books in 1989. Originally, I wrote *The Eyes of the Eagle* and *Eyes Behind the Lines* with the intention of leaving behind a written journal of my experiences as an LRP/Ranger during the Vietnam War that someday my sons might enjoy reading. Kenn Miller, a fellow F/58th LRP and L/75th Ranger and a good friend, talked me into submitting that original manuscript to Owen Lock at Random House. I was completely and totally surprised when Owen called me a few days later to tell me he would publish the books. Unfortunately, the next five years brought more fame than fortune, but with the recognition I had attained as a military author came a strange sense of accomplishment, the feeling that maybe I had achieved something even greater—the gratitude of my comrades for including them in my story.

How could I have not included them? They were the reason for my pride in having been one of them. I had come home from the war extremely proud of my service, only to run into the same insensitive lack of interest that most Vietnam veterans had faced upon his or her return. Like most of us, I was quick to hide the pain, shove the memories back into the furthest recesses of my mind, and attempt to get on with my life. I even managed to convince myself that I had succeeded in achieving the great American dream. A wonderful wife, a college education, a successful business, and outstanding sons lulled me into a false sense of security that I had not only survived the Vietnam War, but I had managed to bury it where it could no longer do me any harm. How wrong I was! Something still seemed missing in my life—something that kept me from being a whole man. But not once did I associate this sense of personal insufficiency with my military experience.

Over the years, memories of those days and the deeds we had done together began to surface more and more frequently in my daily thoughts. Occasionally, I would think about those events so long ago, or recall some special moment that had left an indelible mark on me, and then I would wonder what the guys were doing.

Then, seventeen long years after my return from the war, my comrades in the LRRPs and Rangers of the 101st Airborne Division began assembling once again. There was to be a reunion at Fort Campbell, Kentucky. I soon realized that "they" had been the missing part of my psyche that kept me from feeling fulfilled. How can you live with men like those, sharing their humor, pain, joy, grief, life, and death, and then turn and walk away without leaving a part of yourself behind? Well, you can't, and neither could I.

Not long after my return from that first "gathering of Eagles" in 1986, I began to write about my experiences in Vietnam. It was good for me, and I could almost sense the healing it brought on. But as I began to tell my own story, their stories came to life on each sheet of paper I filled, and when the project was complete I knew that I had done a good thing. Because of those books, others would know about the courageous young men who asked for so little and gave so much.

When those two books were finally published, I was amazed at the number of "missing" comrades who surfaced after reading "their" story. Many of the soldiers I had served with during that single year in Vietnam wrote or called to thank me for giving them "credibility." I was puzzled at first, but soon realized that they, like me, had kept their experiences inside for nearly two decades, a period during which, it seemed, no one really wanted to hear about what we had done during the war. And even if we were fortunate enough to find someone from the outside who did, there was no way to show them the camaraderie, the loyalty, the dedication, and especially the trauma of the experiences we had shared and still make it sound believable. It was so much easier just to keep our stories to ourselves and let the memories fade.

The books changed everything. For some reason, when people read something in print, they have a tendency to believe it; tell them the same story face to face, and they think you're making it up. Yes, the books helped to give us credibility that we could never have achieved on our own.

Over the next few years a large number of my comrades published their own war memoirs, preserving forever segments of the legacy we had left behind. Larry Chambers, John Burford, Bill Grant, Jim Walker, and Bill Meacham did their part to preserve our legacy. Others, like Pathfinder Richie Burns, are still at work. Each biography ties the individual stories closer together.

In 1994, Kenn Miller, Rey Martinez, and I decided it

was time to write a composite history of the 101st Airborne Division's long-range patrol companies, consisting of the 1st Brigade LRRP Detachment (1965–68); Company F, 58th Inf. (LRP) (1967–69); and Company L, 75th Inf. (Ranger) (1969–71). Seven years in Vietnam, fifty-eight of our number killed in action, and numerous medals for valor and wounds, added up to a story that needed to be told—a history that had to be recorded. The subsequent publishing of a three-book series entitled *Six Silent Men,* Books One, Two, and Three, completed the legacy of the long-range patrollers of the 101st Airborne Division. It is a work that honors our company and our comrades.

In 1996, I realized that my mission was not yet complete. Over the years I had made numerous friends among the men from other LRRP, LRP, and Ranger units that had served so well during the Vietnam War. Sharing in their experiences soon led me to understand that my company was not the only company that had earned a place in history. I soon convinced Owen Lock to allow me the opportunity to write one final book. It was to be a composite work honoring the men of the other long-range patrol companies who had served during the Vietnam War. With contract in hand, I began a project that has taken me nearly five years to complete.

Predictably, the stories were too many and too long to publish in a single book. It required two volumes to do the job. And yet, our combined histories are so extraordinary that there is still room for a hundred more.

This is the second of two books titled *Phantom Warriors*. It is my final work. Every LRRP, LRP, and Ranger company that served during the Vietnam War has at least now been recognized, however briefly. I have offered but a sliver of their legacy. It is now up to each of them to complete his own history. As for me—well, I'm just proud to have been one of them.

Mission accomplished.

   —Gary A. Linderer
    F/58th (LRP), L/75th (Ranger),
    101st Airborne Division
    "Rangers Lead the Way"

Republic of Vietnam

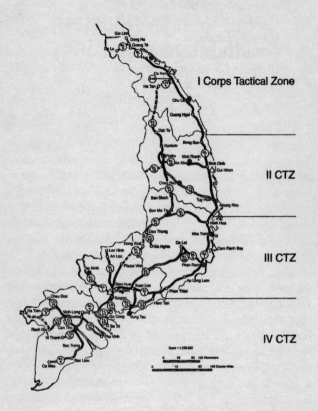

I Corps Tactical Zone

II CTZ

III CTZ

IV CTZ

Scale 1:1,250,000

☆ ☆ ☆ ☆ ☆

Company E,
75th Infantry (Ranger),
9th Infantry Division

The 9th Infantry Division was the only major U.S. Army unit to operate in the Mekong Delta during the Vietnam War. Faced with a hostile environment unlike anything they had trained for back in the States, the infantrymen of the 9th Division were forced to develop new techniques to carry on operations within the watery world of the Delta. Like its parent organization, the division's long-range patrol unit, Company E, 75th Infantry (Ranger), had to adapt to operate inside the swamps and along the canals and rivers that crisscrossed the area. The predecessor of the division's Ranger unit, E Company, 50th Infantry (LRP), had pioneered a concept that proved especially effective in meeting and defeating the enemy on his own terms. "Parakeet flights" were aerial combat raids consisting of a Huey slick carrying a six- or seven-man contingent of Army Rangers, a Cobra gunship, and a LOH (pronounced "loach") scout helicopter. The job of the LOH was to fly around at treetop level until it located enemy troops or emplacements. Then, pinpointing the location by dropping smoke grenades or directing tracer fire on the target, the LOH stood back while the Huey slick moved in to launch its Ranger element as close to the enemy as possible. The Cobra gunship orbited nearby to support the ground forces with rockets, miniguns, and 40mm

1

grenade fire. The entire operation was based on catching the enemy by surprise and hitting them before they could flee or mount a defense. When it worked, it worked very well. But when it didn't, the frequently outnumbered Rangers often found themselves in the middle of an angry hornets' nest.

On the morning of 12 June 1969, Capt. Al Zapata, the commanding officer of Company E, based at Tan An, approached SFC Jimmy Booth and told him that he needed him to fly C&C (see Glossary for an explanation of abbreviations and other terms) on a parakeet flight later that morning. Sheepishly, Zapata admitted that he had been drinking with a Navy SEAL officer the night before and had gotten a little carried away swapping boasts with the swabby. The Ranger CO smirked when he said, "Sergeant Booth, let's get some action for this guy. Let's show this SEAL lieutenant what Rangers can do."

Booth returned the officer's smile and said, "Can do, sir."

While Sergeant First Class Booth left to make arrangements with the aviation unit, Captain Zapata went to look for S.Sgt. Jim Thayer and his boys to fill out the Ranger team. Zapata had already decided that he would lead the ground element himself, and he had invited the SEAL officer along to observe the operation.

He quickly located Thayer and asked the NCO if he would like to go out on a Ranger raid. When Thayer said yes, Zapata told him to select three men from his Ranger Team 1–1. With Zapata, his RTO, and the SEAL lieutenant already in on the raid, there would be room for only four others.

Jim Thayer had been back with the company only two months since spending some time in Japan recovering from wounds received on an earlier patrol. Thayer's original team had been broken up and reassigned to other team leaders while he was away. Sergeant Laurer, his former ATL, had long since ETS'd back to the World, and Sergeant O'Day was too short to go out in the field anymore. Private First Class Boone had been transferred to another team, and Specialist Fourth Class Bellwood, his senior radio operator, had been killed on the mission when Thayer had been hit. Bellwood's death on that patrol was something the Ranger team leader was still trying to deal with.

With the exception of the team leader himself, everyone on Thayer's new team was relatively new to the game. All of his teammates had been in the Rangers only a couple of months. There had been a lot of switching personnel around between teams since the company had changed from a long-range patrol unit to a Ranger company back in February 1969.

Unlike most Ranger companies in Vietnam, it was not an uncommon practice in Company E for an officer to lead a team in the field, especially during parakeet flights. Since parakeet flights were nothing more than quick, hard-hitting raids, trained infantry officers were an asset rather than the liability they often proved on typical LRP/Ranger missions. Therefore, no one on Thayer's team questioned him when he announced that Captain Zapata would be in charge of the patrol during the raid.

The Rangers quickly changed into cammies and painted their faces, hands, and necks for the raid. Camouflage face paint was not a necessity for a parakeet operation, but the 9th Division LRP/Rangers wore it anyway almost like war paint to let the enemy know exactly who was after them. Thayer slipped on a sleeveless tiger-stripe shirt and taped his pants legs around his bare ankles. The veteran Ranger team leader had long ago stopped wearing boots on patrol, ever since he had been outrun by a barefoot VC he was attempting to capture. He had sworn that it would never happen again.

Zapata, Thayer, and the SEAL officer carried CAR-15s on the raid, while the two radio operators and Sp4. Sef Galardo, the senior scout, toted M-16s. The other Ranger from Thayer's team humped an M-79 grenade launcher along with nearly forty HE rounds for it. For a backup the team leader hung a Colt .45 revolver around his waist. Most Rangers wore a couple of bandoliers of ammo across their chest. A few wore their full LBEs (load bearing equipment). The two radio operators carried PRC-25 radios strapped to shortened pack frames on their backs. The idea on a raid was to travel light and hit the enemy hard and fast.

Sergeant First Class Booth returned to the team hootch and announced that everything was a go. The aviation assets would be available and waiting at the helipad at 1030 hours. The parakeet flight would then fly west out of Tan An into Long An Province to search for the enemy. It was typical Delta country—flat and soupy, with lots of rice paddies and steamy, single-canopy jungle. It was tough terrain for ground troops to operate in, but ideal for fast, hard-hitting heliborne raids.

The parakeet flight was scheduled to lift off at 1045 hours. However, with the Cobra gunship already airborne, the LOH pilot radioed that he was having engine problems and was unable to take off. Seated at the end of the fold-down seat in the cabin of the Huey slick, Captain Zapata turned to Thayer and said, "Jimmy, let's take off. They can catch up." Seconds later the

Huey joined up with the lone gunship, and the two air-craft headed west toward the Cambodian border.

A few minutes into the flight, Thayer was sitting in his favorite spot, on the floor of the chopper next to the port-side door gunner. He was smoking a final cigarette and enjoying the feel of the wind blowing against his legs as they dangled outside the helicopter. Suddenly he had a brief, unexplainable premonition that he was go-ing to get hit in the chest sitting in that spot. He stood up, tossed out the cigarette, and moved to a new posi-tion up on the end of the fold-down seat jutting from the back wall of the cabin. The experience was new to the veteran Ranger and quite discomforting.

Ten minutes out they were over the target area look-ing for VC, and it didn't take long to spot some. Flying low over an area full of rice paddies and scattered patches of jungle, they saw two hootches sitting on a slight rise of high ground backed up to an abandoned rice paddy. The hootches faced a dense patch of jungle perhaps twenty meters away. The larger hootch had a red tile roof, the smaller was covered in thatch.

As the Huey swung around for a closer look, Booth saw a VC soldier, weapon in hand, run out of the larger building. When the man saw the slick hovering nearby, he quickly turned and ran back inside the building.

Aboard the Huey, Booth advised the pilot, "We have VC down in that hootch. Put us down at treetop level."

The pilot made a quick circle out over the rice pad-dies a half mile from the hootches, then came back in fifty feet off the ground. As the chopper flared over the rice paddy, the Rangers spotted several VC sitting on the ground cleaning their weapons under a dilapidated porch. Thayer, sitting on the floor next to the starboard door gunner's hellhole, immediately opened up on the surprised VC. Seconds later everyone aboard the chopper who could get a clear shot followed suit. Immediately a large number of VC broke from the hootches and tried to escape toward the jungle. Some of them stopped to return fire.

As the helicopter touched down thirty meters away from the two buildings, the six Rangers and the SEAL leaped from the skids on both sides of the aircraft and scattered out into attack formation. Firing from the waist as they slopped through the muck, Thayer and his grenadier headed for a spot between the two hootches. Captain Zapata, the SEAL officer, and Zapata's RTO moved to the right approximately thirty meters and took up covered firing positions just behind the high ground where the hootches were sitting. Galardo and the other RTO moved twenty meters to the left and set up to support the assault.

Aboard the departing Huey, Booth flinched as enemy bullets from the edge of the jungle suddenly found the aircraft's range. Realizing that Zapata and Thayer had more than they could handle, Booth notified the pilot to head back toward Tan An for a backup team.

As Thayer and his grenadier neared the two enemy structures, over a dozen VC broke from the hootches and sprinted for the trees. Some were unarmed, but others with weapons turned as they ran and fired back over their shoulders at the Rangers and the departing helicopter.

Thayer opened fire first and immediately saw a VC go down. The Ranger team leader and his grenadier were the only ones who could see the VC breaking for the jungle so they continued putting rounds into the enemy soldiers as fast as they could load and fire. The two Rangers on Thayer's left opened fire into the rear of the larger hootch and flushed a VC out the front door.

The enemy soldier was carrying an armload of weapons when he was hit in the back by a burst of fire from Galardo's M-16, sending him somersaulting and scattering the weapons everywhere.

By then several of the VC, some of them unarmed, had reached the trees. Protected by the cover and concealment of the thick jungle vegetation, a few VC turned around and opened fire on the Rangers from only forty meters away. Thayer, realizing that he was exposed, did the only thing he could under the circumstances—he started to assault the two VC structures.

To his right the grenadier shouted, "Where should I put my rounds?"

Thayer responded, "Fire ahead of the ones still running for the jungle."

As the two Rangers charged between the two hootches, Thayer fired from the waist on "rock 'n' roll" at the last of the VC still fleeing toward the trees. He hit the enemy soldier just as the VC turned and opened up. The VC missed low, but Thayer felt a ricochet slam into his chest, fragmenting as it hit his sternum.

Screaming "Oh, shit!" Thayer went down backwards and lay momentarily stunned. The grenadier stopped and knelt beside his wounded team leader, grabbed a floppy hat from the head of a VC he had just killed, and pressed it down over the wound in his team leader's chest. Thayer, believing he had a sucking chest wound, looked up and told the man to find a piece of plastic to put over the entrance hole.

Unable to find any, the grenadier pulled out a field dressing and pushed it down hard in an attempt to seal the wound. There was nothing else he could do for the moment. Thayer, lying helplessly exposed to the enemy fire still coming from the jungle, waited for a minute or two to see if his situation worsened, then coughed and spit into his left hand to see if there was any blood in the sputum. When he discovered that the sputum was clear, he realized that he had probably not been hit as badly as he first thought. Knowing that he was more likely to die of "exposure" lying there in the open than he was from his wound, he asked the grenadier to hand him his CAR-15 lying nearby. Thayer took the weapon and slammed a fresh magazine into it, then, holding the dressing down tight with his left hand, began firing the CAR-15 with his right.

Thirty meters to Thayer's right, Captain Zapata had seen his team leader take a hit in the chest and go down. Without waiting to ascertain the extent of his injuries, Zapata radioed the C&C helicopter to request a medevac for "Sergeant Tango," who had "a sucking chest wound." SFC Booth in the insertion aircraft, on its way back to Tan An to pick up a backup team, immediately relayed the request for a medevac. Two minutes later he was told that the dustoff would arrive in fifteen minutes, but would not come in for the pickup if the LZ was hot.

Booth shook his head and muttered to himself, "There is no way I'll let Jim Thayer die," then told the pilot of the insertion slick to turn around and go back to the LZ.

The pilot nodded and said, "Let's go."

As the aircraft approached the area of the hootches, Booth contacted Zapata and told him that he was landing to pick up Thayer. Zapata misunderstood the transmission and, thinking they were about to be extracted, screamed for his teammates to prepare to board the aircraft when it touched down.

At that point, Thayer had decided that he was going to stay and fight. He was still firing into the trees when he heard the Huey slick touch down in the paddy behind them. When Captain Zapata shouted, "Let's go! Let's mount up!" he turned and shuffled back toward the waiting aircraft.

Exchanging fire with the remaining VC, the six Rangers and the SEAL executed a fighting withdrawal toward the Huey, where Sergeant First Class Booth, hanging out of the chopper, was firing at the VC in the trees with his 9mm pistol. After everyone had climbed aboard, the Huey lifted out of the rice paddy, did a ninety-degree pedal turn, and dropped its nose to pick up forward airspeed to get out of range of the enemy fire, which was diminishing.

Aboard the aircraft, Jim Thayer was pissed about leaving the fight. Weaponless, he was lying flat on the floor, where he had ended up after climbing aboard. A sudden, burning pain across his back alerted him to the location of his CAR-15 and made him painfully aware that not enough time had elapsed to allow the barrel of the weapon to cool down. But every time he tried to lift himself off the searing metal, his comrades, concerned about his "sucking" chest wound, kept pushing him back down onto the scalding barrel. But eventually he was able to get the point across to them that he was lying on his weapon. Someone reached behind him and removed the offending branding iron.

As the aircraft swiftly departed the area, a rifle platoon from the 9th Infantry Division's 3d Brigade combat-assaulted into the rice paddy the Rangers had just abandoned. They could see the bodies of several dead VC lying about as they charged past the hootches. During a search of the immediate area they found eighteen dead enemy soldiers and recovered a quantity of enemy weapons. Later, under pressure and not out of "generosity," they reluctantly gave the Rangers a couple of beat-up M-2 (full-auto) carbines they had recovered.

When the aircraft landed at the 3d Brigade aid station at Tan An, Thayer was quickly taken into x-ray to determine the extent of his wound and the location of the bullet. The aid station was full at the time with a large number of casualties from a 9th Division infantry company that had been hit earlier that morning. But eventually Thayer was lifted onto a chest-high worktable and given a local anesthetic. Minutes later a doctor climbed up on the table, straddled the wounded Ranger's hips, and cut a three-inch vertical slit down the center of his chest. Cutting through the muscle tissue to expose the path of the bullet, he reached in with a pair of forceps and lifted out a piece of metal. Seemingly satisfied with his work, he calmly told the shocked Ranger that another piece of metal was lodged in his sternum, but it wasn't life threatening and in his opinion didn't need to be removed. The doctor added that he was going to send the wounded Ranger to the division surgical hospital at Dong Tam to have the wound sewn up. Thayer was then given a strong sedative to knock him out during the medevac flight to Dong Tam.

He awoke at 0800 hours the next morning and noticed that he had an IV tube in his arm. Seeing about six inches of air halfway down the tube, he shouted to a nearby medic, "Get over here and get this rather large air bubble out of my IV!"

"Don't worry about it, Sarge," the medic said. "See that VC next to you?" For the first time Thayer saw the wounded Vietnamese in the bed next to him. The medic continued, "We've pumped two bottles of air into him and we haven't killed him yet."

"Get the damn thing out of my arm *now*," Thayer muttered angrily. When the medic didn't comply immediately, he raised up to yank it out himself. The medic quickly urged him to wait and called for a nearby captain, a doctor. Thayer repeated to the medical officer that he wanted the IV out of his arm, and then demanded a landline to call his company commander. The doctor reluctantly agreed to remove the IV and, shaking his head in frustration, finally returned to what he had been doing.

Free of the dangling IV tube, Thayer got out of bed and went to the front desk to call Captain Zapata at the company TOC. When he got his CO on the line, he asked the officer to send a jeep for him. Zapata said he'd have one outside the hospital in ten minutes. Thirty minutes later, S.Sgt. Jim Thayer was back at his unit, wearing a pair of blue pajamas. He went to his hootch and quickly changed into a pair of shorts. One of his comrades walked in while he was changing and noticed the dressing on his chest and another on his back and asked him if the bullet had gone all the way through. Thayer responded, "No, the bandage on my back is from the barrel of my CAR-15."

The pilot of the aircraft who returned under fire to pick up the Ranger team later received the Distinguished Flying Cross. Sergeant First Class Jimmy Booth was awarded an Air Medal with "V" device, a most unusual award for an Army Ranger.

Division LRRP Detachment, 4th Infantry Division

It was typical for long-range reconnaissance patrols to be given a day or two to prepare for a mission after receiving a "warning order" that a mission had been scheduled and assigned to the team. There was an excellent reason for this as it usually took that much time to properly ready a team for a patrol physically, mentally, and emotionally. However, it was not uncommon for a team to receive a warning order for a mission scheduled for that very same day. It was often during such "last minute" patrols that the term "time is of the essence" took on real meaning, and LRRPs had the opportunity to demonstrate their mettle. On nearly every such occasion they set their jaws, clenched their teeth, and carried on accordingly, successfully preparing themselves and their equipment in short order for what could easily be a tough, harrowing, life-threatening experience. One such mission occurred on 28 June 1967 when a pair of three-man teams from the Division LRRP Company, 4th Infantry Division, were tasked to perform five-day patrols with little more than four hours' advance notice.

Major General William R. Peers, commanding officer of the 4th Infantry Division, had personally sent the warning order down to 1st Lt. Louis Garavaglia, operations officer of the Division LRRP Company. It was only days before the onset of the monsoon season, and

12

Division had just received word that one of its aero-
scouts had spotted a column of two hundred NVA on
the move in the open nineteen klicks (kilometers) southwest of Pleiku City. This message was quickly followed
by SPAR (aerial reconnaissance) reports of forty to sixty
NVA occupying a nearby village, and two full platoons
of NVA troops moving in the direction of Pleiku, one of
them in camouflage uniforms. That information was
enough to get the attention of the division staff. The
NVA were up to something, and there was no time to
lose if countermeasures were to be taken to stop them.

Lieutenant Garavaglia quickly notified Sgt. Bill
Steffens that his three-man team was one of the two
hunter/killer teams selected for the patrol. Staging out
of the 1st of the 10th Cavalry Squadron's headquarters
at Cateckta Tea Plantation (straddling Highway 19
twenty miles west of Pleiku), the patrol was to insert
into the target area just eight klicks south of the base
camp. Four kilometers apart, the two three-man teams
were to find the enemy units and report their location.
Each team was told to take an ample supply of M-14
antipersonnel mines and white phosphorous (WP)
grenades for booby traps along the enemy's route of
march. They were also ordered to direct artillery and air
strikes on targets of opportunity.

Steffens, a Division-trained sniper, decided to carry a
scope-mounted XM-21 on the patrol just in case he got
the chance to make a long-range kill. His two teammates, Sp4. James Burke and Sp4. Butch Franzcobiak,
would be carrying CAR-15s. All three LRRPs packed
their own PRC-25 radio in case they became separated
and had to E&E.

At 1630 hours that afternoon, the flight of five Huey
helicopters—two B-model gunships, a C&C slick, a
chase ship, and the insertion aircraft—flew off the

1/10th Cav's helipad and headed southwest. Ten minutes later they were over the target area, faking a couple of insertions before approaching the team's LZ. The terrain in the patrol's recon zone consisted of rolling savanna broken occasionally by single-canopy wood lots and ragged tree lines. There were also a small number of active Montagnard rice paddies throughout the area, but for the most part they were in virgin territory—a good place to look for NVA units trying to avoid contact.

The insertion aircraft soon neared the north end of a large field. Nearby was an expansive area of single-canopy forest unusual for its size in that part of the country. As the helicopter slowed to a hover ten to fifteen feet above the ground, the three LRRPs exited the left side of the aircraft and landed hard in the thick grass below. While the helicopter climbed steeply out of the field, Steffens spotted what he thought was a gray floppy hat partially hidden behind a bush some two hundred meters south/southeast of the LZ. He quickly got out his sniper scope and observed a single individual dressed in a gray uniform watching the departing helicopter. Steffens could not see a weapon in the man's possession, but concluded that he was most likely an enemy LZ watcher. Astonishingly, the man didn't appear to notice the three LRRPs who had just dropped from the skids of the helicopter. But he was definitely interested in the aircraft.

While observing the enemy soldier, Steffens realized that the crosshairs centered in his sight picture had somehow become detached during the insertion, rendering the scope totally useless. There would be no long-range kill on the mission.

As the distant insertion ship and its two accompanying gunships faked a couple more insertions, Steffens cranked up his radio for a brief commo check and to report sighting the probable enemy soldier. When asked if he thought the team had been compromised and needed to be extracted, Steffens reported that he felt there was a good chance the man had missed spotting the three LRRPs. He said they would remain on the ground and continue the mission. Satisfied that he had done the right thing, he released the choppers.

The three LRRPs moved quickly into the nearby woods where they "lay dog" for another fifteen to twenty minutes. It was already beginning to grow dark, but Steffens wanted to put some distance between the team and the LZ. Earlier he had decided to move the patrol directly to the southwest, but sighting the LZ watcher set up in that direction had changed his plans. Instead he signaled for Burke to head east to avoid a confrontation with the VC.

Fifteen minutes later, as darkness settled in, the team set up an NDP under the cover of a large tree to wait out the night. Steffens divided up the guard shifts among the three of them then settled back to watch and listen as the night creatures came awake. Hidden in the deepening shadows, Steffens couldn't help wondering if he had done the right thing in not asking for an extraction.

Early the next morning, the men packed up their gear and moved out, patrolling slowly through the woods as the sun rose in the eastern sky. It wasn't long before the temperature climbed to the 100-degree-plus mark and the LRRPs began to suffer from the heat. But they pressed on, knowing that it had to be just as hot for the enemy as it was for them.

It was 1000 hours when the patrol encountered a heavily used trail running north to south that wasn't marked on any of their maps. To the east side of the trail was an area of dense overgrowth and bamboo that backed up to an old, abandoned deadwood fence. Just beyond the fence, the ground dropped away sharply to a rice paddy. However, the patrol was unaware of the nature of the terrain that lay beyond the deadwood fence.

To the west side of the trail was an extended level area covered with dried grass and thick brush dotted with a few scattered single-canopy trees. There was not enough cover on that side of the trail to conceal the team and protect the men from the blazing sun.

As the three men stood along the side of the trail, deciding what to do, they heard heavy firing to their north, a mixture of AKs and CAR-15s punctuated by the steady bark of an M-14. Even before confirming the engagement on the radio, Steffens knew that the other hunter/killer team was in heavy contact. That was a dangerous moment for Steffens's patrol, because if they were also hit there would not be enough helicopter assets available to simultaneously support both teams. And since the other team was already calling for an extraction, Steffens knew that his team would have to wait until the other team had been safely pulled before any help would arrive for them.

Steffens quickly decided to go to ground right there in the heavy cover off the east side of the trail. He set up the patrol with himself in the center, Burke four feet away on his left, and Franzcobiak an arm's length away on his right. The three were completely hidden back in the brush four feet off a dogleg in the trail. They were situated on the outside of the curve, able to see down the trail a short distance in both directions. It wasn't long before they heard over the radio that the other team had been successfully extracted and was on its way back to the base camp. However, they never managed to get the full picture of just what kind of trouble it had run into.

In spite of the thick vegetation, it was still incredibly hot in the thick cover away from the trail. Steffens had just come off his twenty-ninth mission, and he and his teammates were still physically and emotionally exhausted. The team had not even been given time to stand down and recover from that last mission, and the broiling heat had collaborated with the stress of the recent patrol to completely drain them. Since inserting, Steffens had already downed a couple of the issue dextroamphetamines to help him through the rough spots.

The team was scheduled to make two situation reports—sitreps—per day, one in the morning and one in the evening. However, they had been in touch with their TOC at midmorning to get details on the other patrol's contact and to report that they were setting up over a fresh enemy trail. But since then they had had no commo with anyone.

By 1400 hours the heat was becoming unbearable. Somehow, Steffens had managed to fight off the dex high and dozed off into a fitful sleep. He was dreaming of home when the sudden roar of a nearby CAR-15 on full automatic jarred him back to reality. When he jerked his head from side to side to see what was going on, Franzcobiak was changing magazines in his still-smoking weapon. When Steffens finally caught his eye, the young LRRP pointed to a bloody body in a khaki uniform lying on the far side of the trail. The dead man had a canvas bag strapped over his shoulders. He had fallen back against the trunk of a tree on the opposite side of the trail. Steffens rolled up to his knees and was about to crawl out in the trail to retrieve the bag when he suddenly heard the drumming of running footsteps coming down the trail from the north. Whoever it was was no more than forty meters away and closing fast.

Steffens froze, then sank slowly back to the ground. Suddenly an NVA officer in OD fatigues and a floppy hat with two red stars on it arrived at the side of the dead NVA soldier and looked down at his body. Seconds later another NVA, perhaps a senior NCO, joined the officer. The NCO said something to the officer, who nodded then turned and signaled up the trail. A minute later twenty NVA soldiers jogged around the bend carrying their weapons at port arms. They continued on until they were strung out down the path thirty or forty meters. Then they stopped. While they waited for orders, still more NVA arrived and began setting up along the section of trail to the north.

While the LRRPs waited breathlessly, ten Montagnards jogged past carrying tubes wrapped in cloth— five tubes, two men to a tube. Steffens and his companions could not tell for certain what the tubes contained, but they knew they were not barber poles. The 'Yards, wearing only their traditional loincloths, soon moved out of sight down the trail heading south. Then everything grew eerily quiet.

The hidden LRRPs were less than twenty-five feet from the NVA officer, and only fifteen feet from the nearest enemy soldiers. Suddenly the officer drew his pistol and started looking around. Never once making eye contact with the heavily camouflaged LRRPs, he began walking slowly down the trail to the south. Abruptly, he stopped and stepped off the path on the same side of the trail where they lay hidden. The officer was still looking south, giving Steffens the impression that the NVA was interested in something his point man had discovered out of sight somewhere down the trail.

Without turning around, the officer began backing

up slowly toward the team with his pistol raised at a 45-degree angle to his front. He kept backing up, backing up, until he finally came up against some old dead brush just off the bend in the trail. Unfortunately, Burke was lying on his back at the base of the dead brush.

Steffens swallowed hard and quietly took his weapon off safe. He sensed at that moment that their cover had just been blown. The NVA officer took another short step backward, then suddenly tensed. There was no longer any doubt—the enemy officer was indeed aware of their presence. With that, the man turned slowly to the right and looked directly at Steffens. Steffens didn't even see the officer pull the trigger on his pistol. Nor did he feel the round blast through the left cargo pocket on his tiger-stripe fatigue pants. He had been too busy reacting to the burst of Burke's CAR-15 as it stitched the enemy officer from his crotch to his chin and blood from the dead officer splashed all over him. To his credit, the dying NVA had managed to get off a second shot that knocked Burke's hat from his head.

Burke's full magazine at point-blank range had blown the NVA officer back across the trail, where he collapsed in a loose heap against the flanking brush. Before the NVA soldiers standing in the middle of the footpath could respond, Franzcobiak, Steffens, and Burke opened fire. Steffens saw eight NVA out in the trail at that point, and was pleased when most of them went down hard in the opening barrage. The XM-21 with its duplex ammo was shredding the trees on the other side of the trail.

But when Steffens heard the dull pounding of a BAR and the noisy, throaty popping of multiple AK-47s, he knew that the enemy had recovered from their initial surprise. However, because debris was falling on them from the overhead cover, he sensed that the NVA were firing blind and, for the moment, shooting high.

The close-range firefight went on for a full twenty minutes before the LRRP team leader realized that they were beginning to run low on ammunition. Steffens had already gone through 280 rounds—about fourteen magazines—of ammo, and he knew that his comrades were in no better shape. He also realized that the NVA were finally adjusting their fire and getting the range. However, he couldn't understand why the enemy soldiers had not yet maneuvered to flank the three LRRPs and overrun their position. Then it occurred to Steffens that the troops they were facing were not infantry. It was the only logical explanation for why he and his men had not been overrun in the few minutes following the opening fire.

At that moment, Steffens simply "lost it." Leaping to his feet, he jumped out on the trail and began screaming and firing into the enemy soldiers, scattering them before his onrush. Franzcobiak heard someone up the trail to the north yelling "Surrender . . . surrender!" in English and couldn't tell if it was Steffens or the enemy. It wasn't Steffens.

Burke and Franzcobiak momentarily lost sight of their team leader as they struggled to their feet and started to pull back toward the deadwood fence behind them. Almost simultaneously, Steffens recovered his senses and began falling back through the dense undergrowth, dragging his rucksack behind him with his left hand. In his right hand he held his radio handset to his ear and was frantically screaming "Mayday . . . Mayday!" In the heat of the battle he had forgotten the team's extraction code.

The retreating LRRPs soon found that the bamboo behind them was too thick to penetrate. Steffens kept falling when his rucksack got entangled in the brush.

He fought to jerk it free and continued falling back toward the fence. The last time it caught in the brush he was unable to free it at all. Backing away with the handset cord stretched as far as it would go, he shouted one last time to let the TOC know that they needed help, then fired several rounds into his ruck to destroy the radio, not thinking about the mines, claymores, and grenades inside the main storage compartment.

Finally he dropped the handset and continued backing up, firing into the brush around the trail. It was then that he caught up with his comrades, backing into Franzcobiak. Burke, on the other side of Franzcobiak, was caught in the thick bamboo and unable to free himself even though enemy rounds were chopping the tops of the bamboo overhead. Steffens, still firing toward the trail, turned around to see what was holding up Burke and Franzcobiak and spotted the radio on Burke's back. He saw that the whip antenna was still folded double, so he reached over Franzcobiak and broke the trip wire to deploy the antenna.

At that same instant, Burke and Franzcobiak finally punched a hole through the bamboo and dived over the wooden fence. By the time Steffens reached the spot and started to climb over the fence, it was shot away beneath him, sending the LRRP team leader rolling head over heels down the hillside, out of control. It was ten or fifteen feet to the bottom, which turned out to be a flooded rice paddy. Twenty meters out in the paddy was a small, brush-covered island with a large, fallen tree lying across it. There was nothing else for cover or concealment for several hundred meters. Just open rice paddies.

At that moment there was no sign of pursuit from the enemy soldiers back on the trail, although there was still a heavy volume of fire coming through the bamboo above them. As the three LRRPs splashed across the shallow paddy then dived behind the fallen tree, the firing from above stopped altogether.

The LRRPs pulled out Burke's claymore and primed it with a fifteen-second fuse so they could throw it like a giant grenade. Taking stock of their situation, they realized just how low on ammo they were. If the enemy soldiers broke through the bamboo and came down after them, they were going to find themselves in an instant world of hurt.

Finally, Burke raised an unknown station on his radio. Someone out there had heard the team's frantic "maydays." But it wasn't any of their people. Lieutenant Garavaglia had been busy inserting another team at the time, and whoever had picked up Steffens's calls for help had managed to reach Garavaglia by radio and report to him that he had a recon team in trouble somewhere out there. Garavaglia immediately dropped off the team he was preparing to insert along a nearby road, then raced towards Steffens's AO.

Back in the rice paddy, Steffens spotted choppers flying off to the west, but they were heading due north. Frustrated that the helicopters he saw were going to miss his position by several klicks, he grabbed Burke's radio and shouted some very nasty things over the team's frequency.

At that moment, something up hill from the team drew his attention. By the time he returned to the radio, a Huey slick was flaring up over a paddy dike to their east and preparing to land fifteen meters away from the team on a yellow smoke grenade tossed out by Burke or Franzcobiak. Steffens couldn't understand how the aircraft had managed to cover the distance so quickly.

Burke and Franzcobiak leaped to their feet and sprinted for the helicopter. When he jumped through the open door, Burke was so wet he slid damn near all the way out the other side of the Huey. Franzcobiak piled on next with Steffens right behind him. The pilot wasted no time lifting out of the rice paddy, banking sharply to the southeast to put some distance between the aircraft and the enemy soldiers on the high ground. As the helicopter climbed for altitude, a pair of Huey B-model gunships raced in to make their first run against the NVA soldiers still scattered along the trail.

When the emotionally drained team landed back at base camp, they could only think of the sleep they would get after their debriefing. Steffens made the shocking discovery that he was down to his last magazine. Back at the company area, their fellow LRRPs began teasing the three survivors about why they hadn't thrown any of their grenades. It was a question none of them was able to answer; in the heat of the battle it had not even occurred to them to use their fragmentation grenades. On 30 June, during the team's subsequent stand-down, someone came down from operations to get Steffens to attend a briefing over at G-2. On the way, the soldier told Steffens that an aero-rifle troop had just gone into the patrol's AO, but had not been able to locate the battleground.

At Division, a colonel told Steffens that he wanted the LRRP team leader to show the Blues where the firefight had occurred. So Steffens grabbed his weapon and flew out to join the aero-rifle troop. When the captain commanding the Blues told Steffens that he didn't believe the action had even taken place, Steffens flew off the handle. Minutes later the helicopter landed again and pulled him back out of the field. The aero-rifle troop had been two klicks northeast of where the battle had occurred and was moving due west.

Early the next day, 1 July, a Division intelligence

officer accompanied Steffens, Burke, and Franzcobiak back out to the LRRP's old AO. They landed near the spot where the firefight had taken place and walked right to it. They could smell the scene long before they reached it. When they reached the site, the place looked like total war had recently gone down there. Unfortunately, the enemy had long since policed the battlefield so there were no bodies to be found, no weapons, and no equipment left behind. However, there were numerous pools of coagulated, sticky blood scattered around the dogleg in the trail. Even the NVA sanitizing teams couldn't hide that. Searching through the brush, the LRRPs soon found a can of C ration peaches that had been blown up.

When they returned to their base camp, the situation was soon put behind them. But a report issued later confirmed seven enemy bodies at the site of the battle. Each of the LRRPs was later awarded a Bronze Star with "V" device for his actions that day.

Long Range Reconnaissance Patrol Platoon, 3/506th Infantry, 101st Airborne Division

During the Vietnam War, the 3/506th was called the Bastard Battalion of the 101st Airborne Division. The battalion landed in South Vietnam in October 1967, two months before the Division arrived. After disembarking at Cam Ranh Bay the battalion moved to Phan Rang, where it joined the Division's 1st Brigade which had been in country since 1965. At the time, the 1st Brigade was preparing to move north, to I Corps. However, the 3/506th was not slated to make the trip north with the 1st Brigade. Instead, it was assigned to remain behind in II Corps as a task force. Shortly thereafter, the battalion moved to Phan Thiet to begin operations.

The battalion's reconnaissance element, which was attached to Headquarters, was known as "Shock Force," but it was not destined to remain a battalion recon element for long. On 2 March 1968, just after the Tet Offensive, Shock Force's platoon leader, Lt. Mike Pearce, went to the battalion commander, Colonel DeRoussey, and suggested converting Shock Force to a bona fide LRRP detachment. Colonel DeRoussey had been so impressed with the 1st Brigade LRRPs during the brief interval the 3/506th was collocated with them, that it took very little to convince him to establish his own battalion long range reconnaissance patrol unit.

In April 1968 the battalion moved into the mountains

around Da Lat to conduct operations, returning to Phan Thiet in June. At that time the newly formed LRRP platoon had established and staffed a recondo school at Go Boy, a small ARVN compound five miles north of Phan Thiet. Its mission was to train ARVN airborne forces in the fine art of long range reconnaissance patrolling. Often, the school cadre took anywhere from two to seven ARVN trainees out on patrols to test them. After graduation, the ARVNs returned to their parent units to set up their own LRRP capabilities.

Also in April 1968 battalion Headquarters combined the LRRP platoon, the 4.2-inch mortar platoon, and the 81mm mortar platoon into Company E, a move that appeared to be a great improvement over having the separate platoons serving as components of Headquarters Company.

On the morning of 22 December 1968, battalion S-2 (intelligence) sent a patrol order down to the LRRP platoon. The platoon leader at the time, Lieutenant Roos, happened to be absent from the unit that day, so Platoon Sergeant Payne selected the team and notified the men of their impending mission.

Platoon Sergeant Payne soon ran into Sgt. Gene Carne as he was walking through the platoon area. With only thirty-one days left in country, Carne, a veteran LRRP from North Carolina, was "short." Carne had already made up his mind that he wasn't going out in the field again although he was considering extending for six more months in the Nam.

Platoon Sergeant Payne wasted no time. He told Carne that a mission had just come down from S-2 and, since most of the teams were out in the field, he was going to have to put together a "scratch" team to handle it. He intended to put Connie "Tennessee" Taylor in charge of the team, but because Taylor had only been in country five months and had just made sergeant (E-5), Payne wanted Carne to go along as his ATL. Someone with seasoning had to be along to make sure Taylor didn't screw up during his first outing in charge of a team.

Carne hesitated for a long moment as he considered all the negatives, and the old fears flooded back. Given his state of mind, he knew he would be pushing the envelope if he went out again, yet he owed it to Payne. Sergeant Payne was a great guy and had always taken care of his men, and Carne just didn't have it in his heart to let the senior NCO down when he needed help. He also realized that the unit was going through a difficult period of transition in manpower and leadership. Taylor just didn't have enough experience to handle a mission by himself. Some of his fellow LRRPs thought he had been given his stripes a little too early and figured he was still too wet behind the ears to be leading a team. Reluctantly, Carne agreed to go out as the number-two man on the patrol. In the back of his mind he could see his parents getting the wire from Western Union on Christmas Day.

Although the LRRP platoon once had a wealth of good people, just then there happened to be a shortage of experienced team leaders. Most of the original LRRPs who had come over with the battalion had DEROS'd or ETS'd just a month earlier.

Besides Taylor and Carne, the rest of the team consisted of Sp4. Gary Curtis, the RTO, in the number four position, Sgt. Chris "Kip" Rolland at slack, Sp4. Morgan at point, and PFC John "Cherry" Mendoza in the number five slot.

Curtis was a fourteen-month veteran of the Vietnam

theater. He was popular among the troops but always seemed to be getting into trouble over petty things, like arriving late for formation or being out of uniform.

Kip Rolland hailed from New Jersey and had already been in country six months. A dropout from the Special Forces medic course, he had completed enough training to qualify as the team medic. Although he constantly volunteered to walk point on patrol, his medical expertise was too important to the platoon to permit him to get any closer to the front of the team than the slack position.

Morgan was a short, streetwise black kid from New York City. Feisty as hell and tough as nails, he was just as good in the jungles of Vietnam as he claimed he had been in the asphalt jungles of the Big Apple. It was a foregone conclusion that he would walk point on patrol, a position he excelled at. Mendoza, in country only a couple of months, had been out on four patrols, all without contact. He was a quiet, likable guy.

The mission was scheduled for a rugged, mountainous area approximately forty-five miles northwest of Phan Thiet. None of the men could ever recall pulling missions in that part of the country before, but there was a first time for everything. Payne informed Taylor that his six-man patrol would be designated Papa-Three, and told them to prepare for a reconnaissance patrol lasting four days.

Early on the morning of the 23d, Tennessee Taylor got in an O-1 Bird Dog and flew out over the team's recon zone to see firsthand the kind of terrain they would be working in. While he was gone, the rest of the team packed their gear. Most of them had not worked together before, so there was a degree of uncertainty that would only be dealt with out in the bush.

When Taylor returned from the overflight two hours

later, he informed his teammates that their mission would indeed be back in the rugged mountains northwest of Phan Thiet. Since all of the suitable LZs appeared to be down low in the valleys, they would have to do some climbing to reach an OP high enough to observe their entire recon zone.

The battalion executive officer came down to the LRRP compound at midday to conduct the mission briefing. He told the team that they would be going into an area designated MR-6. Little was known about the area, but the officer assured them that it had all the potential of being a real hot spot.

At 1403 hours that afternoon the team went through a final equipment check before heading down to the chopper pad to wait for the arrival of their lift ship. It had always been the custom in the 3/506th for the battalion commander to come down to the helipad to see the LRRP teams off. This time was no different.

At 1445 hours the insertion slick arrived at the LRRP helipad to pick up the waiting team. Taylor stood to one side as his teammates climbed aboard. He was anxious to get under way; he wanted to prove that he could lead a patrol in the bush.

The aircraft lifted off and was quickly joined by the chase ship and a pair of Cobra gunships for the forty-five-minute trip to MR-6. Thirty minutes into the flight, the four aircraft touched down at an ARVN Petroleum, Oil and Lubrication (POL) point to refuel. After topping off their tanks, the choppers resumed their flight on the final leg out to the LRRPs' AO.

When the four aircraft reached the recon zone the Cobras went into a high orbit over MR-6 and the two slicks quickly lost altitude and dropped down into the valley. After making a number of false insertions on some secondary ridgelines, they approached a low knoll rising from the valley floor. As the chase ship staged an insertion on the crest of the knoll, the insertion aircraft hovered a hundred meters away just off the north side of the hill. In seconds the team was out the near side of the aircraft, dropping into the six-foot-high elephant grass covering the ground. As the six LRRPs ran down-hill away from the LZ, the two slicks lifted out of the valley to rejoin the circling gunships.

The lower slope of the knoll opened up into low shrubs and sparse thickets running into a dry creek bed. When the patrol reached the "blue line," as streams were called because of their representation on maps, they split into two elements ten meters apart and set up security. They lay dog while Taylor established commo and quickly released the aircraft. A short time later, as he was checking his map to see if they were in the right spot, he called Carne over to assist him. When Carne looked at the map, he decided that although the terrain *looked* pretty close to what was shown at the insertion point on the map, something was not quite right. He suggested that Taylor call in a smoke round set for air burst, then shoot an azimuth to it to establish their actual position. Taylor agreed and immediately radioed for a single marker round.

When they had neither seen nor heard anything three minutes after being given a "shot" by the FDO on the distant firebase, the six LRRPs realized that something had gone wrong.

When Taylor called for a repeat shot, the results were the same—absolutely nothing. The NCO realized that they were nowhere close to where they were supposed to be.

Taylor and Carne decided to move to higher ground in order to get a better look at the surrounding terrain.

They selected a hill approximately seven hundred meters to the north, where they thought they might be able to get a view of the entire valley.

Two hours later they reached the crest of the hill. They quickly set up a defense perimeter and called for a third smoke round. Once again the results were negative. They now knew they had been inserted into the wrong LZ.

It was growing dark when Taylor finally established commo with the team's radio relay site and warned them of their situation. The radio relay team ordered the LRRPs to sit tight and wait until morning, when battalion would send an aircraft to locate them.

The patrol was situated on an open, sparsely vegetated hilltop with a few scrubby trees scattered here and there. It afforded a wonderful view of the valley from the north side, but it dropped quickly off into triple-canopy jungle on the reverse slope. In spite of the close proximity of the dense cover, the top of the hill was still as good a place to defend as they were apt to find. Although it was only twenty meters across the crest, to defend both sides of the hill, the team was forced to divide into two elements ten meters apart to take advantage of two natural depressions. Even though the patrol would be without friendly artillery or tac air support during the night, they still felt fairly secure.

Just before dark the LRRPs slipped out of their tiny perimeter to set up claymores in a circle around the crest of the hill. Checking out the reverse slope for the first time, they discovered that a trail ran up to the crest from the triple-canopy jungle. Although Carne and Taylor felt that it was most likely just an animal trail, they decided to set out a few trip flares and booby traps along it just in case.

At dusk Taylor called for 50 percent security during the night. Not long after dark, everyone began to grow a little concerned when they realized that if they got hit at any time before daylight, they were entirely on their own. By midnight no one had yet managed to fall asleep.

When a flare suddenly went off down by the trail, everyone froze; no one fired or attempted to blow a claymore. LRRPs knew fire discipline. No one would fire without a valid target. Although the trip flare had been only thirty meters from the nearest LRRP, it was far enough away that they were unable to spot anything moving in its pulsing glow. Wisely, they did not react. Until morning, stealth and the cover of darkness would be their only allies.

At first light they attempted to reach the radio relay but were unable to establish commo. It was very foggy that morning and the dense blanket probably had a lot to do with their signal not getting out. Curtis pulled the long antenna from his ruck and screwed it into the antenna mount on the radio. But even with the ten-foot pole antenna they could barely reach the relay site. Curtis fumbled in his rucksack and came out with a coil of commo wire, climbed a nearby tree, and stretched the wire across some of the branches. When he got back on the ground he secured the "field-expedient" antenna to the radio to boost its signal. That worked and the team immediately had excellent commo with the relay site. When Taylor reported that they were lost and had no idea where they were, and requested an aircraft to do a flyover to give them a fix, battalion responded that a FAC would not be available until later that afternoon. All assigned aircraft were supporting an LRRP team that was in heavy contact outside MR-6.

Nothing happened during the rest of the morning. At

1400 hours a FAC pilot broke in over the airway and radioed that he was approaching MR-6. The pilot radioed that he would begin flying grid patterns from one side of MR-6 to the other. But three long hours passed before Carne finally spotted the aircraft flying five miles away in the opposite direction. Carne grabbed his compass and shot an azimuth toward the aircraft as Taylor got the pilot on the radio. When he gave the pilot the back azimuth and told him to fly on that heading for approximately five miles, the man seemed incredulous.

The LRRPs watched as the plane did a 180-degree turn and flew toward their position. When the aircraft was less than a half mile away, Carne retrieved his signal mirror and flashed the approaching plane. The pilot acknowledged that he had spotted their signal, but it seemed like several more minutes passed before he radioed back and told them that he had some bad news—they were not on his map. As the shocked LRRPs looked hopelessly at each other, the pilot radioed that he would remain on station until the choppers could make it out to pick them up. This had the immediate effect of making the LRRPs feel better about their situation, but that didn't last long. Thirty minutes later, battalion was back on the net, telling them that there were no aircraft available at that time, and no one wanted to risk a night extraction unless the team was in contact. Battalion ordered them to remain in place overnight and they would be extracted the next morning. By that time everyone on the hilltop was pretty tired. To reduce the need for 50 percent security, Taylor pulled the team into a tight wagon-wheel perimeter and assigned one man on guard at a time.

Rolland was on guard shift just before midnight, watching the stars just above the horizon, when he realized that the "stars" he was looking at were actually below the horizon. Concerned by the situation, he woke up the rest of the team and asked them what they thought of this phenomenon. Each man admitted that it did look like stars, but it wasn't long before they realized that what they were looking at were fires or lanterns flickering down in the valley approximately five hundred to a thousand meters away. When they reported the observation to battalion, the radio operator requested an accounting, which proved difficult as the lights kept flickering on and off. Finally the LRRPs concluded that people passing back and forth in front of the lights was giving the impression that they were flickering on and off.

Taylor ordered each man on the patrol to come up with a number. The consensus was that there were at least thirty-five lanterns or campfires scattered over a large area on the far side of the valley. They appeared to extend beyond a distant hill then continue again on the opposite side. Estimating ten men around each fire, and guessing there were probably another thirty-five fires behind the mountain that they could not see, Taylor reported that they had a probable enemy regiment encamped across the valley from their position. He also reported that they had not seen any lights in that area the night before.

Battalion responded by saying that his conclusions were impossible; there was no enemy unit of that size in the vicinity of MR-6.

Everyone on the team was very upset with this new revelation. Carne was especially angry and wanted to know why the hell they were out in MR-6 if S-2 (battalion intelligence) already knew who was in the area. But the LRRPs' venting wouldn't change a thing, and it might get them in trouble. Without accepting the patrol's sighting, battalion signed off the net.

Papa-Three remained awake the rest of the night. Since there was apparently no friendly artillery within range of the team's location, the six LRRPs could only watch the lights and hope that the enemy wouldn't decide to explore their neighborhood.

The remainder of the night was uneventful. When Carne realized that it was Christmas Eve, he whispered the news to his comrades, but no one seemed to appreciate his observation. During the next regularly scheduled sitrep, Curtis reported that they had just sighted reindeer pulling some fat son of a bitch in a sleigh. They figured it had to be some gook Santa Claus. Curtis warned that if the lead reindeer didn't turn off that goddamn red light, they were going to blow his ass right out of the sky. No one back at the relay site saw the humor in Curtis's report.

The next morning, Christmas Day, battalion came up on the net and told the team to move two thousand meters across the valley to the north. When they reached the other side, they would be on the map.

Taylor immediately acknowledged the message and told the radio operator that they would comply. The only thing wrong with this picture was that the suggested route of travel would take them about a thousand meters beyond the string of campfires they had seen across the valley from their perimeter. Obviously battalion had not believed their report. And though a Christmas cease-fire was supposed to be in effect, none of the men believed that an enemy regiment was going to let six armed LRRPs parade through their base camp.

Carne blew his stack. "I'm not going anywhere," he told Taylor. "They can court-martial me, torture me, or shoot me, but any or all of it will have to be done right here."

Taylor contacted battalion and said that they had decided not to move to that point. When he specified his reasons for staying put, battalion came back and ordered the team to move out immediately.

Carne shook his head and told Taylor that he didn't care what battalion threatened, he wasn't going. When everyone else on the team backed up Carne, Taylor called back and told battalion that he was refusing to move his team.

After a very pregnant pause, battalion announced that helicopters would be out to extract the team. They were to move back down to where they had been inserted as it was the only suitable LZ in the area.

Papa-Three was more cautious than normal as it slipped down off the mountain. It took them three hours to cover the seven hundred meters back to the knoll. Although they were greatly relieved when they reached it, their anxiety levels soared when they learned that it would be several more hours before the extraction aircraft could arrive.

Finally at 1600 hours they heard the sound of distant approaching helicopters. They watched with excitement as two Huey slicks appeared over the horizon. Five minutes later the two aircraft touched down on top of the knoll as the six LRRPs broke from cover and climbed aboard, three men on each ship.

When the team reached Phan Thiet they went directly to battalion S-2 for a debriefing. Taylor anticipated a court-martial at best. Carne was also prepared for the worst, but he was ready to blow his stack as soon as the issue was brought up. To their amazement, not one word was mentioned about their refusal to follow a direct order the night before.

Five weeks later, in early February, an NVA regiment engaged 3/506th forces in a major battle thirty miles northwest of Phan Thiet. It was believed that to have reached the battle site, the enemy regiment had infiltrated into the area through MR-6 a month or two earlier.

Sergeant Taylor later became the battalion commander's personal driver. Sergeant Carne went home in January. Sergeant Rolland, Specialists Four Morgan and Curtis, and Private First Class Mendoza continued pulling long range reconnaissance patrols until their time in Vietnam came to an end. Battalion S-2 never acknowledged its error in judgment on that Christmas Eve night.

1st Brigade LRRP Detachment (Provisional), 4th Infantry Division

In 1968, the 4th Infantry Division area of operations covered a larger area than that of any other U.S. infantry division in Vietnam. Of its three brigades, 1st Brigade was at Dak To, 2d Brigade was at Phu My, and 3d Brigade was at Kontum. Due to the distance between the three brigades, each was forced to create its own provisional long range reconnaissance patrol detachment to deal with its need for area ground recon. At that time the 4th Division also maintained a full LRRP company, Company E, 58th Infantry (LRRP), based at division HQ in Pleiku. One would think that with more teams operating in the bush than either of the two oversized Field Force LRRP companies, the division's long range reconnaissance capability would be more than adequate. However, LRRP teams from both the 173d Airborne Brigade and I Field Force had to be brought in to beef up the operational patrols. This was not done to discredit the 4th Division's patrols, but because of the extent and complexity of the division's operational area. In 1968, for the men in all the LRRP units operating in the Central Highlands, the missions were coming hot and heavy.

On 31 October, as the monsoon season began drawing to a close, a warning order from the 4th Division's 1st Brigade S-2 shop came down to the brigade's LRRP detachment located just off the airstrip at Dak To. The detachment first sergeant immediately contacted Sgt. Mort McBain, the team leader of long-range patrol Team Lima-One-Hotel, and notified him that he had a mission for the following day. McBain immediately went down to the unit TOC to attend a briefing by the detachment commander, Capt. Forest Kay, then departed in a single Huey slick to overfly his recon zone. Later that day, McBain called a team meeting and briefed his two teammates, Specialists Fourth Class Glen Aoki and Bill Manderfeld, on the mission. He told them that they had been scheduled to go into an area west of Dak To, not far from the Special Forces A-camp at Ben Het. It would be a five-day reconnaissance patrol to check out suspicious activity reported in the immediate vicinity of their patrol box. Intel for the area was not good, but that was often the case at brigade level. Around that time, most of their missions had been in areas that somebody "suspected" were hot. Sometimes they were, and sometimes they weren't, but for the long-range patrollers who drew the job of going in to find out what was there, it seemed that no one was worrying about the risk to them.

The overflight revealed that the team's recon zone contained the rugged, hilly terrain typical of the area. The vegetation ran from kunai grass and brush in the valleys to single-canopy forest at the base of the slopes with thicker double-canopy at higher elevations and along the crests of the ridges. LZs were not a problem, and McBain selected a large clearing located at the base of one of the secondary finger ridges that ran two-thirds of the way up to the crest of the major terrain feature in his AO. The insertion, scheduled for 1330 hours the next day, 01 November 1968, would be an easy touchdown for the aircrew. A single Huey slick, escorted by a pair of C-model gunships, would be used to get the team on the ground. The extended weather forecast promised hot, humid, and clear conditions for the entire mission, and McBain anticipated a good mission with no surprises. However, the fact that it was McBain's first mission as a team leader and Manderfeld's first mission as a LRRP was a little disconcerting.

Because of the low numbers of qualified volunteers for the detachment and the demand by brigade for more teams in the field, the unit had long ago gone to three and four-man teams. It wasn't the SOP for team strength taught at MACV Recondo School, but the 4th Division's brigade LRRP detachments had proved that it worked.

Sergeant Mort McBain, a native of Glasgow, Scotland, had come to the U.S. at the age of sixteen to join his mother and two sisters, who had made the trip a year earlier. After spending a couple of years in California with his family, McBain attempted to enlist in the U.S. Navy right out of high school, only to be rejected when the Navy discovered that he had problems with his vision. His father had been a seaman in the Royal Navy, and it was only natural for McBain to follow in his footsteps. Disappointed but undaunted, the young Scotsman enlisted in the U.S. Army and soon found himself serving as an MP in an armored cavalry squadron at Fort Carson, Colorado. After six months of enjoying the evening shade of the Rocky Mountains, McBain was sent overseas as a replacement in an armored cavalry unit attached to the 1st Infantry Division.

Two months later he was for some reason pulled out of the Big Red One and sent north to the Central Highlands to the 1st Brigade of the 4th Infantry

Division, where he immediately volunteered for the LRRPs. When his infantry company commander kept telling him that his paperwork had been lost, McBain finally decided to take matters into his own hands by personally carrying his paperwork to the LRRP detachment to make certain that it reached the unit and got into the right hands. When he arrived at the long-range patrol detachment he was told that they had never seen his paperwork, but that was typical. Not wanting to lose their best people to the LRRPs, infantry officers often ordered their company clerks to file the priority paperwork in "Circular File #13," and then blamed its loss on the unreliable U.S. Army postal service. The LRRP detachment first sergeant told McBain to find a place to hang his gear. He promised McBain that he wouldn't be going back to his old unit. McBain went out on a number of patrols before getting his own team. He walked point on missions and carried a CAR-15.

Specialist Four Glen Aoki was Hawaiian-born, of Japanese descent. He had been in Vietnam and the LRRPs for four months and was a good man to have on a team. He was the team's RTO, walked rear security on patrol, and carried an M-16 as his weapon of choice.

Specialist Four Bill Manderfeld grew up in Oregon, and the Central Highlands was not his first experience in the mountains. Although he was new to the LRRPs, Manderfeld had spent a considerable amount of time in a line company before volunteering for recon. On patrol he walked slack, behind McBain at point, and carried an M-79 loaded with buckshot to back up his team leader.

At 1230 hours the next day, LRRP Team Lima-One-Hotel arrived at the helipad just outside the LRRP compound where they found the three helicopters assigned to them waiting on the tarmac. Thirty minutes later the aircraft lifted off with the LRRPs aboard, then headed west toward the tri-border area. In less than a half hour they were over the team's AO, where the insertion aircraft dropped back while the gunships circled to look over the area. Satisfied that everything appeared normal, the gunships called for the slick to put the team in. Minutes later the insertion aircraft flared briefly over the designated LZ on the east side of the north/south-running primary ridgeline, while the three LRRPs exited the right side of the aircraft, facing uphill.

McBain, Aoki, and Manderfeld squatted in the knee-high grass until the aircraft departed the area and silence returned to the valley. Then they were up and moving quickly into the nearby brush, where they set up security and called to establish communication with the radio relay team set up on a distant firebase. Satisfied that they had good commo and had gotten in undetected, McBain released the helicopters and signaled for his teammates to follow him as he began to move uphill to the west.

They moved for nearly two hours, patrolling slowly and cautiously as they had been trained. As they angled higher up the secondary ridge, McBain noticed that the cover had gradually changed from brush to single-canopy and finally double-canopy.

Just inside the double-canopy, some five hundred or six hundred meters above the LZ, McBain struck a narrow trail that ran directly uphill from down in the valley. There didn't appear to be any fresh sign on the trail so McBain decided to follow it to see where it led. He didn't move more than a few steps before spotting strands of blue-and-black commo wire hidden on the ground along the right side of the trail. Attempts had been made to conceal the wire, but there were areas where time and the elements had exposed it.

McBain stopped the patrol in place and called in his find to the relay team. Satisfied that he still had good commo, he continued up the trail, moving even more slowly and cautiously than before. He soon noticed old fighting positions along both sides of the trail. From their size and composition he figured they had been dug by an American line unit operating in the area more than a year earlier.

At 1538 hours the patrol was only a hundred meters from the crest of the main ridge when they suddenly began to receive small-arms fire from their right front flank. The fire had come from a single AK-47, a long, steady burst. Although none of the LRRPs heard the rounds impact, they could tell that the weapon was definitely firing in their direction.

McBain reacted quickly and dived into one of the old fighting positions to his right a fraction of a second before Manderfeld jumped into the same hole. There was no sign of Aoki, who had been farther down the trail when the enemy weapon opened up. The two LRRPs immediately thought their RTO had been hit. Fearing the worst, McBain shouted his name and Aoki answered immediately. Satisfied that Aoki was alive and unharmed, McBain told him to get his ass up to them with the radio.

Minutes later Aoki piled into the hole. McBain grabbed the handset, called the relay team to report that they were in contact, and asked for immediate support. McBain knew they were outside the artillery fan, so the relay team was their only lifeline if the shit really hit the fan.

Within minutes of his call for support, an Army O-1 Bird Dog arrived on the scene and began circling overhead. While McBain was attempting to make contact with the Bird Dog, he spotted an NVA soldier crawling through the trees toward the team. He grabbed a white phosphorous grenade from his web gear and pulled the pin. Satisfied that the Willy Pete would take care of the enemy soldier sneaking up on them and at the same time mark their position for the O-1 Bird Dog, McBain tossed the grenade uphill toward the hidden NVA. He was horrified when the canister-shaped device bounced off a tree and rolled back downhill to within ten feet of the team's position. The LRRPs had two seconds to cover up in the bottom of the hole before the grenade detonated, showering the jungle with a deadly spray of burning phosphorous. The chemicals set fire to jungle, sending a thick plume of white smoke boiling up through the trees and effectively marking their position for the spotter plane. Amazingly, none of the phosphorous fell back on the three LRRPs.

Relieved that he and his comrades were still alive, McBain sat up in the hole and called in a target azimuth line from the source of the smoke to the target. He reported that the enemy was northwest of his position on an azimuth of 290 degrees at a distance of forty meters.

At this time a pair of Huey gunships arrived overhead and were quickly directed by the Bird Dog to commence their gun runs uphill on a northwest azimuth. The gunships made several runs, firing 2.75-inch rockets into the jungle on all sides of the smoke except where the team was located. Then, climbing up over the top of the ridge, they put in a few more rockets south to north along the crest for good measure.

At this time the patrol was catching glimpses of enemy troops moving around in the shadows uphill from their position. They seemed to be climbing in and out of well-hidden bunkers and fighting positions back in the trees. The LRRPs thought their movements strange; the

NVA had to know exactly where they were, yet showed no inclination to come down and get them.

At 1600 hours McBain reported that the enemy was still directing occasional small-arms fire at the team's position and had just thrown a couple of grenades that detonated less than fifteen feet away. Although the LRRPs were far from being pinned down, they knew that the NVA were very likely maneuvering to encircle them at that very minute.

While Aoki and Manderfeld provided perimeter security, McBain continued to adjust the supporting fire of the gunships.

Finally the Bird Dog radioed that he had to leave to refuel, but told McBain that he would request an Air Force FAC to replace him on station until he could return.

As the gunships continued to shoot up the area, an extraction aircraft rigged with a ladder arrived on the scene. Captain Kay was aboard the helicopter and radioed that he was standing by to pick up the team as soon as the gunships had suppressed the enemy fire. Minutes later the Air Force FAC arrived and went on station over the team.

As the Huey circled the ridgeline at altitude, the LRRPs heard the distinct sound of a .51-caliber heavy machine gun open up somewhere up along the crest of the ridge. Immediately the aircraft commander reported that he was taking fire. Within seconds the peter pilot (copilot) reported in an excited voice that the aircraft had taken hits and the aircraft commander had been wounded in the shoulder. The peter pilot was in control of the aircraft. McBain heard him radio that he was going to attempt to fly the aircraft to Ben Het, the nearest friendly base.

The two gunships radioed that they were breaking off

their attack to escort the damaged aircraft back to the firebase. The slick, callsign Alligator Five-One-Niner, was forced down several minutes later just short of Ben Het, snapping off its tail boom and flattening both skids on impact. One of the gunships quickly landed alongside the wrecked aircraft to pick up the crew and the wounded pilot.

Back at the team's position the FAC pilot contacted McBain and reported that he had a flight of fast movers—jets—fully loaded with five-hundred-pound, high-drag ordnance standing by, and asked the LRRP team leader where he wanted it. McBain told him to drop the bombs above and on the uphill flanks of the smoke.

As the three LRRPs tried to dig deeper into their hole, a pair of F-4 Phantoms came in low over their position and dropped ordnance less than forty meters above the team. The ground shook violently as dust and debris showered down on the patrol. The ordnance had been uncomfortably close but was right on the money. Each fighter-bomber made a single run, dropping two five-hundred-pounders just below the crest of the ridge.

As the jets circled around to get into position for a second run, the FAC called McBain and told him that the fast movers still had 20mm cannons and asked if he needed more support. McBain answered, "Yeah, keep it coming."

The F-4s came in again, cannons firing like heavy machine guns, and the bamboo around the team exploded into a million slivers. The sudden shower of bamboo splinters and bits and pieces of wood blew back over the team, causing Aoki and Manderfeld to scream that they were hit. McBain immediately contacted the FAC and shouted, "They're too close; call them off!"

The FAC pilot radioed back, "No problem."

Satisfied for the moment that there would be no repeat performance, McBain turned to his two comrades to see how badly they had been hit. Both men had numerous cuts, and wood slivers were embedded in their faces and arms, but nothing was disabling or life threatening.

The two Air Force fighters left the AO to return to base, but the FAC stayed overhead circling the team. Suddenly the three LRRPs felt terribly alone. For the moment everything around them was quiet, but they knew that the enemy was still out there—waiting and biding his time.

McBain knew that they had to get out of there before dark. He radioed the FAC pilot overhead and asked him to find the nearest LZ. Minutes later the FAC radioed back that when he flew over the team's position, they should move out in the direction that he was heading. McBain radioed that he understood the message and would comply.

Minutes later the O-1 came in from the north at treetop level, paralleling the crest of the ridge and passing directly over the team's position, flying from north to south. Instantly the three LRRPs jumped from the hole, crossed the trail, and began running away from the spot where they had spotted the NVA, paralleling the crest of the ridge above them. There was a spattering of small-arms fire behind them and they heard NVA shouting and breaking brush in hot pursuit.

The patrol ran through the jungle for twenty or thirty minutes, the men stopping three or four times just long enough to catch their breath, look to see if they were being followed, and pump a few rounds downrange to give the enemy reason to pause.

Overhead, the FAC radioed to tell them that he was

calling another extraction slick to recover the team. Unfortunately the only set of ladders available was sitting in the wrecked Huey slick somewhere between the team and Ben Het. McBain understood that they would have to E&E until they reached a clearing large enough to accommodate a Huey.

A thousand meters south of their initial point of contact, they suddenly broke out of the trees into the middle of the prettiest clearing any of them ever saw. Looking up, they observed a single Huey slick circling high above them. Aoki immediately popped a smoke grenade and tossed it into the middle of the clearing to let the chopper crew know that they had arrived, but the pilot had already spotted them in the open and was beginning his final descent to pick them up.

Seconds later the slick was in the clearing and the LRRPs were dashing for the open cabin. Safely aboard, the three LRRPs and both door gunners opened fire as the slick began to lift out of the tiny opening in the jungle. Firing to the north, they were attempting to suppress any fire the enemy might be throwing their way. NVA gunners had already brought down one aircraft over the area, and no one wanted to give them another opportunity to repeat the performance. They continued to burn ammo until their barrels grew hot, but they could not tell if they were taking fire coming out.

The aircraft flew back to Dak To, where the team was dropped off outside its compound. McBain told Aoki and Manderfeld to drop their gear and report to the dispensary to have their wounds attended to, then went over to the S-3 (Operations) shop, where he was debriefed by the brigade commander. When McBain verified that the enemy had used a .51-caliber heavy machine gun to shoot down the first extraction aircraft, then reported hardened fighting positions and the camouflaged commo wire they had followed up the side of the ridge, the brigade commander got excited. He immediately requested that another LRRP team be inserted on the west side of the ridge the following day to verify Team Lima-One-Hotel's intel.

The next morning, Sgt. Roy Leising's team, Team Lima-One-Alpha, was picked for the mission. They were to be inserted at approximately 1520 hours. Since Sergeant McBain was somewhat familiar with the area and because he had cut his teeth serving under Leising before taking over his own team, it was only natural for him to volunteer to go back out the next day with Leising's team.

At 1522 hours the patrol was inserted into a bomb crater just below the military crest of the ridge on the opposite side from McBain's insertion the day before. The patrol called in a quick sitrep and established commo with the relay team, then began to move off to the south, paralleling the ridge crest. The ground ahead of them was brushy and open, showing the extreme ravages of a prior B-52 arc-light carpet-bombing mission. McBain was walking point for the patrol. Leising walked his slack.

Almost immediately they noticed that a trail had been cut through the heavily damaged terrain sometime after the devastating arc-light. Black-and-blue commo wire was running right up the middle of the trail. Cautious and fully alert, the patrol continued moving up the trail until McBain slowly raised his arm to stop them. Ahead of them in a nearby tree line, he had spotted movement. Without turning around, he gave the signal that he had movement up front, and Leising immediately motioned for the team to turn about and go back to the crater.

Safely inside the bomb crater, Leising called the relay

team and reported the movement to their south. Captain Kay instructed him to move out to the north and continue the mission.

The patrol once again left the crater, moving out the backside and heading in the opposite direction. McBain was bringing up the rear. No sooner had they left the crater than the new point man spotted movement to his immediate front and held up the team.

Once again the patrol returned to the safety of the crater and Leising requested an emergency extraction. They had accomplished their mission, verifying that there was indeed a pisspotful of NVA soldiers on both sides of the ridge.

The insertion aircraft had not yet reached Dak To when Leising's request for extraction was called in. Not waiting for an explanation, the aircraft commander radioed the relay team that he would turn around for them.

At that point, the LRRP patrol saw a number of NVA moving around in the trees on both sides of the crater, less than forty meters away. However, the enemy showed no inclination to open fire. Leising and McBain knew that the NVA were fully aware of their presence and the two team leaders were concerned about how they could get out without having the extraction aircraft shot to pieces.

As the aircraft approached the team's AO, Leising worked out a plan with the commander of the extraction ship. The three aircraft would come in from the west, or downhill side, with the slick in trail, making three gun runs, firing rockets on each run as they disappeared over the crest. On the third run the extraction ship would move up into the number two spot, and the three aircraft would spread the formation out a little more than on the previous runs. As the first gunship approached the crest, firing rockets to keep the enemy's heads down, the slick would slip in to pick up the team as the third aircraft brought up the rear, firing rockets on either side of the crater as the extraction ship lifted out. The ballet made sense to everyone concerned. If only the NVA understood their role in the performance.

The plan worked. On the third rocket run, the extraction slick dropped out of formation and flared to a hover directly over the crater while the four LRRPs climbed out of the hole and leaped aboard the aircraft from both sides. The extraction was completed in record time.

The NVA finally realized what was happening and stood up to open fire as the slick was coming out of the crater. As the four LRRPs and the door gunners returned fire, the second gunship came up behind the slick and joined in the fun, launching a number of rockets at close range into the fully exposed NVA. It was a textbook extraction, and not one of the good guys got hit, except the extraction aircraft, which managed to accumulate a number of perfectly round holes in its tail boom.

The men of the rescued patrol were very grateful for their salvation and highly appreciative of the heroism and high level of ability displayed by the chopper crews who came back to rescue them from a very sticky situation.

It was a custom in the LRRPs to have cold beer waiting for teams returning from a particularly hairy mission. McBain, a devout Mormon, was handed a cold beer on his return from each of the two back-to-back patrols. Although he did not routinely drink alcoholic beverages, he made an exception to the rule on both occasions.

After their return to Dak To, Leising was debriefed

on the latest mission. No member of the two teams was ever informed of any action taken as a result of the intelligence gathered on the missions into what was probably at least a battalion-size or larger NVA base camp.

McBain was put in for a Bronze Star with "V" for the first day's actions, but never received the award. This was typical among the brigade-size LRRP units in Vietnam, whose decorations and promotions had to pass through the greedy and envious hands of a parent unit. In time, Manderfeld and Aoki both became successful LRRP team leaders.

LRRP Detachment,
25th Infantry Division

One of the finest provisional LRRP units in Vietnam was the 25th Infantry Division's Long Range Reconnaissance Patrol detachment based at Cu Chi. Billeted with D Troop, 3/4th Cav, the tiny, platoon-size element did its best to locate and gather intelligence against enemy forces operating within the division's TAOR.

In the middle of November 1966, a warning order came down from Division G-2 requesting a reconnaissance patrol into War Zone C to locate a trail that had been reported by aerial scouts. Once the patrol was able to confirm the existence and location of the trail, it was to set up an OP to establish the nature and composition of the traffic passing over it. It was the kind of mission that LRRPs had been trained for.

The patrol was scheduled to go in barely a week later, and the seven-day mission was assigned to "The Animal Team" led by Sgt. Leo Miller. Miller, from Portland, Oregon, was MACV Recondo School graduate number 13 and the son of a career soldier who was a first sergeant on active duty in Korea while Miller was serving with the LRRPs in Vietnam. Miller had been a fire-team leader with the 4/23d, when he and his entire team had signed up for the LRRPs after division headquarters had posted a directive on the company bulletin board asking for "volunteers for hazardous duty." The affable young NCO immediately began working on growing a handlebar mustache, a luxury not permitted in the line companies. On patrol, Miller always carried his own radio and walked slack for the point man so he could be up front to see what was going on.

The rest of Miller's five-man team consisted of PFC David Stanfield at point; Sp4. Samuel Wright at the number three spot; Sp4. Rick Ellison in the number four slot; and Sp4. Dutchey Lane bringing up the rear.

Stanfield, a native Californian, was not as "cherry" as his low rank indicated. He had signed on for a hitch in the army after serving four years in the U.S. Marine Corps. MACV Recondo School graduate number 11, Stanfield walked point for the team, carrying a five-shot Remington 12-gauge Model 870.

Sam Wright, Recondo School graduate number 25, was a diminutive, redheaded ball of fire from Brunswick, Georgia. Like most guys of small stature in the LRRPs, and specifically "carrot tops," he had a hyper personality and was always spoiling for a fight. Backing down from a good scrap was not part of his game plan, and his warlike disposition carried over into the field, making him especially good in a firefight.

Rick Ellison was a quiet, southern boy from South Carolina. Recondo School graduate number 32, he was the first LRRP assigned to the detachment. Although as experienced as anyone in the unit, he was the newest man in "the Animals," having been bounced around from team to team during the first part of his tour.

"Dutch" Lane, Recondo School graduate number 26, was another southern lad, hailing from Church Hill, Tennessee. A dedicated team member, reliable and aggressive in a firefight, Lane humped both an M-16 and an M-79 grenade launcher along with a double basic load of ammo for each weapon.

No overflight was conducted prior to the patrol, and Miller wasn't able to find out if there was a problem getting aircraft, or if G-2 had wanted to avoid arousing the suspicion of enemy forces in the area. For whatever reason, the team would be going in totally blind. Scheduled to last seven days, the mission would begin with a last-light insertion into a single-ship clearing. The patrol would be dropped off next to a large expanse of dense subtropical forest, then, moving only at night, it would infiltrate into the area where the suspected trail was located.

It was common practice in the 25th Division LRRP detachment for teams to be given several days' notice between warning order and mission launch. That gave the designated patrol members time to avoid taking showers for two or three days before going out in the field. In the rear it was considered "bad form" to wash one's tiger fatigues, instead allowing Mother Nature the privilege of taking care of the task in the bush at her convenience. Since nearly everyone in the detachment was Recondo School–trained, what each man wanted to take out on patrol was left up to him. With the exception of Lane, every man carried a basic load of ammo for his weapon of choice. Each team member also carried a pair of two-gallon water bladders and three or four one-quart canteens. Food consisted of dehydrated Chinese rations—rice and minnows. Since no cooking was allowed in the field, they simply mixed water with the dried rice-and-minnows, then sat back to wait.

Early during the U.S. involvement in Vietnam, the LRRPs had a problem obtaining proper equipment. And even if an LRRP team was fortunate enough to get the right equipment, it was rarely lucky enough to get all it needed. So far, support from the "three-quarter Cav" had been more than adequate. D Troop provided not only slicks and gunships for transportation and air support, it also made available an aero-rifle "Blues" platoon as a ready reaction force should a patrol need reinforcement or rescue in the field. Although they had their own building, the LRRPs lived in the same compound as the Cav troops.

On the day of the mission, one hour before sunset, the five-man LRRP patrol walked one hundred meters down to the D Troop chopper pad to board the waiting slick. Escorted by a single Charlie-model gunship, the insertion aircraft lifted off and flew for thirty minutes out toward War Zone C. As the two aircraft approached the target area at altitude, the slick dropped out of formation and corkscrewed down into the team's AO. While the gunship remained at altitude, the insertion aircraft made three false insertions before flaring to a quick hover no more than five feet above the team's designated LZ. The five LRRPs immediately dropped to the ground from both sides of the aircraft and took up prone firing positions facing away from the chopper. As the aircraft departed the area, the team was up and running for the tree line thirty meters away.

When they reached the protection of the forest, they moved into the single-canopy cover and set up in a tight circular perimeter. While Miller got his bearings, established commo with the LRRP relay team at Tay Ninh, and called in a sitrep, the rest of the team scanned the jungle around them. Finally, satisfied that they had gotten in without being detected, Miller radioed that he was releasing the helicopters.

The patrol lay dog for another ten minutes, waiting until it was fully dark. Then, rising as one and with

Stanfield in the lead, they began moving out to the west. They had covered nearly two klicks when Miller signaled his point man to hold up the team for a short break. While the five men rested, they listened in silence for suspicious sounds. Hearing nothing, ten minutes later they moved on. Every fifteen to twenty minutes they paused for a five-minute break to watch and listen. They repeated this procedure the rest of the night, moving slowly and cautiously through the dense undergrowth, making sure they left no discernible trail.

Just before first light the patrol moved into a particularly thick patch of cover and set up in a circular defensive position. There they spent the entire day resting, watching, and waiting for the security of the night to cover them once again as they neared their objective.

Just after dark, Miller signaled for the team to ruck up and prepare to move out. They patrolled for the remainder of the night, always moving to the west in the general direction of the trail.

They reached their objective just before 0500 hours. The point man had stepped through a thin screen of trees when he saw the edge of a forest to his front. He could barely make out an expanse of open rice paddy just beyond the trees. Suddenly he threw up his left hand to stop the team. In the dim illumination of the false dawn he had spotted movement less than a hundred feet away. There it was, right in front of them, running north to south—the main trail they had been sent to find. And moving about on it were a number of Vietnamese.

The LRRPs remained in place for the next hour and a half, watching in silence as twenty to thirty people carrying boxes and pushing loaded bicycles passed back and forth over the trail. Most of the items they were hauling were stored in canvas and burlap bags.

All the activity to the team's front took place before the sun rose over the horizon. From the dark shadows among the trees, the LRRPs were unable to tell if the people were armed or not, and although they were dressed in native attire, all were men of military age.

Between the brief lulls in activity out on the trail, the team had taken the opportunity to drop in place and crawl carefully into position on line facing the trail. Lying there in the shadows, they continued to observe the enemy activity.

As the sun began to rise across the rice paddy to their front, Stanfield and Miller were huddled in the underbrush putting together a situation report when the rest of the team spotted a stocky, barefoot Vietnamese male wearing only khaki trousers rolled to the knees and carrying a long-handled cane knife. He was moving parallel to the trail, angling to the northwest, and headed directly for the team. He seemed to be alert and fully aware of the patrol's presence in the woods. As the five heavily camouflaged warriors remained frozen in place, the man stopped fifty feet short of their position, right next to a deadfall lying across the center of a small clearing. Five seconds later he began beating his cane knife against the fallen log and yelling at the top of his lungs.

The LRRPs knew immediately that their game was up. The man was without doubt signaling their presence to others nearby.

Miller leaped to his feet and gave the order, "Lane and Stanfield, go get him, he knows we're here."

The two LRRPs left the perimeter and moved toward the clearing, motioning for the man to come over to them. In heavily accented Vietnamese, Stanfield said, *"Lai dai! Lai dai!"* ("Come here! Come here!") Instead of coming peacefully, the man suddenly charged Lane and Stanfield, waving the cane knife wildly over his head.

Stanfield stopped and attempted to shoot the man with his shotgun, but the weapon failed to fire. The screaming Vietnamese was within twenty feet of the two LRRPs and still coming on when Lane stepped up, shoved Stanfield to the side, and buttstroked the man just as he reached them. The Vietnamese hit the ground hard, losing the cane knife in the process. But before the stunned LRRPs could react, he had recovered the cane knife, jumped back to his feet, and charged directly at Lane. Lane opened fire on full automatic at point-blank range. Most of the rounds caught the Vietnamese across the torso, spinning him around and sending him fleeing in the opposite direction.

Lane hit the release button on the side of his weapon, dropping the empty mag at his feet. He was reloading a fresh one when Stanfield opened up on the fleeing man with his shotgun. The badly wounded Vietnamese continued running, then fell when he stumbled into a depression just before reaching the trail. When he got back to his feet, the man's intestines were hanging out. The man staggered a few more steps then fell back to the ground for good.

At that point the team began hearing a lot of movement in the trees southwest of their position. Seconds later a number of armed VC were visible moving about in the woods. Some of the enemy soldiers, shouting instructions back and forth, were less than a hundred meters away and appeared to be forming up into assault positions.

The five LRRPs then did what, at the time, seemed to be a very stupid thing. On Miller's command they grabbed their gear and sprinted through the woods across the trail and out into the rice paddy beyond.

Their only thought was to get out of the heavy cover and get to a point where they could be extracted should the enemy pursue. Besides, if the enemy was present in large numbers, the LRRPs would give a better account of themselves if they could force the NVA to cross open ground to reach them. Miller was on the radio as they ran, calling for an extraction before they had even cleared the trees. Although the LRRPs had heard a great amount of yelling in the background, no one fired on them as they spilled out into the open rice paddy.

The patrol ran a hundred feet into the open field before diving behind the first low paddy dike they came to. The five LRRPs spread out and took up firing positions over the two-foot-high dike facing the trail to their rear. At that point they realized that the woods formed an open horseshoe around the paddy, flanking the team on both sides. Behind them the paddy opened up into more of the same.

By that time the LRRPs were beginning to take heavy small-arms fire from well back in the trees. And they could occasionally spot what they believed to be NVA soldiers shouting and maneuvering among the shadows in the forest.

Miller once again got through to the x-ray team and repeated his request for an immediate emergency extraction. He was told that all available choppers were being used in a combat assault and it would take at least forty-five minutes to get aircraft out to them. Even if the assault were to be called off, it would still take forty minutes for the ships to reach them.

Miller continued to ask for help of any kind and was informed that the only support available at the time was artillery. He quickly switched to the arty frequency and requested fire from the nearest 105mm battery.

By that time the enemy troops had moved up to the

edge of the woods and were placing accurate fire on the team. The LRRPs began returning fire, pinning down the NVA in the trees. Lane had not yet brought his grenade launcher into play. As the enemy had not yet made any attempt to flank the team, he was saving the blooper for that event.

As the artillery fire began impacting in the wood line, Miller asked for more arty and got a 155mm battery mounted on a U.S. Navy barge anchored out in the Saigon River. Soon the heavier, more powerful rounds were walking back and forth among the trees. Unfortunately the artillery appeared to have little effect on the NVA hidden there.

The artillery barrage continued for thirty or forty minutes before Miller called for a cease-fire to assess the damage. By then the patrol was running low on ammo. Help had to arrive soon if they were to be saved.

Suddenly the LRRPs began taking 61mm mortar fire that appeared to be coming from a tiny wooded area a thousand meters to the team's rear, across the open end of the rice paddy. The small thicket of single-canopy trees and thick underbrush lay within two hundred feet of the main forest south of the team. The initial rounds slammed into the ground right among the LRRPs. One of the deadly bomblets landed within a foot of Lane's position, splashing mud all over him. Fortunately for the LRRPs, none of the rounds exploded on impact, probably because of the soft mud beneath the stagnant water covering the rice paddy.

Lane shouted that they were being bracketed as more rounds continued to fall among their positions. Soon numerous tail fins were sticking up out of the mud and water around them, and other rounds were still coming.

Miller shouted for the team to begin leapfrogging to the rear, angling away from the wooded island where the mortars were being fired. He hoped that moving the team on a diagonal across the open terrain would confound the accuracy of the NVA mortar team.

From time to time during the course of the battle the LRRPs took advantage of the incoming artillery rounds to pull farther back into the open paddy, leapfrogging from dike to dike. No one had yet been hit, but the enemy fire intensified every time a LRRP exposed himself.

Shortly afterwards, Ellison screamed in pain as a rifle grenade or mortar round exploded nearby, peeling off half his face and perforating his chest and right arm with shrapnel. The wounded LRRP lay back against the berm and continued screaming until Lane moved over to check him out. As Lane began to apply a pressure dressing over Ellison's mangled face, the wounded man asked him, "Am I all fucked up?"

Lane quickly said, "No, you'll be okay."

Ellison responded, "Well, then why do I look this way?"

It was only then that Lane realized that one of Ellison's eyeballs had been blown out of its socket and was looking back at him. The wounded man could actually see the horrible damage done to his face. Lane didn't answer as he struggled to get the dressing over the wound. When the displaced eye was finally covered, Ellison began to calm down. Wright moved over to Ellison's position to cover him while Lane slid back to where he'd been before going to Ellison's aid. For the first time he began dropping M-79 high-explosive rounds into the trees where the enemy fire seemed heaviest.

Wright's M-16 kept jamming when he attempted to return fire, so he used Ellison's weapon.

At that point Miller was back on the horn with the x-ray team asking for the extraction ships. He told the relay team that the LRRPs were taking heavy mortar fire, were very low on ammo, were about to be overrun, and had a man badly wounded. Miller warned them that they couldn't hang on much longer.

The relay team radioed back and told the LRRPs to remain calm, and promised that help was on the way. By then the battle had been going on for forty-five or fifty minutes.

The LRRPs had an emergency radio callsign at their disposal to be used only in the most extreme situations. Miller reasoned that his team was at that moment in one of those extreme situations. Without hesitating he switched to the emergency frequency and began calling, "Red Arrow, Red Arrow. Request air support."

Within two minutes the team had an O-1 Bird Dog on station. The Bird Dog pilot told Miller that he had two flights of fast movers on the way and asked him to identify his targets. The Bird Dog pilot could see the team lying out in the open. Miller quickly gave him azimuths and distances to the targets he wanted hit, and within minutes two flights of F-4 Phantoms were on station.

As the LRRPs watched in fascination, the Bird Dog came in low and marked the targets with smoke rockets. As the single-engine aircraft clawed for blue sky, the four Phantoms rolled in on the woods to their front. The forest seemed to lift from the ground as the high-drag ordnance began exploding.

After the four jet fighter-bombers had depleted their ordnance, they climbed back to altitude and returned to base. Seconds later Puff the Magic Dragon arrived on station. Its deadly miniguns were soon turning damaged forest into toothpicks.

It wasn't long before the LRRPs heard the unmistakable *whop . . . whop . . . whop* sounds of approaching

Hueys in the distance. All but Ellison turned to see a flight of five Huey slicks and a pair of gunships coming across the open terrain behind them. The two gunships escorting the slicks broke off and began plastering the thicket concealing the mortars with 2.75-inch rockets as the Hueys circled. Immediately the mortars ceased firing.

Puff was still producing pulp in the woods to the team's front as the Hueys, bearing an aero-rifle platoon, circled five hundred meters away. Finally a single Huey detached itself from the flight and came in to touch down thirty meters behind the trapped team. Stanfield and Lane quickly grabbed Ellison and helped him into the chopper. Miller and Wright remained behind to cover them as they struggled toward the waiting slick. But by that time enemy fire from back in the trees had all but ceased.

After everyone was safely aboard, the Huey retraced its flight path back toward Cu Chi, followed by the rest of the aircraft.

The extraction ship set down at Division Surg to drop off Ellison. Although the LRRPs didn't think his wounds were life threatening, they would later discover that Ellison had taken a lot of shrapnel they were not aware of. As their wounded comrade was being wheeled into triage, the rest of the team began the long walk down to G-2 to be debriefed.

The debriefing was like all debriefings, long and, seemingly, pointless. The intelligence major in charge immediately challenged the team's report, demanding proof that they saw what they reported seeing. They could only look at one another with smirks of indignation all over their filthy faces. Their attitude was typical of LRRPs all over the war zone: no one ever seemed to believe them so they didn't really give a rat's ass what this pompous REMF officer said. They only knew that they had shot up a hell of a lot of ammo and had brought back a badly wounded buddy. It must have been ghosts they had fought out there in the trees. The intel major, safe in the rear in his starched fatigues and smelling of soap and cologne, could believe whatever he wanted.

Disgusted but not disgruntled, the four LRRPs slipped out of the TOC and returned to their compound. Later that day, after refueling and waiting for the smoke of battle to clear away, the Bird Dog pilot flew back over the scene of the conflict. He was able to confirm at least 245 enemy KIA/WIA visible on the field of battle. He also spotted a large number of enemy soldiers moving among the trees, hauling off their dead and wounded. He immediately summoned another flight of fast movers to finish the job. After the second round of air strikes, the pilot reported an additional 165 enemy KIA lying broken and mangled among the trees.

Word soon came down from G-2 to the LRRP compound that the team had likely stumbled into the middle of a full battalion of well-equipped, well-armed NVA. No accompanying apology came from the G-2 major who had doubted them earlier.

All members of the team received Army Commendation medals with "V" device after their eventual return to CONUS (Continental United States). It seemed that the medals had been awarded as an afterthought. Ellison received a Purple Heart in addition to his ARCOM. Scarred but still an LRRP, the wounded GI returned to the detachment a few weeks later. He never went out in the field again.

LRRP Detachment,
1st Cavalry Division

Although the primary mission of U.S. long range reconnaissance patrols was intelligence gathering, they had to be adaptable to unexpected situations. This is aptly demonstrated in the story of a 1st Cavalry Division long range reconnaissance patrol in the fall of 1967.

Sergeant Ron Holte's Team One-Foxtrot received a warning order on 4 November for a mission into the Crow's Foot area of II Corps Tactical Zone. The five-day mission was scheduled to go in the following day. The overflight on the afternoon of the fourth with his ATL and Captain Udder, the C&C, revealed that Holte's recon zone would be a long, dominant ridgeline overlooking the Soui Ca river valley from the east. There was a lot of scattered brush and single-canopy vegetation down in the fertile valley, and the ground cover up higher on the ridgelines ran from spotty single-canopy on the slopes to dense single-canopy just off the ridge crests.

Intel reports indicated that except for an NVA hospital complex somewhere up in the hills, the area was most likely only a transit point for NVA troops coming into the area from across the border. G-2 wanted Holte and his teammates to be on the lookout for NVA units infiltrating through the area.

The weather promised to be warm and clear during

the five-day mission. Of course, under those conditions it would be difficult to infiltrate directly into the valley without being detected. So Holte selected a small clearing high on the reverse slope of the ridgeline, outside his patrol box. Although it was the only LZ on that side of the ridge, Holte felt that the ridge crest running above them would prevent the NVA down in the Soui Ca valley, on the other side, from observing or hearing the insertion. Once on the ground, the LRRPs would move up over the top of the ridge and drop down the reverse slope to set up an OP overlooking the wide, open valley. Five days later, if everything went as planned, they would climb back up to the ridge crest and move north 250 meters to a narrow clearing to be extracted.

It was not Holte's usual recon team, and that caused him some concern. Indeed, both his assistant team leader and his point man were on temporary assignment, for training, from Company E, 3d Battalion, 506th Infantry, 101st Airborne Division. The newly arrived 3d of the 506th had recently taken over the Screaming Eagle 1st Brigade area of operations around Phan Thiet, while the 1st Brigade went to rejoin the division for the first time in over two years. The 3d of the 506th would go on to earn the name of "The Bastard Battalion" of the 101st, operating independently of the division for the next three years.

Holte's patrol flew out of LZ Uplift on the evening of the fifth in preparation for a last-light insertion. There was no time for the usual false insertions. The single slick came in low and hovered briefly as the five members of the patrol went out on the downhill side of the helicopter, dropping ten to twelve feet into three-foot-high kunai grass. As the LRRPs began to climb uphill, the aircraft flew north until it disappeared around the flank of the mountain.

The team continued moving west another fifty meters until Holte signaled the point man to locate decent cover where the team could go to ground and establish commo. They quickly set up a security zone in the underbrush, where they "lay dog" for five to ten minutes. Holte, carrying his own radio, established good commo with the radio relay team and called in a negative sitrep. The patrol was still 150 meters from the crest at that time, and it was beginning to grow late in the day. They were on the western slope of the ridge already deeply hidden in the evening shadows.

Holte gave the signal to move out, had the point man take them another fifty meters up the slope, and halted the team to listen once again. He waited until dark to move them the final hundred meters to the crest.

Once at the crest the LRRPs established a circular perimeter among a cluster of large boulders. In spite of the heavy cover, Holte didn't like setting up in the rocks at all. They were perched so high above the valley they couldn't view it without exposing themselves. Defensively, a grenade battle among the boulders would be difficult to survive, even for the winners. Holte instructed his teammates to keep their claymores in close, plotted a number of Delta Tangos (defensive targets), then set up a security watch, one man on for one hour at a time. Fortunately the night was uneventful.

At first light on the morning of the second day, Holte called in a negative sitrep. Commo was excellent. He told his men to go ahead and eat in shifts, then be prepared to move out at 0800 hours. A short time later the five LRRPs were angling down the slope, moving almost three hundred meters to the east/northeast. They were inside single-canopy jungle for 250 or 300 meters when they suddenly broke out into grass and brush. Scouting around for a suitable OP, Holte discovered a small knoll covered in ten-foot-tall elephant grass. Crawling into it on their hands and knees, the team quickly packed down a suitable sleeping area in the middle, then tunneled back through the grass to an observation point out on the edge of the knoll, overlooking the valley four hundred to six hundred meters below. As a precaution they had tied the grass back together over the top of the observation point so no one in the valley below would be able to spot an opening in the otherwise unbroken screen of elephant grass.

The Soui Ca was a huge valley, six klicks long and four klicks out to the river. Holte couldn't see beyond the river, which was pretty straight at that point. The valley side began to meander somewhat toward the mouth of the river. The nearest bank was choked with heavy vegetation, except for three areas where it thinned along the river. The low, level terrain between the river and the base of the ridgeline was a mixture of thickets, patches of woods, and grass-covered clearings. No roads or trails were visible from the knoll. To the southeast, the valley thinned out to where the cover and concealment were, at best, spotty.

The patrol had a lot of ground to observe, but Holte and his teammates had come prepared. Besides the starlight scope they had brought along, Holte was carrying 10×50-power binoculars and his ATL had a set of 6×30s. The two men would take turns crawling out to the observation point to watch the valley.

It was nearly 1000 hours that morning when Holte came off the first one-hour watch. He was back inside the perimeter when the team medic, Sp4. Ken White, crawled back and reported that the ATL had just spotted some NVA.

"Where?" Holte whispered. Expecting the enemy to be behind them, he was surprised when White told him

that they were down in the valley. Holte quickly moved
up through the passageway in the grass to where the
ATL lay glassing the valley below. Dropping down beside him, Holte took the binoculars. The NVA were
hard to miss, moving in a long column along the near
side of the river. Incredibly, Holte could see that the column was strung out over nearly three full klicks running
back along the river. The NVA soldiers were spread out
at five-meter intervals, trotting along at a comfortable
pace, seemingly unaware that they were being observed.
In the three thinned-out areas along the riverbank to
his front, Holte counted seventy-six NVA regulars moving quickly along, single file. He estimated that the
width of the three openings was no more than a third of
a kilometer long. When Holte looked back to the north
he could not see the end of the enemy column. He immediately calculated that at least an NVA regiment was
moving through the valley. The enemy soldiers were
wearing khaki uniforms and pith helmets, and each carried a heavy rucksack on his back. Nearly every man
had a firearm, yet there did not seem to be any crew-
served weapons like machine guns and mortars. At their
nearest point the NVA were a full klick away, moving
north to south.

Holte grabbed the radio and reported the situation to
his TOC back at LZ Uplift. The voice on the other end
of the line expressed skepticism at the team leader's observations.

Holte didn't have time to play Twenty Questions with
some Doubting Thomas at the rear. It was 1005 hours
when Holte put the TOC on hold, picked out a grid coordinate right in the middle of the NVA column, and
called the FDO (Fire Direction Officer) at the 8-inch
howitzer battery on LZ English. He quickly gave the
grid coordinates for his selected target and requested a

full battery of HE on the deck. After receiving confirmation for the fire mission, he picked up the team's other radio, called the 155mm battery at LZ Uplift, and gave them the same information. Then with Holte adjusting the 8-inch guns and his ATL handling the 155s, they called for the first rounds. It was 1013 hours.

At 1015 the first salvo came in and exploded in the middle of the enemy column, causing a number of casualties and throwing the enemy soldiers into confusion. Holte immediately began adjusting the 8-inch rounds along the river back toward the head of the column while his ATL worked the 155mm rounds downstream in the opposite direction. As the exploding shells marched steadily away from each other, they left dead and dying NVA soldiers littering the ground in their wake. The enemy column quickly broke up and disappeared into the heavy cover along the river, looking very much like ants abandoning a flooded anthill.

Satisfied, Holte began calling over the air, "Dark Marauder Six-Five, Dark Marauder Six-Five, this is Dark Marauder One-Foxtrot . . . something big is coming down . . . something big is coming down . . . something big is coming down. They're all over down there. We need to get a reaction force out here."

The TOC quickly replied, "Dark Marauder One-Foxtrot, this is Dark Marauder Six-Five, too risky, too risky, over."

Holte's tone of voice failed to hide his frustration and anger. "Dark Marauder Six-Five, this is Dark Marauder One-Foxtrot. We can't let them get away. They'll hurt GIs down the road."

The answer came quickly. "Dark Marauder One-Foxtrot, this is Dark Marauder Six-Five. Negative. Out."

Holte knew then that they were on their own. He

immediately went back to adjusting artillery fire on small groups of enemy soldiers attempting to get away from the river. The sounds of the huge 8-inch rounds steamrolling overhead quickly reminded him that his team was directly on the gun-target line from LZ English. One mistake in his adjustments or one short round and they would all be history.

The fire mission went on for several hours until Holte had to stop and take a break. After telling his ATL to keep working out the artillery, he crawled back inside the team's perimeter for a few moments' rest.

For the rest of the day Holte and his ATL took turns adjusting artillery onto every NVA element they spotted moving on the valley floor. Occasionally they gave the overworked "redlegs" a break and called in ARA gunships to take up the slack. There were still plenty of targets to go around for everyone. Later a flight of U.S. Air Force F-4 Phantoms out of Da Nang arrived on the scene. They were returning from an aborted air strike and had some live bombs they didn't want to land with. Holte thanked them and assigned them some targets.

At 1600 hours Holte was once again on the radio, adjusting artillery. Realizing that the remaining enemy soldiers were now avoiding moving about in the open, especially in large numbers, he told his ATL to call for more ARA gunships because the helicopters could work over the killing ground and spot NVA soldiers hidden in the vegetation down in the valley.

At 1615 hours two Huey gunships came in from the north and radioed the LRRPs that they were on station. As they approached the valley they called in their position to Holte, who immediately canceled the artillery fire missions he had going.

While Holte watched the two Hueys coming in over

the target area, a salvo of large shells passed through the air dangerously close to the aircraft.

Suddenly the pilot screamed over the radio, "Christ, they almost shot us out of the sky! What the hell are they doing?" The pilots were mad as hell. Holte, also outraged by the potentially deadly error, broke in over the radio, admonished the artillery FDO for his carelessness, and firmly reminded the man that *he* was calling the fire mission, not the FDO. Holte again demanded an immediate cease-fire. This time the FDO complied, but quickly added, "After they're done, give us another target."

Holte reminded him that they had already shot up half the valley, but the artillery officer came back, "Give us a target when they're done; we still have plenty of ammo." Holte agreed. After all, there were still plenty of live NVA in the valley.

The ARA gunships continued circling the valley like deadly bees, ready to sting anything that moved down below. When they finally ran out of visual targets, they began destroying areas that had enough cover to hide one or more enemy soldiers.

At 1700 hours the ARA aircraft had expended their ordance and radioed Holte that they were returning to base. Holte thanked them and called the artillery FDO and told him he was back in business again. Since there were no longer any visible targets, and there hadn't been any in quite awhile, Holte called for intermittent H&I (harassment and interdiction) fire up and down the target area.

It was growing late in the day, and for the first time Holte realized that his patrol was in great danger. Surely the enemy commanders were aware that the devastating attacks had not been mere acts of God. It didn't take a

Southeast Asian rocket scientist to realize that the
deadly dance in which they had been reluctant partici-
pants was choreographed by someone with a view of
the entire valley. Only a few locations overlooked the
valley where such a masterpiece of destruction could
have been orchestrated. Holte could only hope and pray
that the enemy was so preoccupied tending to the dead
and wounded that they had not yet had time to organize a search for the long-range patrol that had turned
their world to shit.

At 1830 hours Holte called the FDO for a final cease-
fire. Except for the smoke and dust hanging in the air,
the valley below was quiet. While the LRRP team
leader plotted a number of 155mm artillery concentrations closer to the team's perimeter, he told his men to
eat while they could; there might not be time later. With
that task completed, he plotted a second ring of 8-inch
artillery fire farther out around their perimeter. With
darkness falling there was nothing else the LRRPs
could do but wait for whatever was going to come.

Just before midnight, White, the team medic, was on
guard with the starlight scope when he spotted an NVA
force of up to two hundred men massing about a thousand meters north of the LRRPs' perimeter. However,
they quickly disappeared behind a terrain feature before
Holte could get to the radio to adjust artillery fire on
them. Believing that the enemy was preparing to go on
line and sweep the face of the mountain, everyone remained nervous and jittery for the rest of the night.

From the overflight and by studying his map, Holte
knew there were only five possible observation points
situated around the valley. He also knew that any enemy
officer worth his sauce would realize the same thing.
Therefore, it wouldn't take them long to figure out just
where the LRRP team was located. The realization

made for a very anxious night. Fortunately, it remained uneventful.

At first light on the third day of the mission the team ate a quick breakfast while Holte called in the first sitrep of the day. He reported that everything was quiet. Added to the smoke and dust from the previous day's work, a dense ground fog helped cloak the valley below in a thick, opaque blanket. There was not a breath of movement in the air. A heavy dew had collected on the ground around the patrol's position in the grass and down the slope toward the valley.

Holte was up in the OP watching the ground fog, anxious for it to lift out of the valley. Not being able to see if anything was going on down there greatly concerned him. At 0730 hours three VC in black pajamas materialized out of the fog directly below the team and headed straight up the slope for the knoll. They were less than a half-klick away. When they finally reached the heavier vegetation three hundred to four hundred meters below the LRRPs' OP, they simply disappeared from view.

However, while Holte had been watching the enemy soldiers approaching, he had whispered for his assistant team leader to radio the TOC for gunships. They arrived on station just minutes after the three VC disappeared into the thick cover below them.

By then the fog was getting patchy. The two Huey gunships, remaining close to the ground, flew up the valley and headed straight for the team's OP. They passed directly overhead to confirm the patrol's location as Holte flashed them with his signal mirror. Once they had the patrol pinpointed, the team leader gave the gunships an azimuth and a distance to the last location of the three VC.

The gunships swung slowly around over the valley

and made a second low-altitude pass, coming up the slope from below. The pilots radioed that they couldn't see any VC, but they could make out their tracks in the dew-covered grass.

As the gunships came around from the east for a third pass, Holte became concerned that the choppers might flush the VC into the team. His concerns became real when the two gunships began firing their M-60 machine guns to flush out the VC. As the LRRP team leader anxiously scanned the slope below the team's OP, the Hueys worked over every likely piece of cover below them. Finally the choppers flew away from the area and disappeared over the top of the ridge.

At 1005, Holte moved back up into the OP to take another thorough look around the base of the knoll to check for enemy activity. He quickly spotted a column of NVA troops trotting around the base of the knoll from east to west. Moving north up the valley, they seemed intent on skirting the knoll and trying to reach the other side. There were six groups of four NVA in the column, each group carrying a loaded stretcher. The stretchers were camouflaged with brush as were the NVA bearers. They were wearing helmets and heavy rucksacks covered with netting into which branches and leafy vegetation had been inserted. They quickly moved into a large wooded lot approximately fifty meters in diameter located just below and slightly to the right of the patrol's OP and only four hundred meters away.

At 1010, Holte radioed the TOC to report the sighting, then got on the artillery radio to the 8-inch battery at LZ English and told them he had a target. He warned them to prepare for a fire mission. Holte then computed an eight-digit coordinate on the thicket and called it in, asking for high-angle VT (variable time) on the target.

At first the FDO refused to fire the mission, wanting

to open instead with a marker round. Holte flatly refused and told him that he didn't want to alert the enemy that they were a target. Holte requested HE for a marker round, to be followed immediately by a fire for effect. But once again the FDO refused, stating that it was far too dangerous. The FDO then came back on the net recommending WP. This time Holte reluctantly agreed. He didn't have time to argue. It was now 1015.

As the "Willy Pete" round exploded among the trees in the wood lot, Holte quickly called for HE to follow, "fire for effect." As he watched through his binoculars for the rounds to arrive, not one NVA attempted to escape from the tree line. The first full volley screamed overhead and exploded dead in the middle of the wood lot. Holte and his ATL lay there intently watching the target area for the next thirty minutes but saw nothing moving.

Even though things had once again quieted down, Ron Holte knew that the surviving NVA would sooner or later begin searching the high ground for the hidden recon team, and a deadly game of cat and mouse would ensue.

At 1200 hours, Holte told the ATL to take up a position with his binoculars to watch the patrol's back door up along the crest of the ridge. He told the rest of his teammates to provide 360-degree security from that point on. He reasoned that the enemy would probably attempt to get someone on the high ground behind the team, whose only mission would be to visually search for the American recon patrol. It would probably be no more than one or two men. When they spotted the LRRPs they would mark their position and go for help. Then when the main unit arrived on the scene, they would sweep down on the LRRPs from above. It was a discomforting thought, but the move made tactical sense. It was what *he* would do if he were the enemy commander.

At 1215 hours Holte once again spotted movement down along the river. He quickly called FAC and brought in another flight of F-4 Phantoms to deal with the problem. The FAC made a single pass and marked the target with a white phosphorous rocket, then climbed out of the valley to let the fast-burners do their thing.

The first fighter-bomber came down from altitude and dropped his five-hundred-pound iron bomb (HE) right on the money. As the pilot pulled out of his dive he did a victory roll, then climbed for altitude. The flight of two jets made three more runs, dropping a five-hundred-pounder each time. The enemy movement ceased immediately after the air strikes.

However, it wasn't long before Holte spotted more movement down below, and this time he called in a pair of ARA gunships to deal with the situation. After the Hueys had expended their ordnance on the target, things once more quieted down.

At 1500 hours, Holte's assistant team leader spotted three or four NVA running away from the river about a mile and a half from the OP. They were moving to the east/southeast and heading for the foothills at the base of the ridge. Holte called in artillery, but by the time it arrived the enemy soldiers had made it to cover and gotten away clean.

As soon as the artillery stopped, a single NVA appeared in the brush below the knoll, moving from cover to cover and heading east. He was traveling across Holte's front and going right to left. Holte refrained from calling in artillery because he was fascinated by the individual. The NVA appeared to be shell-shocked. When the man reached a point directly in front of Holte about a mile and a half from the river and still a mile from the base of the ridge, he suddenly disappeared into brushy thicket. Holte watched the thicket for a few minutes until the man finally came back out into the open, but without his weapon, ruck, and helmet. Standing there as if to get his bearings, he suddenly turned and looked straight up at the team's OP, then put his hands above his head. While Holte watched in amazement, the NVA soldier started running directly toward the OP. After about fifty meters he turned to the east and ran for the base of the mountains a mile away. Holte had to smile to himself. The guy had guts! He could still terminate the enemy soldier; the man still had an open mile to cross to reach safety. But Holte couldn't bring himself to call in a fire mission or direct the gunships on him. The guy had guts. He had developed a plan and was, at that moment, executing it. He deserved to survive. Holte decided to let him go.

After a few minutes Holte got on the radio and reported what had just transpired. The CO's radio operator misunderstood the transmission and asked if Holte wanted a lift ship to come out and pick up the NVA soldier. Holte replied, "No!" It would take a helicopter twelve minutes to reach the area and by then the enemy soldier would have already made it into the foothills at the base of the ridgeline. Not even LBJ could cover a mile in twelve minutes.

Holte was still grinning in smug admiration as he watched the NVA soldier make the safety of the trees at the bottom of the ridgeline. Somehow it felt good to let an enemy live.

A short time later, after things had once again quieted down, Holte left the OP unattended and pulled back for a quick bite to eat. It was his third day in the OP, and even though he had been switching back and forth with his ATL, the stress was beginning to get to him.

Only a few minutes had passed before Doc White crawled over to Holte and whispered in his ear, "Gook!"

Holte looked up and asked, "Where?"

The team medic silently motioned for Holte to follow him in a low crawl back to where the assistant team leader was kneeling in the grass, scoping out the ridgeline to the rear of the patrol.

When he got there the ATL told Holte to glass the ridgeline above them, scanning to the right until he reached a particular tree. Holte soon spotted a single VC dressed in black pajamas. The man was about 250 meters above them to the east/southeast, leaning against a tree. He was looking directly at the OP through a set of binoculars. The VC scout had nothing else with him but a carbine slung over his shoulder and a bandolier of magazines. Noticing that his ATL had drawn a bead on the enemy soldier, Holte whispered to him not to shoot. It was already too late; the enemy soldier had spotted them. It was 1615 hours.

Holte quickly returned to his radio in the center of the perimeter and called the TOC to report the incident. Minutes later he was informed by Doc White that the VC scout had disappeared into the trees. Holte had a pretty good idea where the guy was heading. Getting back to the radio, he called the TOC and requested an immediate extraction. But the TOC failed to confirm his request.

Holte didn't have time to play games. Without taking the time to sterilize their OP and hide site, he ordered his teammates to break camp. He then quickly pulled his team back three hundred meters, up into the boulders where the patrol had spent its first night on the ground. While his teammates set up perimeter security, he once again called for an immediate extraction. Again there was no confirmation from the rear. It was pretty clear that Major Gooding, the LRRP company commander, wanted Holte's patrol to remain in the bush another night.

Holte was irate at this obvious lack of concern for the safety of his team. The extraction should have been his call, not the major's, but he was being preempted by his "higher," who was not present on the ground to assess the danger. Holte couldn't believe the decision had been made to leave them in. It served no logical purpose to keep the patrol on the ground any longer. The LRRPs had managed to pull off a very successful mission. But after being compromised, their effectiveness on the ground had come to an end. Meaning every bit of disrespect, he angrily let his CO know exactly how he felt, then just as quickly dropped the subject. Venting his anger and frustration over a bad call by his commanding officer would not get his team out of trouble.

The team's designated PZ (pick-up zone) was only 250 meters down the crest of the ridge to the north, where from a very narrow stretch of ridge top, it looked like five men could hold off an army.

At 1750 hours Holte reported his intent to move down to the narrow part of the ridge to set up a defensive perimeter. Without waiting for a yea or a nay, he sent his point man ahead as they dropped out of the boulders and slipped down the crest of the ridge.

When they reached the spot a half hour later, they found that they couldn't have designed a better site to defend. An area of dense cover fifteen meters in diameter sat right on top of the narrow crest. Along the edge of the ridge someone had dug a series of five foxholes out in the open. The holes were three feet deep, just right for protected fighting positions. Holte couldn't help but wonder what they had been used for—possibly a radio relay site or something similar. The flanks were steep bluffs, impossible to climb. The only way a determined enemy force could reach them would be from the direction of the boulders up the ridge the LRRPs had just vacated.

In the growing dusk the LRRPs quickly set out their claymores while Holte called in a number of artillery preplots on the first night's NDP up the crest in the rocks and along both flanks of the ridge. They spent a strangely quiet evening on top of the narrow crest, hearing nothing from the enemy during the night.

In the morning the team went out to check their claymores to make sure they had not been tampered with in the darkness. When they returned to the perimeter they ate chow while Holte called in a sitrep, then once again requested an extraction.

The TOC radioed back that Holte was to move his patrol back up to the rocks at the higher elevation on the ridge, cross to where they had spotted the VC watching them the day before, make their way down past their old OP, then drop down to where the team had last spotted the NVA stretcher bearers and check to see if an underground hospital was there.

Holte flatly refused, stating that doing this assignment would be to commit suicide. He pointed out that they would be right in the middle of the NVA and unable to return to the high ground if they were compromised. Nothing else was said.

At 0930 the choppers arrived over the valley. The four helicopters swooped down to the narrow spot on the ridgeline to pluck the team off the crest. Captain Udder was aboard the C&C slick, controlling the extraction.

Holte popped a yellow smoke grenade as the aircraft

approached. The two ARA gunships orbited the PZ but held their fire. As the lift ship approached the PZ, the team blew its claymores in place and fired half their magazines down the sides of the ridge. Then the Huey was upon them.

The team landed at LZ Uplift and went through a lengthy debriefing conducted by Captain Udder. The only thing good about the debriefing was that Major Gooding was not present.

When the debriefing had ended and the rest of his teammates were headed for the showers, Captain Udder took the LRRP team leader to the side and asked, "Sergeant Holte, you really didn't see all that out there, did you?"

The officer was red in the face from embarrassment, and Holte knew immediately that the question hadn't come from the junior officer. It was more of Major Gooding's poor leadership.

Holte stood there looking at Captain Udder for a moment, wondering what the hell was going on. He could only stare at the officer in disbelief. After deliberating for a moment, he finally muttered a reply. "Sir, maybe I didn't see what I saw, but I certainly won't tell my men that they didn't see what they saw."

Captain Udder seemed embarrassed by the situation and didn't respond to the team leader's statement. Satisfied that he had said and done all he could, Sergeant Holte snapped the officer a sharp salute, pivoted, and walked out of the tent.

Holte showered, changed clothes, and then lay back on his cot, reflecting on the events of the mission, and its aftermath. For Sergeant Ron Holte, things would never be the same.

Company L, 75th Infantry (Ranger), 101st Airborne Division

The initial ravages of the Tet Offensive had finally been overcome by U.S. and allied forces throughout South Vietnam by the second day of February 1968. However, North Vietnamese Army regulars were still holding out inside the fortified city of Hue, located along the coast in central I Corps. They remained in control of the city in spite of concentrated efforts by overpowering American forces to dislodge them. Not until the twenty-fifth of the month were they finally driven away. Suffering over five thousand casualties at the hands of attacking U.S. Marines and several brigades of U.S. Army paratroopers and cavalrymen encircling the city and patrolling the surrounding countryside, the defeated NVA survivors finally withdrew across the rolling piedmont west of Hue and disappeared into the densely forested mountains of the Annamite Cordillera. The high, rugged peaks, extending all the way to the Laotian border, provided a safe haven for the enemy troops as they licked their wounds and rebuilt their shattered forces. A year later they were as strong as ever and once again threatening the territory around the ancient imperial city of Hue. The 101st Airborne Division, deployed throughout the area previously held by the 1st Marine Division, was assigned the unenviable tasks of securing the area and eliminating the threat.

Into that nearly impassable terrain the Screaming Eagles began sending out five- and six-man long-range patrols from its reconnaissance element, L Company, 75th Infantry (Ranger), to monitor high-speed trails, gather intelligence on enemy units using them, and locate the numerous fortified NVA base camps and staging areas in and around the A Shau Valley. It was not a job for the faint of heart.

Rugged mountains two to three thousand feet high, thickly covered in double- and triple-canopy vegetation, their peaks often hidden among the clouds, had swallowed up entire infantry companies during previous operations. Small successes had usually come at a high price. But the enemy had to be found and confronted. Aerial reconnaissance flights over the area were seldom able to locate the well-camouflaged and heavily protected enemy encampments, making ground surveillance by the small, silent, long-range patrols a necessary fact of life.

In August 1969, during the final month of unmercifully dry and arid heat before the annual monsoon rains, Lima Company's commanding officer, Capt. Robert Guy, made the tough decision to deploy as many of his patrols in the field as possible to keep infiltrating NVA units off balance. Division G-2 had put out the word that while the weather was good, the enemy would be busy moving 122mm rockets, mortars, and supplies up into the "Rocket Belt" west of Hue, Phu Bai, and the division's forward combat base at Camp Eagle. Those areas, secured by the 101st Airborne Division, had been pounded frequently during the previous monsoon season. If the Ranger

commanding officer could help it, 1969 was not going
to be a repeat performance.

It was early in August when Staff Sergeant John
Luchow received a warning order to prepare his team
for a five-day reconnaissance patrol into an area tradi-
tionally known as the "Game Preserve." The Rangers
and their predecessors from Company F, 58th Infantry
(LRP), called it that because of the large number of
successful combat patrols conducted into the area. The
hunting was always good in the Game Preserve. Now it
was Luchow's turn to have a go at it.

Temporarily without a full team of his own, Luchow
was ordered to select any Ranger he needed from the
men remaining in the company area. He quickly chose
two men, Sgt. Larry Saenz and PFC Ken Fagel, both
from S.Sgt. Robert Tingley's team. Tingley was away in
Hawaii on R&R and would not be back for a week so
his team was nonoperational. Luchow assigned Saenz,
a veteran LRRP with a lot of combat experience, as his
ATL and point man, and Fagel, a new man who had
shown a lot of promise, as the junior RTO walking in
the fourth spot on the patrol. Specialist Four Leslie,
Luchow's senior RTO, would carry the primary radio
and walk the third slot behind the team leader, while
Sp4. Dave Weeks manned his usual spot at the rear of
the patrol. All in all it was a team that Luchow felt good
about taking into the Game Preserve.

The next day Luchow and Saenz departed the Ranger
helipad in an unescorted Huey slick to overfly the
team's recon zone (RZ). As the helicopter made a high-
altitude pass over the team's area of operations, the two
Rangers quickly selected a likely spot in the southwest
corner of the RZ to serve as the primary LZ. The site
was a small clearing nestled in the floor of a wide valley.
No sooner had they marked their selection with grease

pencils on the acetate covers of their maps than they spotted movement down in the clearing. Circling around for a better look, they quickly discovered that the movement was a large number of NVA troops jogging along a well-hidden high-speed trail that passed through the edge of the clearing.

The helicopter immediately returned to base where, after discussing the situation with Captain Guy, the two Rangers decided to select a new primary LZ, preferably one as far away from the initial landing zone as possible. The premission briefing at G-2 had indicated the likelihood of heavy enemy foot traffic through the area, a fact confirmed by this sighting of NVA soldiers at the primary LZ.

During the second overflight, Staff Sergeant Luchow quickly settled on a small clearing located east of the initial LZ at the opposite corner of the AO. Luchow estimated that it would take the LRRPs at least two full days to hump into their target area, but he knew that it was better to cover some ground and get in unobserved than be set down in the middle of a hostile welcoming party. Fully satisfied that they had selected an LZ that would give them a good chance for a successful infiltration, the two men rejoined their teammates and began making final preparations for the insertion, scheduled for 0900 hours the next morning.

But there were still some bugs in the works. Later that evening, without any explanation, the patrol was told that there was a good possibility the mission would be scrubbed before morning.

With more anxiety than usual, the team checked their equipment one more time and turned in for the night.

Awake at 0630, the five Rangers silently applied camouflage face paint, slipped into web gear, grabbed weapons and rucks, and moved down the slope to the company's chopper pad. When they reached the area they dropped their rucks and sat or squatted along the earthen embankment just above the PSP pad to await the arrival of the aircraft. At 0800 two Huey slicks left the 2/17th Cav compound and approached the Ranger helipad to land one behind the other. Seconds later the pilots shut their engines down. The wait to find out if the mission was a go began.

Thirty minutes later the radios crackled to life and the aircraft commanders announced that they had just been ordered to crank up their birds. The mission was on. Quickly buckling their web gear, then slipping their arms through the straps of heavy rucks, the five men struggled to their feet and waddled across the chopper pad to climb aboard the first aircraft. The second bird on the pad was the chase ship. Its job was to orbit the AO in case the first aircraft went down. If that occurred, the chase ship was to move in and quickly extricate the survivors.

The two aircraft flew west, then were joined near the edge of the mountains by a third Huey carrying Captain Guy. His helicopter was to be the command & control aircraft during the insertion. The Ranger company commander had departed Camp Eagle earlier that morning to drop off the radio relay team at Fire Support Base Birmingham.

As the three aircraft approached the team's AO, Staff Sergeant Luchow had a sudden, unexplainable change of heart and made the decision to attempt a landing at the original LZ. Captain Guy, flying overhead in the C&C aircraft, considered the request and quickly okayed the change.

The insertion helicopter dropped out of formation as it approached the tiny clearing in the valley floor, but one hundred feet out began taking small-arms fire from the jungle around and above the LZ. The door gunners held their fire as the pilot flared the ship away from the clearing, taking a couple of minor hits in the process but suffering no damage.

As the pilot continued east, Luchow instructed him to drop the team into its secondary LZ, five minutes farther down the valley. The aircraft commander nodded, then flew directly to the spot. Soon the aircraft was hovering over a clearing located near the southern edge of the valley at the base of a steep secondary ridgeline. The small, open area was just large enough for a single Huey and appeared to be choked with four-foot-high elephant grass.

The team was out of the aircraft in seconds, three Rangers hitting the ground on the port side, two on the starboard. They sprinted west around the nose of the aircraft and dashed forty meters through the thick grass toward the nearby jungle. They reached it just as the Huey lifted out of the valley and disappeared into the distance. Once inside the tree line the team went to ground, setting up in a circular perimeter while the senior RTO established radio contact with the insertion ship, the C&C aircraft, and the radio relay team back on Birmingham and gave a sitrep. While he was handling the patrol's commo needs, the remaining Rangers watched and listened for any sign of unfriendly intruders. The jungle around them remained silent. So far everything seemed to be going according to plan.

Thirty minutes later Luchow gave the hand-signal for Saenz to move out up the ridge to the west. The Ranger point man led the team out in a slow, deliberate, zigzag route, climbing higher and higher as they moved. Saenz knew what he was doing. On his watch, the enemy would have a tough time setting up a hasty ambush along the team's route of march. The swarthy Michigan native was excellent on point. Luchow had gotten the scoop on Saenz before selecting him for the patrol. He knew the man had been on a number of hairy patrols and learned how to walk point with the best of them.

The first day in the mountains proved uneventful. The weather remained hot and dry, and the patrol made good time moving into its recon zone. They found no trails, old or new, nor any other sign that would indicate the presence of enemy soldiers. Finally, toward the end of the day, they set up a night defense position just off the crest of the ridge overlooking the valley they had inserted into that morning. The patrol had put nearly four klicks between themselves and the LZ. Silently they set up a tight, circular perimeter and put out four claymore antipersonnel mines for added security—three facing the top of the ridge and one pointing down their backtrail. Luchow then posted a single-man guard shift beginning at 2300 hours and took the first one-and-a-half-hour shift himself. The night passed quietly.

The patrol was awake and alert as the false dawn began to illuminate the jungle around them. After a cold breakfast of LRRP rations, the Rangers sterilized their NDP and slipped into their rucks. They took a second look around their perimeter to make sure that none but the best enemy trackers could tell that anyone had been there, then sat back to wait for Luchow's signal to move out.

At 0700 hours the team leader snapped his fingers quietly, pointed uphill to indicate their direction of movement, then nodded to Saenz to lead the way. Dropping quietly over the crest of the ridge and down the reverse slope, they continued to head west into the area they were to recon. Cautiously, they crossed the valley at the bottom of the slope and began zigzagging up the next ridgeline. After another unproductive day, the patrol set up its NDP and spent a second night on the ground just below the crest of the second ridge. With no changes in their mission nor the enemy situation, the second night was a repeat of the first.

The patrol moved out the next morning at 0700 and finally neared their intended recon zone just before 1500 hours. As soon as they reached it, Saenz hit a major, well-worn, high-speed trail running north/south and paralleling the ridge. The trail was bare and hard-packed, but there were a lot of fresh footprints in the areas where dust had collected—enough to convince Luchow that they had found what they were looking for.

Silently, Luchow motioned for the team to pull back downhill ten meters off the trail. They held up in a cluster of dense vegetation on the side of the ridge. He took the radio from his senior RTO and, barely whispering, called the radio relay team to report their discovery. Minutes later the relay team called back and told him that he was to set up an OP close enough to the trail to monitor enemy traffic. Luchow signed off and moved the team back up the side of the ridge. When he found a spot suitable for the OP, he set the patrol in a fan-shaped linear formation with three claymores to their front aimed in an arc at the trail, and a single claymore covering their E&E route back down the ridge. It was already 1530 hours by the time they had finished, but Luchow didn't expect any traffic out on the trail until after dusk. To be safe, he kept the team on full alert the rest of the afternoon.

His diligence was rewarded when at 2030 hours the Rangers heard movement coming down the trail from the north, less than forty meters away. At first they could only hear the dull sounds of equipment banging together, but it wasn't long before they could pick up the murmur of human voices—and they weren't speaking English!

Soon the first enemy soldiers stepped into view. In the fading light the Rangers could see well-disciplined NVA troops walking in patrol file, spaced out three to four meters apart. There was no point element out front, a good indication that they felt secure and were confident that no American forces were in the area. Since the NVA were using no illumination to aid them in their travel, Luchow guessed they were familiar with the terrain and knew where they were going. He also noticed that they were carrying only small arms and only a few wore even light rucksacks. They were hatless, dressed in black pajamas and Ho Chi Minh sandals.

Barely breathing, the team stayed in position another hour and a half after the enemy soldiers had passed their location. Finally, satisfied that the NVA had moved on, Luchow gave the signal for the team to move silently fifty meters back down from the trail.

At 2200 hours Luchow had his teammates set up a circular NDP while he called in a sitrep to report the latest bit of intelligence. The five Rangers had compared notes on what they had seen and came to an agreement that there were between fifty and sixty enemy soldiers in the column. Captain Guy seemed very pleased with their intel and told them to remain in place for the remainder of the night, then move back up into the OP the next morning to continue monitoring the trail. Luchow acknowledged and signed off.

Everything was quiet for an hour or so, but just before 2300 hours the team heard the sounds of enemy soldiers talking, banging gear, and moving around approximately 150 meters away at a spot uphill and south of their NDP. It sounded like the NVA were setting up an overnight camp along the trail. Silently the Rangers remained in place, listening to the enemy.

The noise finally died down sometime around midnight. Luchow had come to the conclusion that these NVA soldiers were most likely a different group than the ones they had spotted earlier in the evening. It was discomforting to know that so many enemy troops were in their immediate area, but that was the very reason the AO had been selected for a recon patrol. In hushed tones Luchow passed the order around the perimeter for his teammates to remain on 100 percent alert for the rest of the night. That didn't prove to be much of a problem since no one was able to sleep anyway.

During the faint illumination of false dawn, Luchow looked up through the trees in the direction of the trail and spotted an NVA soldier sitting on the ground less than twenty-five meters in front of one of the team's claymores. The enemy soldier, armed with an AK-47, was sitting quietly, facing south, apparently pulling security for the NVA unit camped up on the hillside. He seemed totally unaware of the fact that he was sitting right in the center of a claymore's kill zone.

Luchow slowly picked up the radio handset and called the radio relay team. In hushed tones he reported that there was a "dink in front of their claymore, and we're going to waste him." Without waiting for a confirmation, he carefully picked up the clacker, gave his teammates a thumbs-up, and squeezed the detonator. The massive explosion tore apart the jungle uphill from the team. The enemy soldier disappeared in a pink mist as bits and pieces of the jungle began to rain down on the patrol. Luchow knew it was a "good kill."

Instantly the Rangers were on their feet, pulling in the rest of their claymores. Securing the mines, they began backing rapidly down the hill to the east. Since it was the fourth day of their mission, Luchow had already decided not to attempt a return to the original LZ. Instead they would climb the ridge to their rear. When they reached the top he would request a Maguire rig extraction.

Ten minutes later they were still moving downhill when they heard the faint sounds of pursuit only a hundred meters above them. Luchow was shocked that the enemy had responded so quickly to their claymore. He had figured they would have at least fifteen minutes to clear the area before the NVA could gather their wits and come down the hill to see what had happened to their flank security guard. Then it would likely take another twenty to thirty minutes for them to mount any kind of search. By then the team would be moving up the reverse slope toward their extraction point. At least, that's what he thought.

There was no time to question his error in judgment because the NVA were already sweeping the hillside above them, shouting and reconning by fire. And he didn't have to stop and spell out the situation to the rest of his teammates to convince them that there was, at that moment, a very real sense of urgency to their movement.

The team began running "balls to the wall" to put as much distance as possible between themselves and their pursuers. Without stopping for a breather they plunged down the side of the slope toward the bottom of the ridge. An hour later they broke out onto the wide floor of the valley and began breaking brush toward the opposite side. Each time Luchow stopped the team to catch a breath and listen for sounds of pursuit, they heard the enemy forces behind them.

The Rangers continued fleeing as the shadows shortened toward midday. Finally, early in the afternoon, they reached the slope of the opposite ridge and began climbing. Hesitating for only a moment to catch their breath and listen once again, the Rangers heard the NVA soldiers back in the trees, no longer reconning by fire, but still coming hard less than a hundred meters away.

Luchow guessed that the enemy soldiers had moved out on line and were maintaining their distance from the team no more than twenty minutes behind the Rangers, still too far back in the trees to get a visual but close enough to hear their progress. Suddenly the Ranger team leader realized that the NVA were herding them in a direction they wanted the LRRPs to go. Luchow was aware that the enemy's commo was just as good as their own, and he knew there was the likelihood that somewhere up ahead a well-planned ambush was waiting. But there was no time to deal with that. They would have to take their chances that they could make it to the top of the ridge and be extracted before they fell into the ambush or their pursuers caught up.

Off and running again, the team continued up the steep slope, no longer zigzagging. That tactic would only allow the enemy force behind them to cut off the angles and gain on them. Finally, late in the afternoon, exhausted and gasping for air, they reached the top of the ridge.

Momentarily satisfied that they had put some distance between themselves and their pursuers, the patrol set up security in heavy cover and Luchow called in a sitrep and asked for an extraction. However, that was not to be. After considering the odds against a "night" Maguire Rig extraction, Captain Guy ordered the team to go to ground and remain hidden until first light the next morning. Guy promised Luchow that he would be there at that time with gunships and two Hueys complete with Maguire rigs to pull them out. It wasn't what Luchow wanted, but he fully understood the dangers of a night string extraction and had to agree with his commanding officer.

Not satisfied with their present location, the team moved a short distance away and set up a night defense perimeter in a cluster of dense vegetation. While the rest of the patrol put out claymores, Luchow took Weeks and moved out on an area recon to locate a suitable site for their extraction the next morning. They soon found a likely spot just off the crest of the ridge on the reverse slope, only seventy-five meters northeast of their NDP.

When Luchow and Weeks returned to the patrol's defense perimeter, the team leader wasted no time calling FSB (fire support base) Birmingham and FSB Bastogne to give them artillery preplots covering all the likely avenues of approach to their position. After he finished calling those in, he called in artillery concentrations on their first point of contact with the enemy, then began walking three-round salvos along the patrol's E&E route to within a hundred meters of their location. By the time Luchow finally called off the artillery fire, it was nearly 1730 hours.

The team had good concealment in their NDP and fairly good cover. Fagel, Saenz, and Leslie had done a good job placing the claymores. Three were fanned out facing downhill in the direction of their pursuers, while the fourth claymore was pointed over the crest, facing down the reverse slope.

They spent the rest of that night on full alert. In spite of their exhaustion and the fact that they all had averaged less than four hours of sleep a day since the patrol began, none of them had any trouble staying awake.

Outside of the normal sounds of the Annamese jungle, the Rangers heard nothing to indicate that the enemy had located them. Had they given up? It wasn't like them to throw in the towel so quickly.

At first light Luchow called in a final sitrep and was told by the relay team that the extraction was on for 0800 hours. At 0730 the relay team radioed that the helicopters were on the way. The patrol quietly pulled in the claymores, then moved out of their NDP and proceeded cautiously toward their PZ.

To the team members, it seemed to take hours to cover the seventy-five meters to the extraction site. Each step they took, they expected the jungle to explode all around them. But when twenty minutes had gone by and they reached their goal without making contact, they began to breathe a little easier.

Luchow signaled the team to break up into two groups for the string extraction. The first group out—Saenz, Fagel, and Weeks—took up positions facing uphill. The second group—Leslie and Luchow—faced downhill. They waited breathlessly as the luminous hands on Luchow's watch passed 0800.

Nearly twenty minutes after the hour, the five Rangers heard the approaching Hueys. Soon they spotted the C&C aircraft and an escorting Cobra gunship followed close behind by a pair of slicks. Fagel pulled the pin on a purple smoke grenade and tossed it into the jungle between the two groups of Rangers to mark their location. Immediately the aircraft commander identified "Goofy Grape" and waited as the RTO acknowledged the sighting over the radio.

The first slick came in low and hovered right over the team's location. Three weighted sandbags dropped from the open cabin, uncoiling umbilical cords of nylon rope behind them as they fell through the jungle canopy. The first part of the extraction went like a dress rehearsal. Just over a hundred feet below the hovering chopper, the first three Rangers stepped through the nylon loops at the end of their Maguire rigs and attached the D-rings on their harnesses to the ropes.

Suddenly the aircraft commander radioed that he was taking fire. Without waiting for a response from the Ranger team leader the aircraft began to rise, pulling the three men out of the jungle. The enemy fire seemed to be coming from the reverse slope of the ridge they were on, uncomfortably near the crest. Apparently it was only small-arms fire, but it was enough to force the pilot to take immediate evasive action. Picking up speed, the aircraft commander swung wide out over the open valley to put some distance between his aircraft and the enemy gunners on the ridgeline.

Locked together during the lift phase of the extraction, the three Rangers dangling beneath the helicopter released their grips and began swinging back and forth beneath the aircraft while the pilot was making his evasive maneuvers. This made it nearly impossible for the pilot to control the aircraft in flight. As he fought to stabilize the Huey, the ship drifted far enough away from the enemy fire to eliminate that threat. Soon the pendulum effect caused by the three Rangers swinging about on the ends of the ropes was also brought under control and the aircraft began a slow flight back to Camp Eagle.

Back on the top of the ridgeline, as soon as the first extraction aircraft had cleared the PZ, the second ship moved in to recover Luchow and Leslie as the Cobra circled desperately, trying to suppress NVA small-arms fire with rockets and miniguns. Even so, eight to ten enemy weapons were still shooting at the second lift ship as it carefully pulled the last two Rangers from the jaws of death and departed the AO. The frustrated NVA soldiers continued to fire at the departing helicopter long after it was out of range.

When the two Hueys finally reached the Ranger helipad at Camp Eagle, nearly the entire company was waiting on the PSP to make sure that their buddies were gently lowered to the ground. Finally safe, the five Rangers allowed themselves to realize just how close they had come to "losing one." The enemy forces that had fired on the extraction ships had been waiting in ambush on the reverse slope of the ridge where the patrol had spent the night. The NVA had indeed used the old "hammer and anvil" tactics against the Rangers, and without the assistance of a Maguire-rig extraction, the team would have been slaughtered when they attempted to move down off the crest away from their pursuers.

☆ ☆ ☆ ☆ ☆

Company N,
75th Infantry (Ranger),
173d Airborne Brigade

The 173d Airborne Brigade's long range reconnaissance patrols had become legendary by early 1969. When the Department of the Army established Ranger companies to replace the U.S. Army long-range patrol units operating in South Vietnam, the brigade's 74th LRP Detachment reluctantly cased its colors and reemerged as Company N, 75th Infantry (Ranger). The new designation may have legitimized the hard-charging, long-range patrol detachment, but it had little effect on its mission, its personnel, or its ability to perform in the field. Without even a break in the action, the newly designated "Ranger" company continued to carry out operations deep in the forested mountains of South Vietnam's Central Highlands.

However, the company's executive officer, a young first lieutenant named Giantacio, took the unit's new Ranger designation to heart. Somewhat of a glory hound, by long range reconnaissance patrol standards anyway, he had always demonstrated that he was more than ready and willing to lead "his" men out on any kind of mission that might bring him fame and fortune—fortune that would mean a medal or two for him.

An incident had occurred a few months before that dramatically characterized the young officer's overzealousness. Staff Sergeant Patrick Tadina, a living legend among the brigade LRRPs, had previously come up with the idea of using long-range patrols as "hunter/killer" teams. The concept was implemented and had proven rather successful—that is until a team commanded by SFC Rey Martinez ran afoul of the enemy. The patrol, Hawk Six-Two, had been out on a designated hunter/killer mission and was set up in cover on a hillside overlooking a village suspected of supporting nearby VC units. The team made contact with the enemy and immediately suffered one man killed and two wounded.

Back at the bar in Bong Son, Sp. 4th Class Joe Keshlear, a medic on one of the LRP company's teams, was enjoying a beer when one of his fellow LRPs pulled up in the company jeep and shouted for him to listen to what was happening with Martinez's team. Keshlear went over to the jeep and the driver turned up the volume on the PRC-25 radio. The two LRPs heard Sergeant Martinez calling for an emergency extraction, reporting that he had a KIA and five wounded.

They looked at each other in disbelief when Lieutenant Giantacio answered, "You're good LRPs—stay and fight."

Stunned, Keshlear jumped into the jeep and told the driver to take him over to S-2 to see Major Stang, the Brigade Intel Officer. Keshlear quick-briefed Major Stang on what was happening out in the field, then stood by while the officer dialed up the LRP frequency to listen for himself. He was just in time to hear Giantacio tell Martinez that there were no choppers available. All were being used on battalion supply runs.

Major Stang immediately broke into the transmission and said, "Lieutenant Giantacio, get your ass down to the chopper pad, *now!*" Then he spoke to the wounded team leader: "Boys, I'm coming out to get you."

Changing frequencies, the angry officer called the aviation company and snarled into the handset, "This is Major Stang. Kick the supplies off two of those choppers and warm them up."

Putting down the radio, he turned to Keshlear and said, "Do you want to come with us?"

Keshlear shook his head. "No sir, I'll be waiting for them at the B-med chopper pad."

After the patrol was finally rescued, Major Stang made it a point to royally chew out the aviation unit that had failed to provide helicopters to extract the recon patrol. Although nothing was ever said to Lieutenant Giantacio concerning the matter, the LRPs lost all confidence and trust in him. They knew for certain that when the chips were down, they would never be able to count on him to look out for their safety. They were only glad that they would not have to go out in the field with him, since LRP SOP prevented officers from leading long range patrols in the field. There were exceptions to the rule, but they were uncommon.

However, the action that occurred that day succeeded only in whetting Giantacio's quest for glory. His constant haranguing and pleading to lead a patrol in the field finally elicited a positive response from his commanding officer. In November 1968 he was promised that if a mission ever came down from Brigade that required the full platoon, he would lead it.

Three months later, with the unit's reorganization as a Ranger company complete, Lieutenant Giantacio finally saw his chance for glory. In February 1969, he came up with an idea for a daring mission. He volunteered to take a full platoon of Rangers from their base camp at LZ English into the Fishhook, a particularly dangerous area located in the tri-border region of South Vietnam. It was a longtime sanctuary for NVA troops operating in the area. Giantacio wanted to take his platoon of Rangers into the very heart of the NVA territory and run saturation patrols against the enemy forces operating there. The plan was revealed to be even riskier when it was pointed out that the Fishhook was outside the brigade's artillery fan.

Intel reports had indicated that both the 20th and 22d NVA Regiments were located somewhere inside the Fishhook. There was also evidence that the enemy felt so safe and secure there that they were using the area for an in-country R&R center.

When Brigade S-2 failed either to approve or disapprove the mission, Giantacio kept lobbying for it until they okayed the operation. The mission was set to go in on 16 March, but with only three six-man teams. However, at the very last minute the mission was postponed when saner heads at Brigade headquarters decided that eighteen men were simply not enough to successfully operate inside the Fishhook, especially without fire support.

Unfortunately, S-2 soon changed its mind and decided to allow the mission to go in, but with some minor adjustments. The size of the Rangers' AO would be pared down to an area of five square miles. The number of patrols would be expanded to half a dozen, with each team made up of seven Rangers instead of the usual six. In addition, Brigade decided to reoccupy an abandoned fire support base within range of the patrols in the field. The base would be manned by a battery of 175mm howitzers and secured by a company of infantry. The Rangers were ordered to station a radio relay team on the firebase to provide reliable commo between the teams in the field and the TOC at Bong Son. The mission was rescheduled for 1 April.

On 30 March the actual mission warning order came

down to the Ranger company from Brigade S-2. After the premission briefing, the teams were informed that headquarters expected each of them to make contact sometime during their five-day missions. And just in case the Rangers didn't get the meaning of the term "expected," they were instructed to *initiate* contact with the enemy whenever and wherever they were encountered. It wasn't long before the November Company Rangers began calling themselves the "75th Kamikaze Company" and the "75th Suicide Company."

Team Hotel, led by S.Sgt. John Rae, was one of the six teams that received a warning order for the saturation patrols. Rae, a "shake 'n' bake" NCO, had seven missions under his belt, but only two as a team leader. His veteran ATL was Sp4. Joe Keshlear. Keshlear, a trained medic, carried an AK-47 and always demanded to walk point while out on patrol. With ten months in country he was by far the most experienced man on the team. Keshlear was just returning from the PX at Qui Nhon when he discovered that he and his teammates had been scheduled to pull a mission into the Fishhook with five other teams. He was not happy that Lieutenant Giantacio had been placed in charge of the operation.

The rest of Rae's team consisted of Specialist Four Bennett, the senior RTO, who would walk directly behind Rae on the patrol. Bennett had about as much time in the field as his team leader. Specialist Four Griffin Cherry, a black ranger who had shown a lot of promise on prior patrols, would back up the RTO. Two "cherries" walked the fifth and sixth slots; one of them, a specialist four named Hyde, was slated by Rae to carry the backup radio. The other man would hump the starlight scope and the M-79 grenade launcher. The drag position would be ably manned by Sp4. Fitz, who would also carry a URC-10 UHF radio. In spite of the overall

lack of experience, every man on the team had successfully completed the three-week 173d Airborne Brigade
LRP School back in December and January.

On the morning of 1 April, the mission was postponed for one day. Everyone was so elated over that
good news that they decided to party hard that night to
celebrate their unexpected good luck. Their attitudes,
somewhere between "fully dejected" and "totally de-
pressed," were greatly improved by news of their
twenty-four-hour respite.

Staff Sergeant Rae decided to take advantage of the
delay to pull Specialist Four Hyde from the team. Hyde,
one of the two cherries on the patrol, had recently been
assigned to the team as the junior RTO. But Hyde just
wasn't cut out to be an LRRP; far too noisy in field, he
didn't take the perils of long-range patrolling seriously
enough to satisfy Rae or the rest of his teammates.
However, with Hyde gone Team Hotel would be going
out light, with only six men.

During the overflight on 31 March, Rae had selected
a primary landing zone in a grassy clearing next to a
flooded rice paddy that occupied one of the surrounding hilltops. With six teams inserting into such a small
area of operations, LZs and PZs were at a premium.
Caution had to be exercised to coordinate not only insertions and extractions, but also the movement of each
team once it was on the ground. So many teams operating so close together was a disaster waiting to happen.

The weather during the next five days was expected to
be clear and hot, perfect for conducting hunter/killer
operations against the enemy. Team Hotel's AO consisted of a broad, rounded mountaintop covered with
double-canopy forest.

On the day of the insertion, the six teams climbed
aboard the half dozen waiting Huey slicks strung out

along the helipad. In addition to the lift ships, six Charlie-model gunships and a single Huey command & control aircraft were also present. In pairs, the helicopters began lifting off from the tarmac and climbing for altitude, where they waited in orbit for the remainder of the aircraft to join them. Once all thirteen aircraft were circling at altitude around the airfield, they joined up in a string formation and headed west.

The flight to the mission AO took nearly an hour, and at 0950 the first team was inserted. Everyone aboard the orbiting Hueys held their breath until the team was safely on the ground. So far the operation was going according to plan.

Aboard their aircraft the men of Team Hotel locked and loaded their weapons. They were scheduled to go in third. As their slick approached the LZ situated high on the wide mountaintop, the Rangers quickly realized that the pilot was going in without taking any of the usual evasive maneuvers. That was against SOP, but it was too late to do anything about it. Escorted by a pair of gunships, the helicopter flared out over a patch of three-foot-high elephant grass next to a flooded rice paddy.

As the ship touched down, the six Rangers leaped from the starboard side of the aircraft and set up in a tight circle in the windblown grass. Dropping to one knee as the insertion ship departed the LZ, they waited for the noise to subside. The men cast anxious glances around the perimeter when they saw that the flooded rice paddy was being actively farmed. There were no friendlies living in the Fishhook, so whoever was tending the rice paddy had to be on the other side.

As the sounds of the insertion aircraft faded into the distance, the patrol suddenly became aware of a pair of LOH scout helicopters hovering just above the ground twenty meters on either side of them. The two aircraft sat with their miniguns pointing downhill toward the tree line sixty meters south of the Rangers' position. The patrol had no idea where the two birds had come from, or why they were there, but the additional aircraft hanging around their LZ could not help but call attention to the patrol.

Rae ignored the two helicopters and quickly called in a sitrep to establish communication with the C&C aircraft orbiting to the east just out of sight and sound. Satisfied for the moment that they had not yet been compromised, Rae signaled for Keshlear to get the team moving toward the tree line fifty meters to their southwest.

As Keshlear neared the wood line he spotted the thatched roof of a small hootch sticking up just above the elephant grass. He slowly raised his arm to halt the patrol, then began searching around for another approach into the thick forest. As the team continued moving parallel to the wood line, Keshlear ran across a meter-wide high-speed trail that snaked down into the trees. Cautiously, the Ranger point man followed the heavily used trail through the grass. Based on past experience, he expected trouble and possibly even booby traps at the spot where the trail entered the forest.

At that moment the RTO interrupted Rae to whisper that two of the other teams had just made contact and were being extracted, one by Maguire rig. A Hawkeye aircraft had arrived on the scene to assist the two teams during their extractions. When it was discovered that none of the patrols had been able to establish commo with the radio relay team back at the fire support base, the Hawkeye pilot notified them that he would remain on call.

Fortunately, both teams were extracted with a minimum of casualties.

At the tree line, Keshlear saw that the high-speed trail was well used. Checking carefully for booby traps, he continued moving until he had led the patrol fifty meters into the woods. At that point, lying off to one side of the trail, he discovered a pruned tree trunk that the enemy had been using as a worktable for preparing punji stakes. Bundles of stakes lay all around the area. Looking closer, Keshlear saw that the enemy had probably been working at the site when the Rangers had inserted up on the mountaintop. Fortunately for the team, the enemy soldiers had decided that leaving for points unknown was a better idea than remaining to fight whoever had just landed in their area.

The point man stopped the team, then gave the signal for everyone to back slowly out of the area. Within minutes the six Rangers had returned to the edge of the woods. Still staring into the trees, Keshlear motioned for Rae to come up behind him. When Rae was standing close by, Keshlear whispered that he felt if they went back in they might be walking into an ambush. And if they got hit in the jungle and pinned down, they would have to come out on strings (Maguire rigs). Rae quickly agreed and instructed Keshlear to continue paralleling the wood line to the east until he located a better access point down into the valley.

The patrol moved another twenty or thirty meters before running head-on into another paddy dike. While the team held up to observe the area to their front, Specialist Four Cherry passed the word to Rae that he had spotted a man watching the team as it approached the dike. Cherry said that the man had quietly slipped into the woods as the team drew near.

At that point, Keshlear decided that he wanted to get a better feel for the terrain before they went any further. A short distance behind the team to the north, a long finger ran back up toward the top of the ridge. Keshlear decided to move the team through the waist-high elephant grass along the finger and to the top of the hill, where they could get a better look at the area around them.

The finger seemed to broaden considerably as it neared the top of the mountain. It was nearly 1530 hours when the team reached the top and set up an OP. They soon noticed that on the east side of the high ground a very steep cliff dropped down into a narrow valley with an equally steep cliff face on the opposite side.

In the valley, not more than 150 meters from the edge of the near cliff, were four or five hootches laid out in military fashion in the middle of a grove of banana and fruit trees.

The team sat quietly observing the structures for about thirty minutes before spotting ten black pajama–clad NVA parading around on the other side of the hootches in what appeared to be a weapons inspection. They immediately called in a sitrep to report the enemy activity.

A short time later they heard a third patrol radio that it was in contact and requesting an extraction. The team was in heavy jungle and at that moment had a large enemy unit maneuvering to surround it. Once again the extraction had to be performed by Maguire rig, and before the NVA troops could complete the encirclement the team was safely pulled out of harm's way. Only three of the original six teams were still on the ground.

Staff Sergeant Rae realized that the enemy soldiers down by the hootches were apparently not aware they were being observed. So, for the moment, Team Hotel was safe. Rae estimated that it would take several hours for the man who had observed the team earlier to cover the distance to the hootches and inform his comrades that they had company.

Rae and Keshlear discussed the situation and agreed that the area most likely held a large number of enemy troops. But that was the reason they had been sent into the AO. In spite of the obvious dangers of remaining in the vicinity after being spotted, the patrol continued to observe the ten NVA as the soldiers milled around until dark, when whoever was in charge called an end to their activities and the men disappeared into the hootches, most likely to eat and then retire for the evening.

That night the team observed the area around the hootches by starlight scope but saw no activity at all. It was easy to watch what was going on below because a full moon lit up the area as bright as day.

The team remained a bit nervous as they waited for the coming day. The Rangers had set out six claymores facing south and west of their perimeter to cover the likely access points, but they still felt like they were sitting in the middle of a bulls-eye. Thanks to the Hawkeye aircraft orbiting just outside the AO, they still had good commo with their TOC during the night.

Just after first light the next morning the team spotted smoke from a cooking fire in the vicinity of the hootches. During their first sitrep that day they were informed that a fourth team had made contact at daybreak and had to be extracted. The Fishhook was definitely living up to its reputation.

At 1300 hours the team spotted two NVA wearing black pajamas and carrying weapons moving down a trail that ran north to south through the center of the valley. At 1600 they spotted two more. The Rangers were amazed at how lush the valley was, an actual garden spot but an ideal place for an enemy base camp. The second night passed as uneventfully as the first.

During the third day of the operation the fifth team made contact with an enemy element and had to be extracted. Team Hotel was the only Ranger patrol left in the field. They were still getting their commo through the Hawkeye aircraft circling in a long, high, elliptical orbit several kilometers away from the team's AO.

The patrol spotted no enemy troops down in the valley during the day, but they were beginning to run low on water. Specialist Four Griffin Cherry, down to a single one-quart canteen, was worst off.

Sergeant Rae knew that sometime during the next day they would have to leave the safety of the mountaintop and go low to find a source of water. If they didn't they would never get through the fifth and last day of the mission. Everyone was nervous about the prospect of dropping down into the valley because they suspected a trap. They knew that they had been spotted on the first day and realized that the enemy had to have gotten the word of their presence in the area by that time.

Keshlear wanted to tough it out and stay on top of the mountain, but Rae overruled him; he wanted to go down for water that evening. Keshlear successfully argued that they should wait to go down into the valley before first light on the fourth day so they could move under cover of false dawn.

The team got a late start heading down into the valley on the morning of the fourth day. They moved toward where the NVA observer had watched them the first day.

As they were moving through the elephant grass fifty meters from where they had laagered for the past three days, Keshlear felt a tug at his pants. He stopped immediately and looked down. A razor-sharp punji stake had penetrated his pants leg. When he turned and looked back up through the grass behind him he could see a large number of punji stakes pointing uphill toward their laager site.

Turning slowly around, he walked back toward the rest of the team, pulling out the punji stakes as he moved. By the time he reached them he had a large bundle of bamboo stakes. He realized that the enemy had somehow managed to crawl within twenty meters of the team's OP to emplace the stakes. Either the NVA were awfully good or someone on the team had not been very alert while on guard.

It was a certainty that the enemy knew exactly where the team was located. Keshlear pushed Rae to give up on the idea of making a water run and encouraged him to take the patrol back to the OP to "buck it out" until their extraction the next day. The team leader agreed.

On the fourth day the patrol continued to watch the collection of hootches below, but with tighter security on their backside. Although it was only 0830 in the morning, the climbing sun was already promising another blistering day. It would be especially tough on the exposed Rangers who were on their last canteens.

At 1000 hours the team spotted two NVA standing together down near the hootches. One of them was pointing directly up at them. The enemy soldier did not seem nervous or anxious, but it was obvious to the Rangers that he knew exactly where the patrol was hidden.

At 1030 hours the patrol became aware of a grass fire that had started somewhere to the team's southwest. The breeze was just strong enough to push the fire in the direction of the Rangers. At that point Rae seemed momentarily confused and slow to react, prompting Keshlear to take charge. He immediately ordered his teammates to pull in their claymores to prevent the fire from cooking them off. He also realized that the enemy would most likely be following the wall of fire, which was already about thirty meters away and coming directly at them.

Sergeant Rae wanted the men to prepare to flee north down and across a shallow saddle to the higher ground on the other side, but Keshlear quickly convinced him that would be a mistake because it was just what the enemy expected them to do. Before Rae could respond, the veteran assistant team leader grabbed two of his teammates and darted through the flames. When he didn't find anything or anyone waiting on the other side of the fire, he told his two teammates to stay where they were and keep their eyes on the tree line while he ran back through the fire to tell the rest of the patrol that it was safe to move in that direction.

After they were clear of the flames, Keshlear grabbed the radio and contacted the Hawkeye aircraft. He quickly informed the pilot that the team was compromised and needed help. Within minutes the Hawkeye circled over the team's position and radioed back that he had just spotted two dozen NVA waiting in ambush on the high ground across the saddle from the Rangers' perimeter. With the team's approval, the Air Force pilot called in a fire mission on the hidden enemy troops.

While the rounds were on the way, Keshlear squatted in the brush on the side of the mountain, talking with the Hawkeye pilot. Suddenly he heard the loud *crack* of a bullet as it snapped past his head. A split second later the sharp report of a single rifle shot confirmed that he was definitely on someone's gun/target line. The shot had not come from across the saddle but from somewhere down in the valley below them.

Keshlear dropped to the ground and called in to report that the team was not only compromised, but it was now engaged with the enemy. The assistant team leader was no longer whispering; he shouted into the radio handset, "Timber . . . Timber . . . Under fire! Immediate extraction!"

The artillery salvo arrived moments later and was right on the money. Keshlear stayed on the horn with the Hawkeye pilot and kept the artillery pounding the high ground across the saddle from the team's position. It was comforting to know that someone was looking out for them.

At 1210 the Rangers consumed the last of their water. The blazing midday heat had become their worst enemy. They searched the sky as they waited anxiously for the arrival of the extraction ship and its escort. The minutes ticked by slowly. Nearly an hour later the aircraft finally arrived on the scene. The helicopters went into a high orbit about the same time an Air Force Tonto—or FAC—arrived overhead. The Tonto pilot announced that he had a couple of fast movers waiting at altitude to join in the fun.

At that time the Hawkeye pilot called off the artillery fire to allow the FAC to drop down and mark the targets for the fighter-bombers. As the FAC pilot sent a pair of white phosphorous rockets into the forested hilltop that hid the NVA soldiers lying in ambush, the extraction slick slid unmolested into the charred LZ to lift out the team. Amazingly, the aircraft took no fire coming out.

As the team departed the AO, the six Rangers spotted the flight of F-105s arriving. The two aircraft took turns sending shiny napalm canisters tumbling end over end into the enemy ambush positions. After the team was clear and the 105s reported that they were out of ordnance, the Hawkeye pilot once again called in a fire mission. However, this time he adjusted the artillery fire down in the valley to knock out the enemy hootches and the well-tended gardens around them. After a number of salvos it became apparent that the enemy had chosen the site well; the intervening ridges prevented the artillery rounds from impacting anywhere near the hootches.

When the patrol finally arrived back at LZ English, the men were immediately hustled off to Brigade headquarters and debriefed by the brigade S-2, Major Stang. The briefing officer told the exhausted Rangers that though it was not yet confirmed, he believed the NVA had suffered heavy casualties due to the artillery and air strikes they had called in. But because of the heavy enemy activity in the vicinity of the strike, they would not be sending in a reaction force to develop the situation.

All six Ranger teams had escaped with close calls. A number of Rangers had been wounded during the operation, but no one had been killed. The enemy presence in the area was so extensive that during some of the other patrols' contacts, Team Hotel could hear the supporting artillery fire impacting.

Lieutenant Giantacio had gotten his wish, but not one of the Rangers who had survived the "suicide" mission attributed their success—or their luck—to the gung ho officer.

Company E,
50th Infantry (LRP),
9th Infantry Division

The 9th Infantry Division had relocated from Bear Cat to Dong Tam not long after its arrival in Vietnam. It would remain the only U.S. Army Division assigned to work the watery world of South Vietnam's Delta region. The division's 3d Brigade established a base camp at Tan An and began conducting operations in that area. Although based at Dong Tam, Company E, 50th Infantry (LRP), the division's long range reconnaissance patrol company, kept three to four teams down at Tan An to pull missions in the 3d Brigade's area of operations. Because of the open terrain in the brigade's AO, most of the missions were either short-lived reconnaissance patrols or the infamous 9th Division LRP "parakeet" flights, hard-hitting direct-response actions where six-man teams were dropped into a given area based on a hot intel report and were expected to "develop" the situation.

On 25 January 1969, LRP Team One-One was on stand-down at Tan An. Staff Sergeant Jim Thayer's team had just come in from a couple of days in the bush and was taking it easy until its next assignment. Early that morning the LRP officer in charge of the four teams stationed at Tan An approached Thayer to tell him that he had a mission for the team. G-2 had gotten a recent intel report of enemy activity in a wood line twelve klicks north of Tan An. They wanted an LRP patrol to check it out. The lieutenant ordered Thayer to make an overflight of the RZ that morning, select an LZ, then take his team in to see what was out there.

Within the hour Thayer was aboard a 9th Division LOH scout helicopter flying at a thousand feet out toward the LRPs' AO. He instructed the pilot to line up his approach to the RZ from several klicks out to make the enemy think they were on a routine cross-country flight instead of an overflight of the tree line. In addition, he had the pilot make his flyby out away from the woods, flying from southeast to northwest parallel to the direction of the wood line. Flying at normal speed over the open terrain, Thayer was able to look down and see that the wood line was dense single-canopy, approximately seven hundred meters long by one hundred meters wide at its thickest point. A number of heavily used trails ran into and along the woods, but that was not unusual because of the large number of farmers and woodcutters who plied their trades in the vicinity. The terrain was made up of large, abandoned fields, open and level, pockmarked by numerous bomb and artillery craters. Thayer saw no sign of enemy activity in or around the woods.

After making a single pass over the area the LOH circled off in the distance for ten to twelve minutes before returning to Tan An over the same route, with Thayer taking a second look at the wood line in the process. Thayer picked out an LZ on the northwest edge of the woods in a large, open area about fifty meters from the trees. There was no place anywhere in the wide-open terrain where the team could land without being observed, but for some reason the northern end of the wood line appealed to the LRP team leader as the safest point of entry.

Back at Tan An, Thayer quickly briefed his teammates and told them to pack light for the mission—
LBEs, radios, and weapons. He didn't figure they would
be on the ground longer than three or four hours, so
there was no reason to wear their heavy rucksacks.

Thayer had a pair of PRUs on his team who walked
point and drag for him. He had been out with them on a
number of occasions and was completely satisfied with
both their ability and their loyalty. He himself walked
slack—the number two spot on the patrol—while his
senior RTO, PFC Richard Bellwood, took the third
spot, directly behind him. Sp4 Mike O'Day, a veteran
LRP, walked the number four spot with Sp4. Willy
Boone in the fifth position. For Boone, an inexperi-
enced black LRP newly assigned to the company, the
patrol would be only his third. Sp4. Steve Laurer, a veteran LRP from Evansburg, Pennsylvania, and Thayer's
assistant team leader, carried the backup radio and
walked the sixth spot on the team. Except for Thayer,
who carried an M-14 rifle, and the PRU who walked
drag, everyone else on the team was armed with an
M-16.

While Thayer's teammates were getting their gear together, he briefed the two helicopter pilots who would
insert the team. He indicated on a map the direction of
approach to the LZ and the actual spot where he
wanted to be put down. They nodded.

At 1045 hours it was clear and hot as the team
boarded the single Huey slick sitting on the tiny chopper
pad used by the LRPs. In minutes they were airborne,
heading north unescorted toward the patrol's area of operations. The pilot executed a low approach to the LZ as
the seven LRPs stood on the skids, ready to drop to the
ground as soon as the helicopter flared to a hover over
the open field. At three to five feet above the clearing the

pilot felt the aircraft suddenly go light, and knew that his passengers had departed the ship.

It was almost 1100 hours when the team bailed and sprinted for a low mound of earth ten meters away. The meter-high dirt berm lay between the LZ and the wood line and offered the exposed patrol the only available cover in the entire area. The seven long-range patrollers quickly set up in a thin line along the backside of the berm, facing the wood line.

Thayer immediately looked at his wrist compass and realized they had been inserted in the wrong spot. Nothing was where it was supposed to be. He thought they were somewhere along the north end of the tree line, but not at the place he had designated. But he had no time to sort out the problem. His teammates were out in the open, and he had to get them into the cover of the trees fifty meters away.

Two to three minutes later Thayer gave the signal for the team to move out. The point PRU stepped out from behind the shelter of the berm and began walking cautiously toward the tree line. Everyone else fell in behind in patrol formation.

As the team moved up along the outside edge of the wood line the lead PRU turned left, parallel to the trees. The Vietnamese wanted to check them out a little more carefully before moving into the shelter they offered. He hadn't taken more than three steps when Thayer saw an NVA soldier stand up less than ten feet back in the trees. Dressed in a khaki uniform and wearing the standard olive/gray NVA web gear, he carried an AK-47 which he was leveling at the PRU walking point. Before the enemy soldier had a chance to fire, Thayer opened up with a full burst from his M-14 and dropped the NVA.

At that moment all hell broke loose inside the wood

line. At least a full platoon of NVA soldiers opened fire on the LRP team from less than fifteen meters away.

Thayer backed away from the wood line four or five steps but continued to put down a base of fire into the trees. Out of the corner of his eye, twenty meters to his left, he saw an NVA dressed similarly to the one he had just killed stand up and take off running along the edge of the woods. The man was wearing a pith helmet, but Thayer could not tell if he was armed or not. Suddenly he saw O'Day and the point PRU take off in pursuit of the fleeing enemy soldier. Ten meters into the chase, O'Day stopped and put a single round through the back of the soldier's neck, tumbling him into the heavy cover.

By that time nearly everyone on the team was facing to the right, spread out on line, and firing directly into the wood line. Some of the LRPs had dropped to one knee while others were still moving left or right to keep the enemy from drawing a bead on them.

Thayer heard Bellwood holler from somewhere to his right, "What do you want me to do?"

The team leader shouted back, *"Shoot!"*

Bellwood dropped the radio handset and was just starting to bring up his rifle when a round hit him just to the right of his groin and exited his backside. As he fell hard to the ground, he screamed once, "Jim!"

Thayer snapped a glance to the right, saw that his RTO was hit and had gone down, then ran over to him. Dropping to one knee beside the wounded man, Thayer cradled Bellwood's neck in the crook of his left arm. He held his rifle in his right hand, upright, butt to the ground. In severe pain, Bellwood muttered something Thayer could not understand, prompting the LRP team leader to respond, "You've got the million dollar wound, Richard. You're going home. Stay down and I'll be back for you."

At that moment an NVA soldier stood up from behind an earthen berm that Thayer hadn't noticed and opened up on the two LRPs with an AK-47 on full automatic. Thayer winced as two rounds hit Bellwood in the chest, went clear through him, and slammed into the radio on his back. It was a sound Thayer would never forget.

Bellwood was knocked unconscious by the sledge-hammer force of the blows. Thayer sensed that he, too, had been hit by the burst of fire. He had felt the *thump* of a round hitting his right shoulder, but at first thought that since no great pain accompanied the impact he had not been hit too bad.

Thayer immediately dropped and rolled away from Bellwood, coming up to empty the rest of a magazine at the NVA who had shot at him. The man staggered and went down but Thayer did not know how well he had hit him.

Thayer, still under intense fire, knew that he had to get in touch with the relay team before the enemy destroyed his patrol. Realizing that Bellwood's radio had taken hits and was most likely out of commission, he started low-crawling to the right toward where Laurer, with his backup radio, was fighting desperately.

Crawling along the edge of the trees, Thayer was momentarily unable to locate the junior RTO. So he screamed, *"Laurer!"*

Through the noise of the gunfire he heard the RTO yell, *"Here!"*

While he was crawling, Thayer noticed that his weapon was beginning to grow heavy in his right hand. At that point he realized for the first time that he was injured much more severely than he first thought. Shifting the weapon to his left hand, he continued to move toward Laurer.

By this time the two PRUs had somehow managed to join forces. Thayer spotted them off to one side standing out in the open less than ten meters back from the woods. They and the NVA hidden in the trees were shouting back and forth. The team leader couldn't understand what they were saying but occasionally made out the term "Fuck you!" coming from one or the other of the PRUs.

He watched in amazement as the two men yelled at the NVA, emptied a magazine or two into the trees, then ran to one side to reload and opened fire again. The NVA, out of sight in the woods, were yelling back and returning fire. Months later Thayer would discover that the NVA had been trying to convince the PRUs to turn on their American comrades and kill them where they stood. They had promised to spare the PRUs if they did so. However, their tactic failed to impress the loyal Vietnamese and succeeded only in increasing their resolve to fight.

At that point the NVA began maneuvering out toward the edge of the trees. The LRPs could see the enemy soldiers eyeball to eyeball because the battle was being waged at distances of less than ten meters. The LRPs were trapped. There was no place to hide and nothing behind them but wide open terrain. Their only chance for survival was to make the price for taking them out too steep for the NVA to pay.

Over the next few minutes Thayer heard one PRU and then Laurer shout that they had been hit. That left only three LRPs fully able to defend the team. He renewed his effort to crawl to the backup radio. It was their only hope.

When Thayer finally reached Laurer, he discovered that the LRP RTO was on his feet, still moving and fighting. His wound was merely a flesh wound, hardly enough to knock him out of the battle.

Thayer grabbed the radio handset from Laurer and called the relay team back at Tan An. He soon discovered that Laurer had already called in the contact and that help was on the way.

When the relay team asked for a sitrep, Thayer reported, "Bellwood and I have been hit hard. I think we need to *di di mau*." Without waiting for a response he requested artillery support. But when he looked down at his wrist compass to give the artillery FDO an azimuth, he was shocked to discover that a bullet had smashed his compass and knocked the glass facing off his wristwatch. He could only mutter, "Oh shit!"

Laurer squatted down to change magazines and gave Thayer a reading from his compass. He also informed Thayer that they were at the south end of the tree line instead of the north. That was why the LRP team leader had been unable to confirm their position.

Thayer quickly called in a fire mission on the north end of the wood line and requested gunship support. But he was amazed when within seconds of his request Cobra gunships arrived over the embattled team. He couldn't understand how they had arrived so quickly until he stopped to realize that they had probably responded at the first word of the team being in contact.

The Cobra pilots could see the team spread out across the open terrain ten to fifteen meters back from the tree line. It was obvious to them that the LRPs were fighting for their lives. So when the team leader got on the radio and told them to hit anything in the wood line, they wasted no time earning their pay. As the gunships hovered over the patrol like protective mother hens, they began blasting the trees with rockets, miniguns, and 40mm grenades. Amazingly the NVA stood their ground and continued to return fire.

Along the edge of the woods the three mobile LRPs and their PRU teammates continued to move and fire as they fought for their lives. Of the seven LRPs, only Bellwood and Thayer were down and out of the fight.

The PRUs and the NVA were still shouting back and forth at one another Thayer noticed, as he stood once again to rejoin the fight. At this time he discovered he could no longer hold his weapon to his right shoulder. Undaunted, he squeezed the heavy rifle against his left side and got off single shots whenever he spotted an enemy soldier among the trees.

Twenty minutes after the initial contact, the extraction slick arrived on the scene. It came in from the south and set down about eighty meters from the wood line, directly behind the team's position. NVA fire was still coming from the trees, but not as heavy as before. The Cobra gunships were exacting a terrible price from the enemy soldiers.

Thayer shouted for Laurer and O'Day to retrieve Bellwood, then, without waiting to see if they were complying, he turned and ran back toward the helicopter to tell the door gunner to give them some cover fire. When the crewman complied, Thayer moved to rejoin his teammates.

While the two PRUs, Boone, and Thayer continued firing into the trees, O'Day and Laurer grabbed Bellwood under each arm and began dragging him back toward the waiting helicopter. As they passed Thayer's position, the team leader looked over his shoulder and shouted to Boone and the PRUs, *"Mount up!"*

Everyone but Thayer was aboard as O'Day and Laurer slid the unconscious Bellwood into the cabin of the chopper. Thayer reached the chopper just as it started to go light on its skids. He climbed aboard and dropped to one knee next to Bellwood. The eighteen-year-old RTO was pale and not breathing.

On the ride back to Tan An, Thayer believed that his RTO was dead. Until he saw him cough once. Realizing that he might still have a chance, he shouted at the pilot to get them to a hospital.

O'Day caught Thayer's eye and pointed toward his team leader's right sleeve. When Thayer looked down he saw congealed blood dripping from the end of his sleeve and puddling on the cabin floor. Thayer shook his head and muttered, "Don't worry about me," then, nodding toward Bellwood, said, "I think he's still alive." They were only a few minutes away from the aid station at Tan An and he knew that if they could get there quickly, Bellwood might make it.

As soon as the medevac helicopter landed, a half dozen medics slid Bellwood onto a gurney and began wheeling him into triage. The rest of the wounded LRPs followed close behind. They found their platoon leader inside the operating room, waiting for them. As a team of doctors started working on Bellwood, one of the medics turned to help Thayer remove his shirt. When he saw the wound, he frowned and told the LRP team leader to have a seat on the table behind him.

Thayer was sitting on the edge of the table with tears running down his cheeks, watching the doctors working on his friend and teammate, when another doctor walked up to him and said, "You're not hurt that bad, son."

Thayer looked up at the doctor and immediately came unglued. He jumped off the table shouting, *"You think I'm worried about this? That's my friend over there!"* he screamed. *"Get over there and take care of him! Do you even know how close I was to that boy?"*

With that, he charged across the room to grab a

weapon from one of his PRUs, but was stopped by his platoon leader who shouted, "Sergeant Thayer! Just be cool. Don't get upset. Everything's all right!"

The medic, seeing that the situation had been defused, patted Thayer's arm and said, "C'mon, Sarge, get back up here and let me wrap that shoulder." The callous physician, realizing his close call, quickly turned on his heel and left the room. Things began to calm down after that.

After the medic finished wrapping Thayer's shoulder, the bleeding stopped. The medic informed him that the bullet had left no exit wound, that it had to be lodged somewhere in his back. He would have to go to the surgical hospital at Tan Son Nhut to have it removed.

At that time one of the doctors who had been working on Richard Bellwood turned and said, "He's gone. There's nothing else we can do."

Thayer was devastated. Lost in his own personal grief, he was scarcely aware of what was going on when the medics put him on a gurney and took him out to a medevac chopper. They placed him on a litter and slipped it into the bottom rack, tight against the back cabin wall of the helicopter. Another wounded soldier was on the litter just above him. Thayer could see the blond hair on the back of the man's head and thought it was Bellwood. There had been a mistake. Richard Bellwood was still alive. Happily, Thayer reached up with his left arm and grabbed the wounded man's arm. The two soldiers held hands as the chopper lifted off, Thayer muttering, "We're going to make it, Richard, we're going to make it." He continued talking to the wounded man all the way to Saigon.

Stark reality returned a short time later when the wounded were being off-loaded at Tan Son Nhut Air Base. To his horror and grief, Thayer glimpsed the face of the soldier he thought was Richard Bellwood and realized his mistake.

Thayer was immediately taken to surgery, where a medic began cutting away what was left of his uniform. He was still wearing his U.S. Marine Corps K-bar knife in a sheath on his belt, a keepsake that had been with him for a long time. Thayer told the medic, "Don't cut the belt."

The medic stopped what he was doing and looked up at the doctor, who quickly nodded and said, "Just pull it off."

Thayer begged, "Don't take my knife away. I don't want to lose it."

The doctor answered, "No problem; we'll just wrap the belt around the sheath and put it under your bed." Then he told Thayer that he was going to give him a local anesthetic and cut the bullet out of his back.

When the surgery was over and the doctor had rewrapped his shoulder, Thayer once again asked about his knife. The doctor smiled and promised him that he would give it to the ward clerk for safekeeping, then he gave Thayer something to help him sleep.

The next morning after Thayer had awakened, he received a phone call on the landline from fellow 9th Division LRPs Jesse Deleon and Bob Pegram back at Tan An. They asked Thayer how he was feeling and when he was coming back, and then told him that all hell had broken loose out at the wood line after his team had been extracted. Four infantry companies had been fed into the area that afternoon to assault the wood line and the battle was still going on. There were dead NVA everywhere. But to Thayer, all the dead NVA in the world weren't enough to make up for the loss of Richard Bellwood.

The following morning, while Jim Thayer was waiting

for his medevac flight to Japan, the 9th Infantry Division's commanding general and Thayer's company commander, Capt. Dale Dickey, arrived at the surgical hospital in Saigon to see Sergeant Thayer. They praised him for the outstanding job that he and his teammates had done. Then in a brief, casual ceremony, the general presented the wounded LRP the Silver Star and Purple Heart. The NCO was even more surprised when his commanding officer informed him that he had been promoted to the rank of staff sergeant (E-6).

After recovering from his wound at Camp Zama in Japan, S.Sgt. Jim Thayer returned to South Vietnam nine weeks later. He still had his trusty combat knife. When he finally arrived at Tan An five days late, he was shown an article that had appeared in the 9th Division's newspaper, *Old Reliable*. The article described the battle and the heavy casualties inflicted upon the NVA company trapped in the wood line. The four 9th Division infantry companies that combat assaulted into the area and encircled the wood line after the LRPs were extracted completed the annihilation of the NVA company during a two-day battle, killing nearly a hundred enemy soldiers in the process.

Thayer was informed that Spec Fours Mike O'Day and Steve Laurer had also received Silver Stars for their actions that day at the wood line. Laurer's medal was awarded along with a Purple Heart. Both men had also received a promotion to the rank of sergeant (E-5). Sp4. Willy Boone received a Bronze Star with "V" device, as did PFC Richard Bellwood along with a Purple Heart. Bellwood's medals were awarded posthumously.

Company I, 75th Infantry (Ranger), 1st Infantry Division

On 10 January 1970, I Company, 75th Infantry (Ranger), 1st Infantry Division, was still sending reconnaissance teams into the Song Be Corridor, north/northwest of Lai Ke. The area had been a hotbed of enemy activity for years, and extensive infantry operations into the region had not had any lasting effect on the enemy's control of the corridor. Besides monitoring nearly all the likely LZs in the Song Be Corridor, NVA counterrecon units were stationed throughout the entire area of operations.

Sergeant Robert Grose's patrol, Tracker Two-Two, received a warning order for a mission going into the corridor two days later. When he went on the overflight with his ATL, Sgt. Robbie Ballard, the day before the mission, he chose an overgrown rice paddy at the base of a brushy slope that rose to an extensive area of single-canopy for the team's insertion LZ. It appeared the most likely spot from which to search for the enemy if he was anywhere in the AO.

At the premission briefing the G-2 officer told the team that they were scheduled to go in at last light the next day and would spend the following five days reconning the area. That statement caused mumbled comments and eyes to roll among the six Rangers; no one *ever* stayed on the ground in the Song Be Corridor for the entire length of a mission. It was almost a waste of effort to carry a five-day supply of meals and water.

As was usual for that area, the terrain was level to rolling, with a lot of single-canopy jungle and shoulder-high brush. Concealment was never a problem, but the low vegetation provided little in the way of cover. Firefights with large enemy forces usually degenerated quickly into running gun battles, with the Rangers leading the race. On that mission the weather promised to be favorable, with dry, warm days and dry, mild nights.

Besides Grose and Ballard, Tracker Two-Two consisted of Sgt. James Gross, the senior RTO; Sp4. Jerome Tate at point; Sp4. Frank Johnson, the grenadier; and a new "shake 'n' bake" NCO tab-qualified Ranger straight from the States. He was so new in the company that no one even knew his name. But "shake 'n' bakes" were like that. It usually took them a while to get over the enormity of their own egos and settle down to become good NCOs—that is if they managed to live long enough. Grose showed his personal opinion of factory-made staff sergeants by appointing the new guy to fill the role of junior RTO for his first mission.

Grose set up the patrol order with Tate at point carrying a CAR-15. The team leader would walk slack and also tote a CAR. The senior RTO walked third, carrying an M-16, followed by Johnson armed with the "blooper" and a CAR-15. Then the new guy with his M-16 behind Johnson. It was a good spot for the FNG because he would be right in front of Ballard where, from his rear security post, the ATL could keep him out of trouble. Ballard was a giant who looked like he might have lifted a lot of weights and maybe even played some big-time college football before joining the Army. The heavy M-14 he carried looked like a toy in his massive hands.

Nearly an hour before last light, the patrol left Lai Ke heading north/northwest in a formation of five helicopters. Two Cobra gunships provided an escort for the insertion aircraft, the chase ship, and the LOH that flew C&C for the mission. The Ranger's RZ was on the far end of the corridor, nearly forty minutes north of Lai Ke.

Once they reached the area, the chase ship dropped down and made a number of fake insertions before the insertion aircraft leapfrogged ahead and flared over the designated LZ while the chase ship sped past to fake another false insertion. The LZ turned out to be a large, overgrown field that had probably once served as a rice paddy. It was surrounded by thick, brushy tree lines.

When the Huey touched down, the team exited the left side of the aircraft in seconds, then sprinted due east, heading for the nearest tree line which was twenty meters upslope from the LZ. The pilot had done his best to get them in as close as possible to the edge of the clearing. They ran about twenty meters into the trees before dropping silently into a wagon-wheel defense perimeter and laying dog.

While the Rangers caught their second wind and listened for signs of trouble, Sergeant Grose radioed for a quick commo check, gave the patrol's first sitrep, then released the choppers to return to base.

The patrol waited fifteen or twenty minutes before Grose signaled Tate to move out. This was quicker than Grose normally preferred, but the long flight and series of false insertions had used up most of their remaining daylight. Grose wanted to get his team away from the LZ and into some heavy cover while the men could still see.

The patrol had moved fifty or sixty meters up the slope away from the clearing when they began hearing movement in the brush on their right flank. Tate immediately signaled for everyone to halt and go to ground. The movement sounded like one or two individuals trying to make a lot more noise than one or two individuals normally make. It appeared to Grose that whoever was out there was trying to get his patrol to give its position away by opening fire prematurely, a favorite tactic of the enemy of late. They would let American and allied recon teams land, release their aircraft, and move away from their LZs before initiating contact. And the assault was always preceded by the enemy's attempting to get the patrol to betray its location. Fortunately, Grose was aware of the tactic and immediately took the appropriate action to avoid the enemy. He motioned for his team to freeze in place and remain concealed. Each man knew enough to hold his fire until the last moment then, if possible, to respond first with grenades to avoid giving away the team's position.

The enemy attempted two or three more times to entice the team into opening fire or moving, but to no avail. Grose thought that the enemy had either spotted the team inserting or had heard the helicopter departing. But the fact that they were attempting to get the team to betray its position was a good indication that they were unclear about where they were. If the patrol could remain undetected for the next hour or two, the NVA would most likely tire of the game and move on. At least, that's what he hoped!

Soon it was dark enough that everything was in full shadow. The Rangers had not heard any movement around them for fifteen or twenty minutes. It was time to move. They had to get into heavier cover and find a place to set up an NDP (night defense position) if they were to make it through the night without being detected. Grose motioned for Tate to move out and locate a good spot to hole up in. They would have to take the first site he ran across; there was not enough time for the patrol to set up in a false NDP then move out in full darkness to set up again in the actual overnight site. It was already far too dark to attempt that type of maneuver.

Tate soon located a spot that had plenty of concealment in the dense brush on the slope, but the thin, scraggly scrub offered poor cover if they ended up getting into a firefight with an enemy force. The Rangers moved quickly to set up their usual wagon-wheel perimeter about a hundred meters from the LZ. But before they could set claymores out around them, the movement started up again. The enemy was rustling around in the brush both north and east of the patrol's location. The enemy soldiers were shuffling around in the thick cover, deliberately making noise to spook the Rangers. That went on for another forty-five to sixty minutes. By then everyone on the team was pretty much on edge and ready to kick some ass.

Suddenly one of the NVA soldiers broke through the brush at the edge of the Rangers' perimeter and nearly stepped on Tate. The point man had no choice but to open fire at point-blank range. Ballard, to his immediate right, backed him up and put a full magazine from his M-14 into several more NVA who were standing right behind the one that Tate had just killed.

Not knowing for certain what had just occurred, the remainder of the team began putting out suppressive fire downrange to aid their companions. It was just as they had practiced in training and it was paying off.

Tate and Ballard killed two or three NVA in their opening blasts, but there were more NVA up the slope from the team's perimeter. The enemy soldiers who were spread out through the brush immediately returned fire, sending green tracers crisscrossing high and to the left of the Rangers' perimeter. For some reason the remainder of the NVA still had no idea where the American recon team was.

From the number of green tracers flashing through the darkness it appeared that at least three or four enemy soldiers were doing the firing. Grose whispered to his teammates to prepare to throw one frag each straight out in front of their position on his command. When the grenades exploded they were to withdraw back down to the LZ.

Sergeant Grose, the senior RTO, got on the radio and called for an extraction just before the grenades were tossed. By the time the frags exploded through the heavy cover, the patrol was up and running back toward their original insertion point. Just before they reached the clearing, Tate stopped the team at the edge of the brush and motioned everyone to circle up in a wagon-wheel defensive perimeter. They would stand and defend themselves there until the choppers reached them.

It was only minutes before the patrol heard enemy soldiers pursuing them through the brush. At a distance of thirty or forty meters from the team's position, the NVA suddenly slowed down and began to recon by fire. Enemy bullets were coming in high over the team. Once again, the NVA seemed to have no concrete idea of where the Rangers were located.

At the edge of the clearing the long-range patrol waited until the NVA were nearly on top of them before they came up on one knee and tossed six more grenades out into the brush. There was dead silence for several moments after the frags exploded, then the NVA began once again to fire, this time forcing the team out into the open clearing.

The six Rangers broke from cover and sprinted for a waist-high grassy area in the center of the overgrown rice paddy. When they reached the sparse concealment they again quickly dropped down into a defensive circle and prepared to defend themselves to the death.

As they had broken free of the brush, Ballard accidentally tripped over a concealed root and went down hard, tearing the cartilage in his right knee. He was limping badly by the time he reached the grassy area. Not realizing that the patrol's big man was injured, Grose had Ballard switch places with Johnson so that he and his M-14 would be up next to Tate, facing the tree line they had just vacated. He whispered for Johnson to move to the backside of the perimeter with his M-79, so that he could pull security on that side yet still be able to lob indirect fire into the enemy up on the slope if the NVA attacked. From there it would be safer for him to shoot his M-79 over the rest of the team than to use an automatic weapon, which he would have to train lower.

The patrol was only fifty meters from the tree line where the enemy soldiers were located, yet they held their fire until they had targets they could identify. Soon the NVA managed to work up enough courage to come right out to the edge of the brush. They still did not seem to know were the recon team had gone. The six Rangers watched in silence as the enemy soldiers searched the cover looking for them. The NVA paused every now and then to recon by fire, shooting in every direction except where the Rangers lay hidden out in the open field.

Between the bursts of gunfire, Grose continued to

whisper for his teammates to hold their fire. In a hushed voice, Grose reported that he had just been in contact with the C&C aircraft and been told that helicopters were on the way. However, it would still take them nearly an hour to reach the team's AO.

The NVA began to grow desperate and decided to send a couple of their "new guys" out into the open rice paddy with flashlights to look for the American recon team. The two unfortunate soldiers walked back and forth in a zigzag pattern, frantically waving their lights around on the ground. It was obvious they were trying to avoid making easy targets of themselves.

By this time Grose told Ballard and Tate that if the enemy got close to the team's hiding place and they had good targets, to go ahead and open fire. Grose estimated that the NVA in the brush above them now numbered fifteen to twenty men.

Johnson was pulling security in the opposite direction when he heard Ballard and Tate open up behind him. The two Rangers had watched silently as the two NVA with the flashlights had stumbled to within ten meters, too close to the team's perimeter to stay alive. Ballard and Tate opened fire simultaneously and the two enemy soldiers died instantly.

However, their flashlights lived on, casting narrow beams of light along the ground as they rolled from dead fingers.

Their death was the signal for the remaining NVA to open fire. And some of the rounds began impacting very close to the hidden Rangers. Even so, they were wild, random shots. The bright beams of the flashlights served as directional beacons to mark what the surviving NVA believed were their targets. Even though they could see exactly where their two fallen comrades lay dead, they still did not know for certain where the Americans who had killed them were hidden.

When the NVA finally stopped firing to reload their weapons, the Rangers once again broke cover, angling south as they pulled back another fifty meters to set up a third defensive perimeter. Johnson, on the backside of the last position, was now in front, leading the way as they ran.

As soon as the patrol was reestablished in a fighting position, the NVA began moving out into the open rice paddy and commenced to recon by fire once again. This time the team heard a 61mm mortar lob rounds from approximately the location upslope where the patrol had made its furthest penetration from the LZ.

At first they assumed the rounds were headed directly for them, but they were shocked moments later when they heard the first round impact more than five hundred meters off.

The enemy soldiers out in the clearing stopped shooting and began moving forward while the mortar was firing. Grose thought they had to be either the worst shots in the world or, by some strange miracle, they still had no idea where the American recon team had gone.

The mortar fired three more rounds before the choppers arrived over the area. The five aircraft went into a high orbit while the C&C ship made contact with the Rangers and requested them to mark their position with a strobe light. No longer needing to whisper, Ballard shouted for Johnson and told him, ". . . Just do it, man."

Johnson crawled about twenty meters away from the team's perimeter, rolled over on his back, placed his strobe light in the breech of his M-79, then turned it on, pointed it straight up at the sky, and said a silent prayer.

The NVA responded immediately by opening fire in Johnson's direction. Amazingly, that particular group of NVA couldn't hit anything they aimed at, but they managed to put on one hell of a light show with their tracers.

Suddenly, Grose screamed to Johnson that the choppers had a visual on the team's location and were inbound. The senior RTO quickly shot an azimuth to the enemy positions from the team's perimeter and gave the gunships a bearing. The first Cobra came in firing miniguns into the brush on the slope northeast of the team. The NVA immediately stopped firing at Johnson and dashed for cover.

The C&C instructed Grose to have his team ready because, when the second Cobra made its run, the extraction ship would attempt to slip in under the cover of the gunship to pick up the patrol.

Without weighing the possibilities, Grose instructed the C&C to have the slick land directly "on" the strobe light.

The second gunship began its run just as the first gunship was swinging around to begin a second pass and the blacked-out slick came in and flared directly over Johnson, who was lying flat on his back in the field at the time. He could hear the aircraft directly above him but had no visual on it until he saw his strobe light reflecting off the Plexiglas chin bubble in the nose of the aircraft. Johnson had only a second to roll out of the way as the chopper touched down right where he had been lying.

The badly frightened grenadier leaped to his feet and dived aboard the chopper. He ended up flat on his back on the floor, still trying to shut off the damned strobe light. About that time the remainder of the team, pouring in from the other side of the aircraft, swarmed over Johnson.

Before the pilot could lift off from the LZ and vacate the area, a cluster of green tracers passed through the open door of the aircraft and out the other side. Both door gunners immediately opened fire.

Seconds later the two Cobras moved back in to suppress the enemy small-arms fire as the slick pilot lifted his aircraft out of the LZ. Twenty feet off the ground the pilot suddenly dropped the ship's nose and began moving forward to pick up airspeed, then slowly took off to the west, parallel to the brush-covered slope the enemy was still firing from. The courageous pilot kept the helicopter low to the ground while picking up speed until he was well out of the area.

But the danger was not yet over for the Rangers and the aircraft crew. Shortly after the helicopter cleared the vicinity of the firefight, the pilot looked back over his shoulder and shouted that the chopper was losing its hydraulics and he was unable to climb any higher. Then he ordered the Rangers to hang on because he was going to try to reach Highway 13. If he could manage that, he could fly the aircraft at low level all the way to Lai Ke, using the roadbed as his flight path. Turning on his landing lights, he flew the crippled ship at a 150-foot altitude until he reached the highway.

The thoroughly frightened Rangers were sitting in the back of the aircraft, thinking they had managed to survive one hell of a situation with the enemy only to die in a flaming helicopter crash. There just wasn't any justice in the world!

The veteran pilot skillfully nursed the crippled aircraft all the way back to Lai Ke amid the sickening, acrid smell of overheated oil. The chase ship, the C&C aircraft, and both Cobra gunships had moved overhead and to the flanks of the wounded chopper to escort it back to base camp.

When the men in the five-ship formation finally spotted the lights of Lai Ke's airstrip, several crash vehicles were standing by. The pilot shouted for everyone to hang on to anything they could find as he was going to have to make a running approach, whatever that was. At that time none of the Rangers knew that the aircraft had lost its ability to hover.

The chopper bounced several times as it touched down and began to slide along the PSP runway. As the pilot went through the emergency procedures for shutting down the aircraft, the copilot screamed for everyone to get off as soon as it came to a complete stop. No Ranger had to be told twice.

Finally safe on the ground, the recon team met up with some of the guys from the Ranger TOC who were waiting at the side of the runway with a deuce-and-a-half truck. The team members quickly tossed their gear aboard and returned to the Ranger compound, where they were immediately debriefed. At the end of the debriefing they were told that their ride had taken seventeen or eighteen rounds through the tail boom, severing the helicopter's hydraulics.

Ballard and Tate were later given Bronze Stars with "V" device. For holding his strobe light in the open for twenty minutes while serving as a target for numerous enemy marksmen, Johnson was given a box of bad memories and a lifetime of nightmares, and little else. Such was justice in the Rangers.

LRRP Detachment, 3d Brigade, 4th Infantry Division

In the latter part of 1967, the 3d Brigade of the 25th Infantry Division was opcon (operational control) to the 4th Infantry Division, operating in the Central Highlands. Later on MACV would elect to swap the brigade with a similarly detached brigade of the 4th Division rather than return the two brigades to their parent units. But in the meantime the 25th Infantry Division's 3d Brigade continued to work an area of operations that ran west of Pleiku to the Cambodian border.

Due to the immense size of the 4th ID's area of operations, and to the extreme distances between brigade headquarters, each brigade found itself operating independently of the division. Likewise, each brigade found it expedient to form its own provisional LRRP detachment instead of relying on the division's long range reconnaissance patrol company to gather intelligence within the brigade's own area of responsibility.

Drawn from volunteers from the brigade, and usually heavily undermanned, the small long-range patrol detachments developed their own SOPs for equipment, tactics, and weapons. Teams of four Americans became the standard maintained by most of the brigade LRRP units, although some patrols were accompanied by a Montagnard or two. But it was not uncommon to see patrols of three and even two Americans operating alone in the bush.

At the time of the 1968 Tet Offensive, the 4th ID's 3d Brigade was based at Pleiku. However, its LRRP detachment was staging out of Polei Kleng, a Special Forces A-camp not far from the Cambodian border. Hit rather hard by the enemy's recent offensive and suffering from abnormal manpower rotations, the unit was sadly understrength. It was at that point in time that a veteran LRRP team leader, Sgt. Buck Anderson, decided to step up and amend the detachment's SOP.

A couple of years earlier, in April 1966, PFC Buck Anderson had arrived in Vietnam and been assigned to the 25th Infantry Division's 40th Infantry Platoon (Scout Dog Detachment) as a dog handler. The six-foot-one, one-quarter Modoc Indian, raised in the mountains of southern Oregon, had grown up hard, working both as a rancher and logger. Starting at the tender age of eight he had ridden rodeo for recreation. He was still busting wild broncs and riding bulls into the ground when the Vietnam War began to heat up in 1965. Anderson didn't wait for the draft to catch up to him; he enlisted for the infantry.

Seven months into Anderson's first tour, his German shepherd, King, was killed while on patrol. Anderson, heartbroken over the loss of his "best friend," decided to transfer to the division's 3d Brigade LRRPs rather than break in a new dog. It was a decision he would never regret. Anderson, having cut his teeth hunting deer, elk, and mountain lions in the mountains of southern Oregon and northern California, had little trouble adapting to the dangerous work of long-range patrolling in the rugged Central Highlands of South Vietnam. To Anderson the only difference between being an LRRP and hunting game on the West Coast was the prey. He enjoyed recon work so much that he kept extending his tour six months at a time, just to keep his hand in the game.

By early 1968 the understrength LRRP detachment was having a hard time attracting volunteers, and it was becoming increasingly difficult to keep more than four or five teams in the field. It was then that Anderson, by that time a sergeant and one of the most experienced LRRPs in the unit, came up with a plan to help ease the manpower shortage.

Anderson went to his detachment commander, 1st Lt. John W. Chester, and suggested that he be allowed to go out on patrol accompanied only by a Bru Montagnard named Ju. Ju was a member of the PRU force at Polei Kleng and lived with his wife and three children just outside the wire at the Special Forces encampment. He had accompanied Anderson's team on a number of patrols and had so impressed the LRRP with his courage, loyalty, and fighting ability that Anderson had no qualms about going out on patrol accompanied only by the tiny Montagnard.

At first Lieutenant Chester failed to warm up to the idea, but faced with the growing manpower dilemma, he soon agreed to allow Anderson to try out the idea. Many of Anderson's fellow LRRPs thought the big team leader had lost his mind, but Anderson was no fool. Confident of his own ability in the bush, and accepting the tiny Bru as at least his equal, Anderson looked forward to the first mission.

It didn't take long for Anderson to prove his idea in the field. After fifteen highly successful two-man patrols, no one in the detachment questioned his sanity again. At least not when it came to team staffing. Team Dragon Two was well on its way to becoming a legend.

In mid-March, the 3d Brigade was busy mopping up

enemy units that had participated in the ill-conceived Tet Offensive. However, a large number of enemy troops—predominantly NVA—were still operating in the mountains between Pleiku and the Cambodian border. One morning, five klicks west of LZ Mile High, a reconnaissance aircraft pilot patrolling the border spotted a high-speed trail among the trees. When he dropped down for a closer look he spotted a large number of NVA soldiers on it moving west to east, from Cambodia into South Vietnam.

Within hours, efforts were made to combat assault a brigade line company into the area of the sighting, but they met with no success. The terrain in the vicinity of the trail was simply too steep to accommodate a large number of helicopters.

A few hours later a second attempt was made to drop a platoon into the area. It met with the same results. Realizing that a reconnaissance in force was out of the question, Brigade S-2 quickly sent a warning order down to the LRRP detachment requesting a reconnaissance patrol to go in just east of the sighting and set up an OP to monitor enemy activity along the trail.

First Lieutenant Chester was out in the field on a mission when the warning order came down so it fell to 1st Sgt. Gary Howard to select a team for the mission. Because of the steep terrain and the dense jungle, he thought it might be a good mission for Team Dragon Two. He knew that two men would be able to get in and set up with a lot less commotion than a full team. Within minutes he went looking for Sergeant Anderson to notify him that Team Dragon Two had another mission.

When Howard located Anderson, he walked up to him and said, "You and Ju have a mission." Anderson simply nodded and headed toward the TOC to get the details of the patrol. Since it was already beginning to grow late in the day, he decided to conduct an overflight of the recon zone early the next morning.

It was nearly 0900 hours when Anderson, flying high over the AO in the rear seat of an O-1 Bird Dog, scanned the rugged terrain through binoculars. He noted that the area was steep and covered in triple-canopy jungle. No wonder the infantry CAs had been aborted.

As the aircraft made a number of passes over the area, Anderson spotted a section of "hard-pack" that he suspected was part of the trail. With a grease pencil he marked the location on his acetate-covered map, then went back to looking over the terrain far below. As the aircraft circled lazily on the morning thermals, he located an LZ that lay just over a ridgeline two klicks outside his target area. It wasn't much, just a tiny opening in the jungle on the side of a hill, but it was enough for a single Huey to get close enough to the ground to drop off a couple of men. The LZ would also have to serve as Team Dragon Two's pickup point at the end of the patrol. There were no other openings in the jungle for miles around. If they could manage to get in and back out again without being spotted, they would still have a hump of two klicks to get back to the LZ for extraction. If they were compromised during the mission, they would have to come out on strings (Maguire rigs) wherever the chopper could reach them.

The mission was scheduled to last four days, just enough time to allow the patrol to get in and out of the AO. The long-range weather forecast promised a continuation of the hot, humid, clear days typical of that time of the year. Commo would be handled by a radio relay team of two LRRPs set up at the SF camp at Polei Kleng. They would, in turn, relay the patrol's sitreps back to brigade headquarters at Pleiku.

Sergeant Anderson decided to carry his CAR-15 on the mission, taking along plenty of extra ammo. Ju would be armed with an AK-47. If need be, he could always scrounge ammunition from the bodies of enemy dead. In addition, each man carried a half dozen frags and a pair of claymore mines.

The insertion went in without a hitch at 1600 hours the next day. The Huey slick, escorted by a pair of Cobras and a Huey chase ship, executed two false insertions before flaring to a hover just over the designated LZ. Anderson and Ju, riding the skids on opposite sides of the aircraft, dropped ten or fifteen feet down onto the steep hillside. Hitting the ground hard, the two LRRPs rolled to their feet and dashed straight up the hill into the jungle where they quickly dropped to the ground and lay dog.

Carrying his own PRC-25 radio, Anderson grabbed the handset from where he had attached it to his LBE harness and established commo with both the C&C aircraft and the x-ray team back at Polei Kleng. Taking stock of their situation, the team leader decided that they had managed to get in unseen. Seconds later he released the helicopters to return to base. The LRRPs remained where they were until dark, then moved out again, heading uphill to the west.

They covered a full klick during the first night, silently crossing the ridge into their designated AO. They moved steadily down the reverse slope and partway up the opposite side of the next ridge before coming to a stop. They encountered a number of trails crossing the floor of the narrow valley, both Montagnard and game trails, but none seemed recently used.

It was nearly 0200 hours when they finally set up an NDP three hundred to four hundred meters below the crest of the ridge. They quickly set out their claymores and settled down to get a little sleep. The rest of the night was uneventful.

At 0800 hours the next day, the team moved north around the point of the ridge, then back to the south along the reverse slope. It wasn't long before they reached the spot Anderson had preselected for their OP. From that location he thought they would be able to see across the valley. The vegetation down on the floor of the valley was dense, broken here and there by an occasional opening choked with large stands of mature bamboo.

Just before noon they established the OP. Anderson quickly set up radio contact with the x-ray team and reported their position. Then, silently setting out their four claymores around them, the two men expertly booby-trapped them with toe-popper mines and settled in to await the night.

At dusk the LRRPs slipped out of the OP to retrieve their claymores, then silently worked their way down into the valley toward another opening Anderson had spotted earlier from their first OP. He had decided that an OP there would be better for observing the entire width of the valley.

It was fully dark when they finally reached the bottom of the valley. They were moving slowly through the dense jungle when they suddenly heard movement to their immediate right front. Dropping silently to the ground, the two men froze in place.

Over the next thirty minutes they watched in apprehension as a large number of bobbing flashlights moved steadily southeast through the jungle, perpendicular to their position less than seventy-five meters away. The lights were no more than four or five meters apart. Anderson knew there were a lot of people out there. He could not hear any sounds of conversation coming from the enemy soldiers, or any other noise for that matter. They appeared to be maintaining proper intervals, causing Anderson to assume that, at least, a well-disciplined NVA company was passing by. He also came to the obvious conclusion that he and his partner had just located the high-speed trail they had been sent in to observe. However, in the darkness and with heavy enemy activity in front of them, the two LRRPs had no choice but to go to ground.

When the enemy soldiers had finally moved on, Anderson estimated that well over a hundred NVA had passed by them in the darkness. He had counted just over a hundred flashlights flickering through the night, yet he had no way of knowing for certain how many soldiers might have been walking between the lights.

After the danger had finally passed, Ju softly nudged Anderson's leg and pointed back behind them to a shadowy area twenty-five meters away that appeared to be some kind of indentation in the hillside. Appreciating the little Montagnard's foresight, Anderson nodded, and the two men slowly withdrew from the trail and slipped back toward the base of the slope. When they reached it, Anderson saw that it was indeed some sort of cutback into the bank. It almost appeared to be man-made, which for a moment caused Anderson to reconsider. But with enemy forces moving through the valley, the spot offered both cover and concealment until daylight would allow them to see what they were up against. Silently, they once again set out their claymores facing the area to their front where the enemy soldiers had passed.

Safely ensconced in the depression, Anderson established radio contact with the relay team and called in the sighting. Relay immediately asked for coordinates, but Anderson informed them that he was unable to comply because of the darkness and the steep terrain around their position. He promised that he would call in the coordinates at first light, then signed off.

Twice during the night the two men observed single lights that appeared to be lanterns mounted on carts or bicycles passing by their location about one hundred meters out. The first sighting occurred ninety minutes after the infantry company had passed by out on the trail, and the second just two hours later. For some reason the enemy soldiers out on the trail were still maintaining total silence, a fact that was beginning to bother Anderson. Why were the NVA being so cautious in their own backyard? Did they suspect that a U.S. reconnaissance team was in the area?

The two men remained in position until 0900 hours the next morning. Then, retrieving their claymores, they continued moving cautiously toward the second OP site. But as they neared a bamboo thicket close to the trail that traversed the center of the valley, they suddenly heard the muted sounds of Vietnamese voices directly to their front less than fifteen meters away. The LRRPs froze in mid-step and slowly sank to the ground. Only a stand of mature bamboo separated them from the enemy soldiers.

After listening intently for a few moments, Anderson was relieved when he realized that the voices seemed to be carrying on a normal conversation. Ju, able to hear bits and pieces, nodded in agreement. There was no sense of alarm from the enemy soldiers. They appeared to be on the move, heading from right to left as had all the prior traffic out on the trail.

The two LRRPs quietly slipped out of their rucksacks, tied them to their waists with the six-foot sections of nylon rope they always carried, then began crawling slowly down game trails toward the sounds of the

voices. The trails, made by herds of wild pigs foraging in
the bamboo, formed tunnels that snaked through the
dense vegetation. There was adequate cover overhead to
prevent the two men being spotted from above. No one
could see them in the tunnels unless they got down on
hands and knees and crawled down the trails themselves. The trail network meandered back and forth
through the bamboo. Besides making it nearly impossible for anyone to see them, it also prevented the LRRPs
from seeing anything at a distance of more than ten or
fifteen feet. The biggest threat of detection by the enemy was from sound. However, the damp, bare soil
along the floor of the trail made their approach virtu-
ally silent.

After moving less than thirty feet, Anderson spotted
the dark brown streak of a major high-speed trail only
five meters ahead. Peering cautiously through the
hole in the bamboo, he saw bootprints and wheel ruts
in the soft, moist earth of the trail. The two LRRPs
stopped where they were in the middle of the pig trail
while Anderson attempted to establish radio contact
with the relay team back at Polei Kleng. Unable to talk
above a whisper because of their close proximity to the
trail, he finally managed to raise them, only to discover
that he had a commo problem: the radio operator
couldn't understand his message, and Anderson could
barely hear the radio operator. The short whip antenna
was simply not long enough to get the signal out of the
valley.

Back at the Special Forces camp, Lieutenant Chester
was quickly apprised of the situation. The relay team
had notified him that Team Dragon Two was trying to
call in a sitrep but having difficulty transmitting. Aware
that the two-man patrol had reported sighting a large
number of enemy troops near them the night before, the

LRRP commander decided that he had better get up
over the team to find out if they were in some kind of
trouble. Within minutes he was heading west aboard a
LOH scout helicopter in an attempt to establish radio
contact with the patrol.

Ten minutes later Chester was circling a klick outside
the patrol's recon box, trying to raise the team on the
radio. It wasn't long before he managed to make contact with Anderson, who, in a whisper, quickly filled
him in on the previous night's events. Anderson informed Chester that he and Ju were set up on a game
trail less than five meters from the high-speed.

While Anderson was finishing his sitrep, he suddenly
spotted movement directly ahead of him across the
opening to the tunnel. He looked up and spotted the
legs of a number of NVA soldiers passing by out on
the trail. Moving ever so slowly, Anderson turned down
the squelch on his radio and held his breath as approximately fifty NVA walked past his position.

As soon as the enemy soldiers had passed by,
Anderson reported the latest sighting to his commanding officer. Chester, realizing the danger the team was in,
advised him to move back to a safer location immediately. Anderson refused the advice, stating that there was
no way they could safely move back until dark.
Reluctantly, Chester told him to stay put and wait it out.

Down on the ground where Anderson and Ju lay hidden, the dense bamboo bordering both sides of the
trail hid it completely from view of overflying aircraft.
Through the tiny opening where the pig trail intersected
the high-speed, Anderson could tell that the main trail
was much more than a mere footpath. It appeared to be
at least ten feet across, easily wide enough for two carts
to pass each other. For the NVA using it, the trail must
have looked like a national highway.

Chester radioed Anderson and told him he would have to head back to Polei Kleng to refuel, but promised that he would be back out as soon as he could. Anderson acknowledged the transmission and signed off, and the two LRRPs settled down to wait for darkness.

They saw no more activity during the remainder of the day, as the two men tried to stay alert in the humid confines of the pig trail. However, enemy foot traffic began to pick up again as soon as the sun dropped behind the ridgeline to their west.

At 1800 hours another party of fifty NVA passed by their position, moving to the southeast. The enemy soldiers were wearing OD green uniforms with canvas "batta" boots. Anderson immediately got Chester back on the horn and reported the latest intel, advising him that he and Ju were still unable to move back from the edge of the "Redball."

Chester radioed back that he was going to do a fly-over to see if he could spot any lights in the general area of the team. As the officer was finishing his transmission, Anderson spotted more movement out on the trail to his immediate front. With enemy soldiers passing by less than fifteen feet away, he was unable to respond to Chester's last statement.

At that moment Chester's LOH passed over the hidden team. Out on the trail the effect was immediate. The NVA soldiers dropped to the ground on both sides of the trail. From where he lay hidden, Anderson could easily make out a man's arm stretched across the opening to the main trail less than five meters away. The LRRP team leader froze, knowing that the enemy soldier was less than a foot away from being able to look down the wild game trail and spotting him.

The NVA soldiers lay dog for the next thirty minutes

or so while the helicopter circled overhead several times before moving on. Waiting to make sure that the American aircraft did not return, the enemy troops took their time getting back to their feet and even longer moving out of the area. Anderson figured they were either being more cautious than normal or there were more of them than he had first thought. Finally, when the NVA unit had moved beyond the spot where the LRRPs lay hidden, Anderson shoved Ju with his foot to signal him to begin withdrawing back away from the trail.

They had moved to a point five meters beyond the bamboo when they heard more activity out on the trail. The two men dropped to their knees and waited another thirty to forty-five minutes in the darkness while more enemy soldiers moved past. The two LRRPs were too far back to see lights, but they could still hear the muted sounds of the NVA moving down the trail.

After the latest group of enemy soldiers had finally cleared the area, Anderson and Ju got back to their feet and continued moving, paralleling the trail to the west. A short time later they came to a narrow creek and discovered a bamboo bridge where the trail crossed the stream. To reach the point Anderson had selected for their new OP, they would have to cross the stream. There was simply no other choice.

Not wanting to leave any sign of their crossing in the damp earth covering the ten-foot-wide trail, Anderson decided to cross the stream directly under the bridge. The noise of the running water would help drown out any noises they might make. As they neared the bridge, Anderson slipped out of his ruck and signaled for Ju to do the same so the two LRRPs could pass under the low span.

Once they were on the other side of trail, Ju signaled

that he wanted to go back and booby-trap the bridge with an M-14 toe-popper mine. Anderson shook his head; he knew that if the NVA in the area even suspected that there was an American patrol around, they would be all over the valley in minutes trying to flush it from hiding.

After the two men crossed the creek, Anderson halted long enough to call in a current sitrep. He reported continuous heavy enemy activity in the area. At that moment LZ Mile High broke in over the air and reported that it was being hit by mortars and small-arms fire. That was significant to Anderson and Ju because LZ Mile High was only ten or so klicks from the patrol. Rising quickly to his feet, Anderson could make out the sounds of gunfire and explosions to the southeast. For the first time the LRRP team leader thought that he knew the destination of the enemy soldiers who had been moving past them.

Anderson and Ju continued moving cautiously to the east, still paralleling the trail. They were heading for a spot overlooking the high-speed directly across from where they had first observed it. As they neared the general area where Anderson had chosen to set up the new OP, they noticed a large stand of bamboo that appeared to run back from the trail almost directly across from their previous night's OP.

They were skirting it when they heard voices up the slope seventy-five meters to their right. Sandwiched between an enemy unit in bivouac a short distance up the ridge and the trail to their left, the two LRRPs suddenly found themselves in a very dangerous predicament.

Anderson looked at the luminous dial on his watch and marked the time at 0300. It would begin to grow light in less than two and a half hours, and they were in

The Phantom Warriors' Photo Gallery

Company F, 52nd Infantry (LRP) 1st Infantry Division LRPS at Lai Khe in late 1968. *Standing left to right:* Larry Wenzel, Freddie Blankenship, Gary Johnson, Robert Levine, and Dave Flores. *Squatting left to right:* Bill Goshen and Julian Rincon. Johnson and Levine were KIA on 27 February 1969, Goshen and Wenzel were badly wounded. (Courtesy of Bill Goshen)

Company F, 52nd Infantry (LRP), 1st Infantry Division LRPs at Lai Khe, 1968. *Standing left to right:* Sgt. Robert P. Elsner, Sp.4 Thomas McMahon, and Sgt. David Hill. *Squatting:* Sp.4 Richard Chase. (Courtesy of Robert Elsner)

LRRP Detachment, 196th Light Infantry Brigade, 1967, during operation Junction City in Tay Ninh Province. *Standing left to right:* Vic Valeraino, Robert Clark, G. Williams, Paul Rosselle, Earl Toomey. *Kneeling:* Tony Mazzuchi and Mark Brennan. (Courtesy of Vic Valeriano)

LRRP Platoon, 2nd Brigade, 4th Infantry Division, Central Highlands 1967. Sp.4 Ron Coon on patrol in the Ia Drang Valley. (Courtesy of Ron Coon.)

74th LRRP Detachment, 173rd Airborne Brigade, 1967. Team 3 at helipad before a patrol. (Courtesy of Pat Tadina)

74th LRRP Detachment, 173rd Airborne Brigade, 1967. "Bugs" Moran and Fletcher Ruckman in TOC bunker before a briefing. (Courtesy of F. Ruckman)

Project Delta, B-52, 5th Special Forces Group (Abn). Sgt. Charles McDonald resting on patrol. (Courtesy of Charles McDonald)

Project Delta, B-52, 5th Special Forces Group (Abn). *Left to right:* Sgt. Charles McDonald and SFC Paul Tracy. (Courtesy of Charles McDonald)

Project Delta, B-52, 5th Special Forces Group (Abn). SFC Cook. (Courtesy of Charles McDonald)

Project Delta, B-52, 5th Special Forces Group (Abn.) SSG Tafoya and Sgt. McDonald resting during a patrol. (Courtesy of Charles McDonald)

Company D, 151st Infantry (Ranger), Indiana National Guard, II Field Force, 1969. Team 2-5. SP.4 Terry MacDonald (*left*) and Sgt. Jack Jarvis (*right*) in staging area waiting to go out on patrol. (Courtesy of Terry MacDonald)

LRRP Detachment, 1st Calvary Division. Team Dark Marauder Foxtrot. Sgt. Ron Holte directing artillery fire against NVA positions in the 506 Valley. (Courtesy of Ken White)

Company E, 52nd Infantry (LRP), 1st Calvary Division. *Left to right:* Sgt. Rick Tedder, Sp.4 Benny Gentry, Sp.4 Felix Leon Jr. (KIA) on patrol northwest of Hue 1968. (Courtesy of Ken White)

LRRP B-36, 5th Special Forces Group (Abn). Sp.4 Bill Miller, at 18 the youngest American soldier in B-36, waiting on the airstrip at Tay Ninh during Rapid Fire V. (Courtesy of David Spencer)

LRRP Platoon, 3rd Brigade, 4th Infantry Division, 1967. Sgt. Buck Anderson on the right after completing a successful two-man patrol into an enemy held valley. (Courtesy of Buck Anderson).

Company E, 75th Infantry, (Ranger), 9th Infantry Division, 1 June 1969. Foreground left to right: SSG Jim Thayer and 1st Lt. Al Zapata just before a mission where Thayer was wounded in the chest. (Courtesy of Jim Thayer).

Company F, 58th Infantry (LRP), 101st Airborne Division, September 1968. Sp.4 Riley "Dozer" Cox. (Courtesy of Gary Linderer)

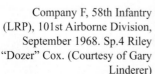

Company L, 75th Infantry (Ranger), 101st Airborne Division, 1970. SSG Jim "Lobo" Bates (3rd from left) team preparing to go out on patrol in the Ruong Ruong Valley. (Courtesy of Robin Kristiansen)

LRRP Detachment, 1st Brigade, 101st Airborne Division, January 1967. Sp.4 Kenn Miller on patrol. (Courtesy of Kenn Miller)

Company F, 58th Infantry (LRP), 101st Airborne Division, September 1968. Sp.4 Mitch Taylor at a river crossing southwest of Hue. (Courtesy of Gary

Company F, 58th Infantry (LRP), 101st Airborne Division, January 1968. William "Raider" Laing preparing to go out on patrol. (Courtesy of Gary Linderer)

Company F, 58th Infantry, 101st Airborne Division, September 1968. Sgt. Tom Brooks helping Sgt. John Burford up a river bank southwest of Hue. (Courtesy of Gary Linderer)

LRRP Detachment, 3/506th battalion 101st Airborne Division. Long range patrol after a tough mission west of Phan Thiet. *Front:* Sp.4 Oliva. *Middle, left to right:* Sp.4 Ohama, Sp.4 Christopher "Kip" Rolland, Sp.4 Seivers, and Sgt. Jerry Gomes. *Rear:* Sp.4 Wilson. (Courtesy of C. Rolland)

Company D, 75th Infantry (Ranger), II Field Force. *Left to right:* Sgt. Pat Brown, PFC Rafael Baez, Sp.4 Ernest "Frisco" Cuyler, Sp.4 Gerald "Slim" Wilson. (Courtesy of Steve Meade)

Company D, 75th Infantry (Ranger), II Field Force. Team 3-5. *Standing left to right:* Sp.4 Tom Delaney, Sp.4 William Fitzgerald, Kit Carson scout (name unknown), Sp.4 Ken Dern. *Sitting:* Sp.4 Richard "Herd" Nelson. (Courtesy of Tom Delaney)

Company F, 52nd Infantry (LRP), 1st Infantry Division, 1968. *Left to right:* Sgt. Robert Elsner, Sp.4 Duke, and Sp.4 Billy Faulkner. (Courtesy of William Faulkner)

Company M, 75th Infantry (Ranger), 199th Infantry Brigade. SSG Sloyer. (Courtesy of Mark Johnston)

Company M, 75th Infantry (Ranger), 199th Brigade. A LRRP takes a break on patrol. (Courtesy of Mark Johnston)

Company M, 75th Infantry (Ranger), 199th Brigade. Sgt. Mark Johnston posing at the entrance of the Company M compound. (Courtesy of Mark Johnston)

A long range patrol's favorite sight—a Huey slick coming in to extract the team. (Courtesy of Gary Linderer).

Screaming Eagle LRP team inserting west of LZ Sally in I Corps, 1968. (Courtesy of Darrol Walker)

Company L, 75th Infantry (Ranger) 101st Airborne Division, March 1969. Sgt. Gary Linderer during a mission outside Firebase Jack northwest of Hue. (Courtesy of Gary Linderer)

LRRP Detachment 3/506th Battalion, 101st Airborne Division. *Left to right:* Sp.4 Christopher "Kip" Rolland, Sgt. Gerry Gomes, and Sp.4 Brown. (Courtesy of Christopher Rolland)

Company C, 75th Infantry (Ranger) I.F.F.V. (1st Field Force). Chuck Vaughn in the bush with rifle at ready. (Courtesy of Chuck Vaughn)

Company C, 75th Infantry (Ranger) J.F.F.V. (1st Field Force). Robert McClure *(facing camera)* talking to Sp.4 Miller. (Courtesy of Chuck Vaughn)

Company F, 58th Infantry (LRP), November 1968. Team 2-2 prepares to depart for a mission west of Hue. (Courtesy of Gary Linderer)

Ranger Memorial at Ft. Benning, Georgia honoring all LRRPs, LRPs, and Rangers from America's wars. (Courtesy of Gary Linderer)

a very exposed position. They would have to find some way to get clear or run the risk of discovery.

Suddenly the voices above them began to grow excited. Ju couldn't quite understand what they were saying, but the words were coming faster and louder. Something or someone had alarmed the enemy soldiers and they were beginning to respond. Seconds later the NVA began running down through the trees, heading toward the trail. It sounded to the two LRRPs as if they were coming right at them. Anderson and Ju turned to face the enemy, hastily preparing to defend themselves to the death, but were relieved a moment later when the NVA ran past them to their left, still moving toward the trail.

The LRRPs went to ground where they were while Anderson quickly radioed in another sitrep, warning of more activity and reporting that the NVA around their position might be on to them. While the two men remained hidden in the darkness, wondering who or what was coming next, the battle for LZ Mile High was still raging to the southeast.

Finally satisfied that the danger had passed, Ju and Anderson moved on, still paralleling the trail to the west, but moving more cautiously than before. They were attempting to put more distance between themselves and the trail by angling away from it when they found themselves in the middle of an NVA base camp. They knew they were in trouble when they began to smell smoke and human feces, then heard people talking in muted voices all around them. At the time they were in an area of dense bamboo less than twenty meters north of the trail. The enemy soldiers around them were in bunkers dug into the openings between the individual stands of bamboo.

The two men stopped immediately when they heard the noises around them. After sizing up the situation, they started backing slowly out of the bamboo, no easy task because there was bamboo not only above them and to their immediate front but also in the dense thicket behind them they had skirted when paralleling the trail.

They continued backpedaling until they reached the patch of bamboo to their rear. Sensing that they were out of the base camp, they turned and crawled into the thickest cover they could find and went to ground.

By then more voices were coming from the area of the base camp. The voices sounded excited and agitated, the way they would sound if they had just spotted something that upset them. Once again Anderson feared they had been compromised.

Ju, squatting on the ground next to Anderson, slowly shook his head, indicating that the NVA were not talking about them. Something else was responsible for the NVAs' excitement. Relieved at that bit of good news, Anderson decided to remain in the cover offered by the bamboo. At that moment they were directly across the trail from the spot where they had hidden the night before. It was nearly 0400 hours, and the sounds of enemy activity continued around them the remainder of the night.

With the coming of first light the two LRRPs hidden in the bamboo were faced with a new problem. It was the final day of their mission and their extraction was scheduled for 1000 hours that morning. However, they were a long way from the LZ. Worse, they were on the wrong side of a heavily used trail. And, with enemy forces all around them, leaving the cover where they lay hidden would be tantamount to suicide.

The only good news was that from their new position,

Anderson had a clear view of both the trail and the wide valley it traversed. No traffic could pass by without being seen. With that in mind he decided that their only option was to postpone the extraction until the next day, stay put, continue reporting on enemy activity in the valley, then attempt an exfiltration during the night.

After calling in the change of plans to the radio relay team, he spotted five more carts coming down the trail, three towed by water buffalo, two by NVA porters. The carts moved past the hidden LRRPs, then left the main trail and proceeded directly to a series of well-hidden bunkers dug in along the base of the opposing slope. Anderson and Ju watched in silence as the enemy soldiers backed the carts right into the earthen storage bunkers and began off-loading crates. Anderson swallowed hard when he realized that the hidden bunkers were indentations in the base of the slope not far from where he and Ju had spent their second night in the bush. The storage bunkers had been freshly dug.

Through his field glasses Anderson saw that the crates, with markings in Chinese, appeared to be the right shape and configuration to contain AK-47s and boxes of ammunition. During the entire off-loading process, enemy activity continued unabated all around the team. The off-loading finally ended at approximately 1500 hours. At that time another party of seventy-five heavily armed NVA infantry passed by on the trail. Carrying RPGs, AKs, and RPDs (light machine guns) and dressed in fresh uniforms and pith helmets, they wore web gear and rucksacks with medical kits attached to them.

Anderson called in a new sitrep to report the latest sighting. With NVA soldiers moving by less than five meters away, Anderson was forced to communicate with the C&C aircraft by using squelch breaks. The newly arrived NVA unit soon linked up with another unit that had been encamped further down the trail almost two hundred meters away—only a hundred meters from the bridge where Anderson and Ju had crossed the stream. The team heard a lot of hoopla and exuberance when the two units came together.

The LRRPs' situation was deteriorating by the minute. NVA soldiers were now encamped on both sides of the stream, above them on the slope, and along the trail next to them. In spite of the overcrowded conditions around them, the night proved uneventful.

During the fifth day of the mission the team remained in position. Between 0800 and 1000 hours, six more carts arrived fully loaded with weapons, mortar rounds, and small-arms ammunition. Enemy soldiers unloaded the cargo in a number of different bunkers carved into the hillside. Anderson also watched as they unloaded a number of 61mm mortars. Someone was in for a real beating if the NVA managed to deploy all the weapons, ammo, and equipment they were caching in the valley. But just then there was little Anderson and Ju could do but watch and wait. With so many enemy soldiers constantly moving about them, the two men were forced to maintain strict radio silence.

By that time Anderson had determined his exact location and computed the coordinates not only for each of the enemy encampments but also for the bunkers and the trail itself. If they could just manage to get out of the enemy complex within the next twenty-four hours, they could guarantee that there would be hell to pay for the NVA troops and emplacements along the trail. But, at the moment, the two men were having other problems. They were already out of food and running dangerously low on water. Somehow they had to break out of the area before hunger and thirst forced them to do something stupid.

Between the hours of 1200 and 1300, fifty new NVA troops moved past them on the trail and Anderson concluded that the two of them were in the middle of a troop buildup of regimental size or larger. He knew that he had erred earlier in believing that these were the enemy forces hitting LZ Mile High. The NVA troops moving into the valley around them were not leaving. They were obviously staging for something else altogether.

During the night of their fifth day in the field the empty carts, now numbering about a dozen, were hauled out of the valley and back up the trail. The only other movement in the valley that night was the normal activity of troops encamped.

Early in the morning of the mission's sixth day, three more carts, all pulled by water buffalo, arrived in the valley. They were loaded with more mortars and cases of mortar rounds. Unlike the previous carts, those three turned around as soon as they were unloaded and went back up the valley. It was nearly 1300 hours.

At 1500 hours another NVA company arrived and began setting up camp a hundred meters away from the hidden LRRPs. Anderson was beginning to get a little worried at the overcrowding in their little valley. It was only a matter of time before someone out looking for a private place to empty his bowels or write a letter would stumble across their location.

That night around 2000 hours, more troops carrying flashlights entered the valley. The NVA camped on the slope above the LRRPs soon heard them arrive and moved down to join them. Their lights reminded Anderson of swarming fireflies, and there seemed to be hundreds of them milling about out on the trail. Enemy soldiers were everywhere, moving around among the bunkers and passing up and down the Redball. Later, at the mission debriefing, Ju would report that at that time the NVA were saddling up to move out.

The valley floor was between five hundred and six hundred meters wide, running to a 60-degree slope up the ridgelines on either side. The creek, one to two meters wide, fast flowing, and mid-calf deep, meandered down the length of the valley. At that time, few places in the valley were free of NVA soldiers.

Late that night, Anderson decided that the area behind him was, for the moment, clear of enemy troops. He signaled for Ju to prepare to move out, and within minutes the two men were out of the bamboo and making their way back to where they had crossed the creek. If they could retrace their steps they would be able to move back up the slope in the direction of their insertion LZ. Without food for the previous two days and water for a full day, they knew they had to get out of the valley while they still had enough strength to climb the steep slope.

Stopping momentarily to refill their empty canteens, they made it across the creek under the bridge without being detected, then moved cautiously through the jungle to the base of the ridge. They spent the rest of the night climbing up over the crest of the ridge and halfway down the reverse slope, reaching the LZ by daylight.

As the faint illumination of false dawn washed over them, Anderson managed to establish radio contact with the x-ray team at Polei Kleng. And a good thing; their fellow LRRPs had just about given them up for lost. Anderson reported that they were out of the valley and requested an immediate extraction.

Within the hour the C&C helicopter was orbiting in the vicinity of the exhausted LRRPs. Lieutenant

Chester advised them that they would have to move about two klicks to another location, then prepare for a Maguire rig extraction. Chester felt there was too much activity in the immediate area to risk returning to the original LZ. The trek nearly killed the two starving LRRPs, but they managed to reach the spot by calling on their last physical reserves.

A short time later the lift ship arrived, escorted by a pair of Cobra gunships. Anderson tossed out a smoke grenade to pinpoint his position for the pilot, and within minutes the weighted sandbags at the ends of the coiled Maguire rigs were dropping through the trees to the LRRPs. The remainder of the extraction was textbook. At 1300 hours they were out of the jungle and on their way back to Polei Kleng.

The two men were immediately debriefed by Lieutenant Chester and the 3d Brigade's S-2, a major who, when he realized that Anderson had plotted the coordinates for a large number of very lucrative targets, was having a difficult time controlling his excitement. The two officers soon came to the conclusion that Anderson and Ju had indeed run into an NVA regiment staging for operations inside South Vietnam.

Chester informed the two men that during the three-night/two-day period when they could only break squelch, the radio relay team was not able to pick them up at all. At that time a colonel at brigade decided that the two-man team was most likely dead and he wanted to call in an arc light strike on the valley. Only Chester's strong intercession to wait until they were certain that the team had been wiped out had kept that from happening. Anderson and Ju could only look at each other and gulp. They were lucky to be alive.

Right after the team had been safely extracted, the 4th Infantry Division set up a TOT (time on target) artillery fire mission by 8-inch batteries located at two firebases several miles from the valley. The rounds were set on delay fuses to allow them time to penetrate the triple-canopy jungle before exploding. After the fire mission was completed, an arc light was put into the same area to finish off any survivors.

The 2d Battalion of the 35th Infantry combat assaulted into the valley immediately after the arc light, but Anderson was never officially told about what they had found. He later managed to talk to grunts from the unit that went in on the operation. They told him they had found a lot of destroyed and shattered equipment scattered through the area. They had also discovered fragments of flesh and bone, but only God or a team of forensic scientists could tell how many people they were from. Immediately after the completion of Team Dragon Two's mission it was reported that the firebases at LZ Virgin, LZ Mile High, and LZ Brillo Pad were no longer getting clobbered on a regular basis.

Lieutenant Chester recommended LRRP team leader Buck Anderson for a Silver Star immediately after the mission. He also saw to it that Ju was put in for an equivalent Vietnamese decoration. But Ju was killed a short time later by a friendly reaction force sent in to look for the survivors of Sergeant Hess's four-man LRRP team. All the Americans on the patrol had been killed. Ju had survived the firefight and was making his way back to friendly lines when he spotted the reaction force coming in. He stood and yelled to them to identify himself and was immediately killed by their point man.

While Sergeant Anderson's Silver Star was pending, he caught a flight from Polei Kleng back to Pleiku, where he ran across an Air Force jeep that someone had foolishly left unattended, and at night. In the darkness, not realizing that the jeep was not Army green,

Anderson drove the "confiscated" vehicle from Pleiku to Kontum, catching three rounds from a disgruntled VC sniper before reaching the LRRP platoon's billets at the large Central Highlands city. The next morning, realizing for the first time that the jeep was gray, the LRRPs tried to repair the damage caused by the VC sniper and repainted the jeep with the only color available on an Army outpost—OD green.

Later on, when it was discovered that the unauthorized LRRP jeep actually belonged to the U.S. Air Force, the brigade higher-ups saw this as an ideal opportunity to burn Lieutenant Chester, who they viewed as a renegade officer leading a band of cutthroats and thieves. Brigade threatened to court-martial the entire platoon unless someone stepped up and admitted his guilt in stealing the jeep. There was also the matter of a missing three-quarter-ton truck that had not yet been settled. Sergeants Anderson, Chrysler, and Garrison, along with Lieutenant Chester, took the hit for the unauthorized use of the two vehicles. The four men were detained, questioned, and threatened with court-martial, then sent back to their unit without any official action being taken. In the confusion of the inquiry, Sgt. Buck Anderson's recommendation for the Silver Star mysteriously disappeared.

LRRP, B-36 Detachment, 5th Special Forces Group (Airborne)

Utilizing six-man LRRP teams furnished by the Army's 1st, 9th, and 25th Divisions, and the 199th Light Infantry Brigade, Special Forces Detachment B-36 had been conducting reconnaissance and prisoner snatch missions throughout western III Corps since 5 September 1967. Calling the operation Rapid Fire I, B-36 worked the Army recon teams alone or in conjunction with twenty-man Hatchet teams made up of Cambodian Khmer Serai volunteers led by U.S. Army Special Forces personnel. The operation was under direct command of II Field Force and was tasked to provide direct intelligence to II Field Force and any other U.S. commands in the area on enemy units operating in the III Corps Tactical Zone.

The 25th Infantry Division sent down a request to B-36 for a special reconnaissance patrol to check out Recon Zone I-99, an expanse of high ground that overlooked the Saigon River. The enemy had recently launched a series of 140mm rocket attacks against the division's base camp at Tay Ninh, and the "Tropic Lightning" Division's G-2 suspected that the rockets were being fired from somewhere inside RZ I-99. The recon team was assigned to go into the enemy-held area and determine where the rockets were being launched from.

Staff Sergeant Dallas Pridemore was given the mission on 14 September. Although he had the authority to put together the best six-man team he could from within the unit, he was not given the normal amount of time to prepare for the mission. He immediately called Sgt. David Spencer into the TOC for a short conference. Spencer, a veteran LRRP, had been going out as assistant team leader on a number of Hatchet missions under Special Forces Sgt. Frank Polk. He was no stranger to combat. Pridemore told Spencer about the mission, then asked him if he would be willing to serve as his assistant team leader on the patrol. Spencer had just returned from a rather hairy Hatchet mission during which Sergeant Polk had been medevacked, so the young ATL was looking for something a little "different" to settle his nerves. He quickly accepted Pridemore's offer.

Pridemore also selected Dan Miller, an eighteen-year-old LRRP who was even a teenager in spirit; Patrick Wesson, a nineteen-year-old recon veteran going on thirty; and two paid Cambodian volunteers the LRRPs affectionately called "Old Man" and "Big Cowboy." They were older than the Americans they were going out with, but they were loyal and could be counted on to perform in a tight situation.

Pridemore and Spencer sat down with the map overlays of their recon zone and plotted a number of artillery concentrations. One was at a trail junction, another on a loop in a creek, and a third at the intersection of two grid lines on the map. When they had finished, Pridemore told his ATL to meet him at the chopper pad at 1400 hours for the overflight.

The overflight that afternoon was high above War Zone C. It was a single, slow pass over the team's AO, but that was enough to confirm that the RZ was a heavily jungled area with only a single LZ near where they wanted to go. That was not good news for the patrol; isolated LZs in heavily used VC/NVA areas were almost always watched by the enemy. Most likely they would have to shake VC trackers right after their insertion.

The next day, it was actually chilly down on the chopper pad a half hour before dawn. Pridemore gave his teammates a last-minute equipment check, then ordered everyone aboard the insertion aircraft. Minutes later the pilot lifted off the tarmac and headed north toward the team's RZ. It wasn't long before the aircraft commander looked back over his shoulder and signaled that they were approaching the LZ.

The aircraft banked sharply, losing altitude as it neared the clearing. Finally the helicopter was hovering just above the ground in a thickly vegetated clearing in the middle of the jungle that didn't look nearly as open or as large as it had on the overflight. But it was good enough to get the team in and the chopper out.

The six LRRPs were out in seconds and sprinting for the nearest tree line. As the sound of the departing helicopter faded, the patrol reached the cover of the forest and dropped to the ground in a tight defensive circle. The six men lay at the edge of the jungle, watching and listening. If enemy soldiers were in the vicinity of the clearing, the two Cambodians would pick up on it in minutes.

Finally, hearing and seeing nothing to alarm them, Pridemore decided that his team had gotten into the recon zone undetected. He called in a quick commo check on the radio and reported a negative sitrep to the TOC. Signing off, he hand-signaled his teammates to move out, with Big Cowboy at point and Miller walking his slack. Pridemore moved into the three slot, followed by

Old Man carrying the PRC-25 radio, Wesson, and Spencer at drag.

Seventy meters from the LZ, Big Cowboy and Old Man began hissing and motioning for the LRRPs to drop down. Squatting in a circle, facing outwards, the six LRRPs waited breathlessly, listening and watching. Pridemore also sensed danger all around them. But only time and patience would reveal it.

Within seconds two VC suddenly appeared from the direction of the landing zone. Only fifty meters away and moving quickly, the men crossed the patrol's back-trail, going diagonally from the team's right rear to their left front. The four Americans and two Cambodians watched as the enemy soldiers moved, until they disappeared into the thick jungle less than thirty meters away.

Ten minutes later, Pridemore gave the signal to move out. As one, the six LRRPs rose from their cover. But before they could take a step, Old Man looked back at Spencer and silently mouthed, "VC," then pointed to where the two enemy soldiers had disappeared. Then he turned and pointed to the rear and repeated his signal. There were VC in front of the team and behind.

Big Cowboy then stepped out cautiously, leading the patrol slowly through the jungle. Everything went well for the next two hours, when Old Man suddenly informed the rest of the team by sign language that they were still being followed, their tracker a single individual, close behind. The team held up in cover and set out security while they held a brief conference to decide the best course of action. After discussing several possibilities, they decided that Spencer would hang back in ambush as the team moved out on its patrol route.

Spencer looked around until he found a good spot in

the brush next to the trail, then lay prone facing the team's backtrail. As he listened for the sounds of the patrol moving away from him, he felt the momentary pang of fear that came with being abandoned. It passed in a second and he refocused his mind on the task at hand. He had a man to kill, preferably with a single, well-placed shot. He only hoped Old Man had been right about there only being one VC on their tail.

Fifteen minutes later, when no one had appeared, Spencer had to give up his ambush and rejoin the patrol. He slipped silently out of his hiding place and eased cautiously back up the trail. The rest of the team would be waiting not far away, yet he was still caught off guard when he pushed aside some brush and found himself looking down the darkened barrel of Old Man's M-16.

After Spencer whispered that he had seen and heard nothing, Old Man indicated that he felt the VC was still back there. He was so certain about it that the Americans couldn't help but believe him. Spencer realized that the VC tracker had to be good. He knew that the VC had not gotten close enough to spot him lying in wait, yet somehow the man had sensed that he was there and intentionally held back. It was going to be tough to shake him.

Pridemore kept the team in position for nearly fifteen minutes, hoping that the VC would close up the distance between himself and the team. But when Big Cowboy and Old Man both expressed their doubts, with hand signals and head shakes, Pridemore understood that the tracker was not taking the bait. It was time to give up and get moving. The longer they waited in one place, the more time enemy troops had to close in on them.

As they continued to patrol, it soon became apparent

that something was missing; nowhere else in War Zone C could one cover so much ground without encountering enemy trails crisscrossing the jungle. Perhaps not all were in active use, but they were everywhere. However, there were no signs of trails, recent or old, anywhere in their recon zone, even though they knew that Viet Cong were all around them.

It was almost noon when they reached a large stream running directly across their route of march. Nearly twenty meters wide, the waterway was bordered on both sides by high, muddy banks. The bank on their side and a good portion of the opposite bank were covered with dense stands of bamboo. Much of the bamboo had fallen over into the sluggish stream, choking the area near the shoreline. Crossing the stream would be difficult. And they had to cross it; their patrol route dictated passage through the RZ on an azimuth of 130 degrees. The stream flowed directly across their path, and if they did not get to the other side they would be unable to cover the southern half of their recon zone.

Without hesitation Big Cowboy and Miller slid down the steep bank into the stream while their teammates provided security behind them and across the waterway. They slowly waded through the sluggish current, getting hung up momentarily in the submerged bamboo. When they finally reached the other side, they had to fight their way through more underwater bamboo and up the opposite bank. After they made it to the far side of the stream and were providing security, Pridemore and Old Man slipped into the water and followed their route across, while Spencer guarded their backtrail and Wesson watched both flanks.

When the first four LRRPs had successfully traversed the waterway, Pridemore signaled Spencer and Wesson to cross. Without waiting, Spencer stepped in, Wesson right behind him. The two LRRPs were surprised at how chilly the water was. As they pushed across, they struggled through the bamboo on the near shore as the water reached up to their chests. Spencer noticed that Wesson was having difficulty getting through the bamboo. Soon he was stuck midstream. The assistant team leader immediately turned back to help him, only to have Wesson whisper at him to go on.

"That's not the way it works," Spencer hissed back as he continued to struggle through the water. He reached out his hand to Wesson, and soon the trapped LRRP was able to extricate himself and continue. The two men finally made the opposite shore and rejoined their companions.

Pridemore decided they were at as good a place as any to take a break. With the stream at the LRRPs' backs, pursuers would have to expose themselves to get at them. This would leave them vulnerable to the patrol's fire and also give the LRRPs a running start if they had to escape and evade. Pridemore signaled Wesson to watch the team's right flank, where the stream disappeared around the bend. He placed Big Cowboy to the patrol's front while Miller watched their left flank. Spencer and Old Man faced the far side of the stream while Pridemore cranked up the radio to call in a sitrep.

After the team leader finished his commo chores, he turned around and whispered that it was okay to eat. Realizing that he was indeed hungry, Spencer pulled a dehydrated LRRP ration from his pack and added water, then set the meal aside to rehydrate. He had just raised up to take another look at the opposite shore when Old Man's low hiss caught his attention. The Cambodian was jabbing at his temple with his right finger and muttering something about VC. He then motioned for Spencer to slide over to one side behind a large tree nearby. When Spencer complied, Old Man seemed relieved and satisfied with his actions.

So that was it—the old Khmer was uncomfortable with the team's ATL sitting out in the open. However, from his new location Spencer could no longer see anything across the river unless he shifted around and poked his head out from behind the tree. That bothered him, but not as much as noticing that Old Man was staring intently down their backtrail with a worried look on his face.

Finally, Spencer's LRRP ration had set long enough to be edible. The assistant team leader looked around before chowing down, and saw that everyone else was busy dividing time between eating and observing their zones of security—everyone, that is, except Old Man, who was still staring intently into the jungle on the opposite side of the stream. Spencer nodded, then held out his LRRP ration to him, but the Cambodian only smiled his tight-lipped smile, squinted his dark eyes, and shook his head.

Everyone had just finished eating when Spencer saw Old Man's expression change. A split second later, cursing in Cambodian, he was on his feet charging toward the stream and firing a long burst across the water. As Spencer turned to support Old Man, return fire from the far side of the stream slammed into the tree he was sitting behind. The ATL slid out to the edge of the tree and tried to open fire, only to discover that his selector switch was frozen on SAFE. He slipped back behind the tree, pulled out a spare magazine, and was using it to pound the selector switch over to FIRE when enemy rounds began coming through the trees from their front.

Immediately, Big Cowboy and Pridemore began fir-

ing at the muzzle flashes blinking in the bamboo to
their southeast. Pausing to jam home a fresh magazine,
Pridemore yelled for Old Man to bring him the radio.

Old Man was still firing into the jungle on the opposite side of the stream, yet he managed to roll to his
side, grab the handset, and hand it to Pridemore. It was
an incredible example of the Cambodian's coolness under fire, but it would go almost unnoticed in the middle
of the battle.

Pridemore lay flat on the ground, calling in the contact to the TOC. He could hardly hear the voice on the
other end of the line over the noise of the intense firing
going on around him. Big Cowboy and Miller were
keeping the enemy pinned down in the bamboo to their
front as Wesson began firing across the creek to the
right of the team.

By then Spencer had managed to free the selector
switch on his weapon and joined in the battle. Raising
up on one knee, he began supporting Pridemore and
Old Man as they chewed up the jungle on the other side
of the stream. Suddenly two rounds smacked into the
tree just above Spencer's head. Old Man shouted something in Cambodian that Spencer failed to understand,
then blasted the enemy soldier who had shot at the
LRRP ATL.

Spencer rolled hard to his right and came up on the
other side of the tree. He spotted a number of shadowy
figures flitting through the thick bamboo on the opposite shore and opened fire at them. The figures scattered, then fled to the west along the stream, leaving
Spencer unsure if he had hit any of them. On the other
side of the tree, Old Man was still hosing down the jungle across the river.

Pridemore was back on the radio, shouting to make
himself heard over the sounds of the gunfire. Suddenly

he turned to his teammates and shouted, "We're going to Maguire rig out." He slapped Spencer's leg and yelled, "You go first."

Spencer shook his head. "Wesson and Miller should go first."

Pridemore disagreed, shouting, "I said you and Wesson go out first."

It was no time to argue; Spencer agreed.

"Pop smoke!" Pridemore yelled.

Spencer pulled the pin on a yellow smoke grenade and pitched it out along the team's backtrail. A sulfur-colored cloud billowed up around the team, hugging the ground because there was no breeze inside the dense bamboo.

Soon the first slick arrived on the scene and spotted the smoke down in the trees. The aircraft commander worked the chopper in over the team and the crew chief kicked out the weighted rigs as the other door gunner fired down into the jungle to keep the enemy heads down.

Over the roar of the Huey and the sounds of battle, Spencer screamed for Wesson to get into one of the Maguire slings. Low-crawling on his belly, the young LRRP slipped his leg through the cargo strap and D-ringed his harness to the rope. Nearby, Spencer discovered that the ropes were tangled in a knot just above the loops. If the aircraft lifted out with the ropes ensnared like that, the two LRRPs ran the risk of being spun out of the rigs and tossed into the jungle.

While Pridemore, Miller, and the two Cambodians fought to hold back the enemy, Spencer worked as fast as he could to untangle the ropes. Ignoring the bullets whizzing past his head, he stood up to untie the final knot. He was taking a risk, but no one was going to make it out unless he could untangle the rig.

Above him in the helicopter, the bellyman, LRRP

Wal Handwerk, was screaming for Spencer to cut the ropes. Spencer couldn't hear him above all the noise, nor did he realize that the aircraft had been taking intense small-arms fire the entire time he was working on the rig. Suddenly the enemy found their target and rounds began striking the unprotected aircraft. Unable to wait any longer, Handwerk sliced through the ropes, letting them fall around Spencer and entangling him helplessly in their folds.

Spencer struggled free of the snarl as Wesson was climbing out of the slack Maguire rig. The two men looked to see what was happening around them, just in time to hear Pridemore shout, "We have to get to an LZ!"

The team leader pointed toward the southwest, then looked back at Spencer and said, "You're on point."

Spencer grimaced then flipped open his lensatic compass cover to shoot an azimuth in the direction they had to go. It led right across the bend in the stream. It was risky to recross the open streambed, but that was their closest route to an LZ. He yelled for Wesson to follow him, then slid down the muddy bank into the stream. As he waded away from the shore, he noticed that Wesson had not followed. He was still up on the bank, firing across the water. Pridemore and Old Man were standing behind him, while Miller and Big Cowboy were hosing down the bamboo toward what had become their rear.

A large explosion erupted at Spencer's feet, slamming him back against the mud bank. Water and debris were raining down around him, and there was an intense pressure inside his eardrums, almost as if he were diving in deep water. He struggled back to his feet, trying to clear the cobwebs out of his head. Then with a sudden lunge he lurched back out into the stream, intent only on reaching the bend fifty feet away. He only half noticed the water spouts kicking up to his right. At the time they had no real significance for him, except they didn't seem natural. Then he spotted the tiny lights blinking madly at the edge of the jungle on the opposite shore. Instinctively he raised his weapon and fired at the lights.

Above and behind him, Old Man and Wesson had also spotted the hidden VC and were blasting away at the bamboo concealing him. Suddenly a limp form detached itself from the shredded bamboo and tumbled into the water. Spencer saw the body of the dead VC submerge beneath the surface of the stream but didn't recognize it for what it was.

No longer seeing the lights, Spencer continued wading toward the bend in the river. When he finally reached the far shore he crawled out of the water and lay half-submerged at the bottom of the bank, sucking air into his lungs. By then his head had cleared somewhat and he was acutely aware that he was taking fire. He raised his weapon and began firing back as he climbed the slope and struggled through the dense bamboo. Seconds later he broke out of the bamboo and into a large clearing on the other side. He'd found the LZ!

Spencer turned to cover the area to the southeast as the first of his teammates began climbing the bank behind him. He spotted a strip of tiger-stripe camouflage back away from the river. He hesitated for a moment, thinking it was one of his teammates, then Big Cowboy blasted the area and it was gone.

The six LRRPs withdrew to the center of the clearing, continuing to place intense fire into the surrounding jungle. They quickly popped another yellow smoke grenade to mark their new position and ducked down as a pair of Huey gunships moved in to rake the jungle around them. While the gunships kept the VCs' heads down, the LRRPs' extraction ship slipped in and recovered the patrol.

The team's debriefing back at the TOC didn't take long. They had failed in their mission to locate the rocket launchers, but they had managed to verify that the enemy was there in great numbers, and they were definitely monitoring all the potential LZs in the area. That information might save the lives of other recon teams trying to infiltrate the area in the future.

1st Brigade LRRP Detachment, 101st Airborne Division

The 1st Brigade of the 101st Airborne Division arrived in South Vietnam on 29 July 1965, landing at the port of Cam Ranh Bay. The crack airborne brigade immediately began clearing operations in the coastal area between Cam Ranh Bay and Nha Trang to the north. Then it was off to An Khe to secure the area for the arrival of the 1st Cavalry Division. From An Khe the brigade moved further north to Qui Nhon during the height of the monsoon. Phan Rang was the next stop for the airborne unit, and when its mission there was completed, it once again departed, this time by LST, traveling up the coast to Tuy Hoa.

After Gen. William Westmoreland authorized the establishment of LRRP detachments, the 1st Brigade became the first Army unit in Vietnam after Special Forces B-52 Detachment (Project Delta) to establish a long range reconnaissance patrol capability. Selection into the 1st Brigade LRRPs was highly competitive and the initial crop of only twenty-two was accepted from more than four hundred fit volunteers. Needless to say, the final selectees were the cream of the crop of a brigade that was the finest in the U.S. Army at the time.

At the beginning of 1966 the 1st Brigade LRRPs moved to Tuy Hoa with the rest of the Screaming Eagles. They set up camp on the east side of the airstrip and began running patrols south, west, and north of the city. But as the brigade kicked off Operation Van Buren in the coastal plains around Tuy Hoa, the LRRP platoon received a call for help from the Special Forces A-camp at Cheo Reo back in the mountains near the Cambodian border. At least a VC Main Force battalion was conducting operations around the CIDG encampment, mortaring and rocketing the base, sending in ground probes at night and ambushing patrols sent after them during the day.

At the beginning of 1966, the 1st Brigade LRRPs had four operational teams based at Tuy Hoa. Two of the teams, One and Two, had inserted into the area around the Cheo Reo on the evening of 13 January but failed to stay in twenty-four hours. When a warning order came down from Brigade S-2 early on the morning of 15 January requesting that two more long-range reconnaissance teams go into the mountains around Cheo Reo for five to seven days to relieve pressure on the beleaguered CIDG encampment, Lt. Joel Stephenson, the LRRP platoon leader, went to find his first sergeant.

Joel Stephenson was an outstanding officer. He had been in Special Forces as an enlisted man before applying for Officer Candidate School at Fort Benning. Upon graduation he had been assigned to the 101st Airborne Division and had come over on the boat with 1st Brigade.

When he found Platoon Sgt. Phillip Chaisson, Stephenson showed him the warning order and, after deliberating, the two men decided that the missions would go to Teams Two and Three. Team Two had just come in from the field but hadn't been on the ground long enough to work up a sweat. Team Three, led by S.Sgt. David Skau, had been on stand-down for better than a week and was anxious to get back out in the field. The missions were scheduled to go in on the evening of the sixteenth with Team Three inserting first, then Team Two twenty minutes later, at last light.

When Sergeant Chaisson found Skau and told him that he had a premission briefing at the CP tent in a few minutes, Skau went to round up his teammates. The short briefing was conducted by Lieutenant Stephenson and S.Sgt. Curtis Herdner, the platoon operations NCO. Immediately after the briefing, Skau and his ATL, Sgt. James Tadlock, along with the TL and the ATL from Team Two, went out on a recon overflight in an unescorted Huey slick. It was a long trip back to the mountains around Cheo Reo, so it was late in the afternoon before they returned to Tuy Hoa.

At 2000 hours the teams went up to Brigade S-2 for the mission briefing. In the presence of members of the S-2 staff, Sergeant Herdner briefed the team and gave them the current intel on the area they would be in. When he was finished, S.Sgt. Ron Bourne, the platoon commo chief, gave the team their SOIs and wished them good hunting. Like Herdner, Bourne had other duties in the platoon, such as flying bellyman during insertions and extractions. Bourne had also been in charge of a number of secured and unsecured three-man radio relay teams. For a month a reinforced Main Force VC battalion had been hitting the CIDG camp with mortars and rockets, probing the perimeter at night, and attacking security patrols conducting sweeps outside the camp during the day. The camp was manned by a Special Forces A-team and two companies of CIDG manned by local Rhade Montagnards.

The rest of the brigade was just kicking off Operation Van Buren in the coastal plains around Tuy Hoa when the request for help had come down to the brigade LRRPs. The reconnaissance patrols were being conducted as an assist operation to the SF encampment in the area.

After the briefing the two teams returned to their tents to relax and talk themselves through the mission. It was a ritual they always performed to help them establish the necessary mindset to go out in the bush in small teams.

The teams spent most of the next day running dry rehearsals, practicing immediate-action drills, test firing their weapons, and conducting last minute checks on their equipment. Late in the afternoon S.Sgt. David Skau gathered his team around him to go over everything one last time. Skau, a native of Pennsylvania, had come over as a member of A Troop, 2/17th Cav in July 1965. A popular, good-natured NCO, he was tall, stocky, and quite athletic. Ranger qualified, he had left a wife and two daughters behind back in the States. Like everyone else on the team he carried an XM-16E1, the earlier version of the M-16, known for its propensity to jam at the worst possible times. He would walk slack on the patrol.

Skau's ATL was Sgt. James Tadlock of Dallas, Texas. Tadlock had been a grunt with the 1/327th before volunteering for LRRPs. Tall, muscular, blond, and blue-eyed, Tadlock was a joker who enjoyed cutting up in the rear. However, he was deadly serious out in the field. Like Skau, Tadlock was married. He would walk point on the patrol and carry an M-79 with a chopped stock in addition to his M-16.

The team senior RTO was Sp4. Tom Payne. Payne was from New Mexico and had come to Vietnam as part of the brigade headquarters commo platoon. Tall, slim, and handsome, Payne had joined the military out of a strong sense of duty. At twenty-five years of age he was older and more mature than everyone else on the team. He was not a strong supporter of military protocol and respected the privacy of others. Perhaps by nature, or because he was going through a nasty divorce, Payne wouldn't take any shit from anyone. An excellent commo man and exceptionally good in the field, he would walk directly behind Skau on the patrol.

The team medic was Sgt. Pascual "Pass" Meza. Pass grew up in Richmond, Texas, and arrived in Vietnam as a member of the FASP, the forward area support platoon, detached from Company B, 501st Signal Battalion. Special Forces–qualified as both a communications specialist and a medic, Meza spent time in both SF Training Group and 7th Group before being assigned to the 101st Airborne Division at Fort Campbell, Kentucky. Outgoing and adventurous, he was popular among his fellow LRRPs. On this particular patrol he would carry an M-5 medical bag and walk the number four slot. He, too, was married and had a son back in Texas.

The junior RTO was Sp4. Tom Camp of Santa Barbara, Texas. Camp had previously served as a sergeant E-5 in 7th SF Group, but had gotten busted over some Stateside malarkey and ended up in the 101st Airborne Division as an E-4. Like Meza, he was daring and ready to try anything once. He had been trained as a communications specialist in Special Forces and would walk the number five slot on patrol. Camp was single.

The rear security spot was in the very capable hands of Sgt. Phillip Henry. Also unmarried, Henry had come to LRRPs from the 2/502d. A quiet professional, Henry brought with him a lot of combat experience. He had served in the 2/502d task force that had gone into the Ia Drang Valley back in '65 with the 1st Cavalry Division.

Of average height and medium build, he was well respected by his teammates.

The LRRP compound was situated just off the
brigade helipad, so at 1500 hours it was only a short
walk for the two teams to go down and climb aboard
their insertion slicks from the 48th Assault Helicopter
Company (AHC). The two aircraft lifted off and joined
the C&C bird and a pair of Charlie-model gunships for
the long flight to Cheo Reo. The five aircraft climbed to
altitude and flew due west for nearly one hour before
reaching the CIDG encampment. The birds set down
on the chopper pad outside the camp, and while the five
aircraft were refueling the LRRPs got off to stretch
their legs. Lieutenant Stephenson and the two bellymen,
staff sergeants Guy Thomlinson and Ron Bourne, entered the camp to coordinate the insertion with the
Special Forces detachment operations NCO. The meeting took nearly an hour.

Just before nautical twilight the five aircraft departed
Cheo Reo and flew directly out to the AO, south of the
encampment. While C&C and the Team Two insertion
slick remained on station, the two gunships and the
Team Three bird approached the LZ from the south,
flying nap of the earth.

As the aircraft slowed to a hover six feet over the
brush-covered LZ, Tadlock, Camp, and Henry exited
on the port side, while Meza, Skau, and Payne
dropped to the ground out the starboard side. The patrol merged on the starboard side of the aircraft as the
Huey lifted out of the LZ and picked up speed as it flew
north. They immediately began moving due north
toward the heavier cover three hundred meters away. As
soon as the sound of the helicopter had faded, they
heard a high-pitched whistle a couple hundred meters
to their left front. The LRRPs suspected that they had

already been compromised by trail watchers, but they continued moving, trying to put some distance between themselves and the LZ.

Suddenly the sound of someone banging on metal was heard coming from the front and rear of the team. Skau immediately raised his clenched fist to signal for the team to go to ground. Setting up in a tight circle, the LRRPs waited and listened. Finally Skau whispered, "Hey, you guys, this doesn't look good. I think we need to do a one-eighty back to the LZ and call for an extraction."

Everyone agreed. The noisemaking was the same tactic the VC had used on Teams One and Two two days earlier. They had been lucky to get out without taking any casualties.

The patrol turned around and began moving back toward the LZ, one hundred meters away. As it moved south, Skau tapped Meza and signaled for him to drop out of the patrol formation to do a stay-behind. He was to delay pursuit so the team could get back to secure the LZ. As the remainder of the team continued on toward the clearing, Skau signaled Henry to drop off twenty meters behind Meza.

Just as the patrol was closing in on the LZ, they heard Meza open up fifty meters to the north. Meza had been down on one knee behind a low bush when he spotted three VC moving down the LRRPs' backtrail less than forty meters away. They were armed, wearing black pajamas, and moving in single file.

Meza opened fire immediately, hitting the point man and knocking him to the ground. As the other two turned around and disappeared into the brush, Meza tried to hit them too but his weapon wouldn't fire. Thinking it had jammed, he looked down to clear it and realized that his magazine was bone dry. In the excitement he had burned through an entire mag. He caught the empty magazine as it dropped out of his weapon and stuck it inside his shirt, then quickly slammed another home. Not able to pick out a target, he began firing three-round bursts into the brush to his north.

Back at the LZ fifty meters behind Meza, the four LRRPs set up just off the clearing suddenly found themselves under intense small-arms fire coming from the north, south, and east. From the large amount of enemy fire, it seemed that an entire platoon was engaged. Fortunately, no LRRPs were hit in the initial onslaught.

Glad that he had not yet released the aircraft, which were still on station, Skau grabbed Camp's handset and called the C&C bird to request an emergency extraction. Team Two had not yet been inserted.

Skau was firing at the surrounding enemy soldiers as he communicated with Lieutenant Stephenson. Suddenly his weapon jammed. Camp grabbed Skau's M-16 and offered his own weapon to the team leader. While Skau went back into action, Camp tried to clear the jammed weapon. Not having a cleaning rod, he looked around for something to use and finally employed the whip antenna on his PRC-25. It worked.

Right after he got the M-16 cleared, Camp took a grazing round along the bicep of his right arm. The wound was not disabling.

Out in the brush, Henry, the other stay-behind, had just decided that the best place to be was back inside the perimeter with the rest of his teammates, so he turned and followed the trail back to the team. He had forgotten that Meza was still behind him.

Thirty meters farther north Meza was conducting a "fighting withdrawal." It was getting dark and the VC were too close for him to turn and run, so he was forced to back away, firing as he moved. Suddenly a brace of 2.75-inch aerial rockets fired from one of the supporting Charlie-model gunships bracketed the LRRP, knocking him to the ground. The gunship had just arrived on the scene and was attempting to suppress the enemy fire.

Back at the perimeter, Skau was shocked when he saw the first gunship fire four rockets directly into the area were Meza was still holding off the VC who were attempting to move up their backtrail. Believing that Meza had just been killed, Skau told Tadlock and Henry to go out and recover his body.

The two men soon reached the spot where the smoke and dust from the aerial rockets was just beginning to dissipate. They began yelling to see if Meza might still be alive, but never really expected a response. Then they heard him scream "Over here!" They looked at each other with grins on their faces, then turned to enter the impact area, only to stop again when Meza staggered out of the smoke, saying, "Goddamn that was close."

Satisfied that Meza could walk on his own, the three LRRPs closed back into the team perimeter, adding their weapons to the base of fire being put down by the rest of the patrol.

It was growing pretty dark by that time, and Skau had to use his red-lens flashlight to mark the team's perimeter. Minutes later they saw the slick approaching the LZ. The aircraft was totally blacked out as it came in through the gathering dusk. The pilot was just about to set down twenty meters from the team when all hell broke loose from everywhere around the perimeter. The LRRPs had never seen anything like it.

All the enemy fire was being directed at the chopper. The enemy had been using the team as bait to get to the extraction aircraft. The Huey began taking hits, but in spite of that the pilot still managed to set the aircraft down among the waist-high scrub.

Skau immediately hollered, "Make it back to the chopper! Let's go!"

Just as they had practiced in immediate-action drills, the team began to leapfrog back toward the aircraft, each man firing an entire magazine as he pulled out. As they neared the ship the team split in two and boarded the chopper on the same side they had inserted from.

When Meza reached the aircraft Skau was standing out next to the skid, trying to get a final head count as the door gunners swept the surrounding brush to keep the enemy at bay. When the team leader spotted Meza pushing through the brush, he shouted "Get in here!"

Picking up the heavily loaded LRRP, Skau threw Meza aboard the waiting aircraft and jumped in right behind him. The fully loaded chopper struggled mightily to lift up out of the LZ, and the pilot expected at any moment to hear the engine seize up and force the stricken ship back into the kill zone.

Both gunships were making rocket and machine-gun runs around the extraction bird as it lifted out of the brush, and the LRRPs let their breath out slowly when the Huey dropped its nose to pick up forward airspeed, then climbed out of the LZ, heading north. On board the aircraft the rescued team overcame the terror of their near demise and the men began to laugh at the way Skau had tossed Meza into the cabin.

In the dark of night the five aircraft made the long flight back to Tuy Hoa. Once on the ground the crew discovered that the extraction aircraft had taken seven rounds through its tail boom, just missing the rotor shaft. Miraculously, only Camp had sustained a wound in the ferocious action back at the LZ. The first thing the six LRRPs did after reaching the ground was to express their extreme gratitude to the pilot for pulling them out of a hot LZ.

The aircraft commander only smiled and said, "Hey, glad to be of service."

Chaisson was there to meet them when they walked away from the chopper pad. Lieutenant Stephenson was already out of his aircraft and quickly trotted over to see if any of his LRRPs had been hit. Relieved to see that they were all right, he smiled when he heard Sergeant Chaisson say, "Well, that was a close one."

The patrol went to the platoon CP tent where Stephenson debriefed them. It was a chore that had to be done, and everyone wanted to get it over with. With the mission behind them, the LRRPs were soon heading for their tent to drop their gear and partake of their mission bonus, Carling Black Label beer. It wasn't their favorite brew, but none of them would have any difficulty sleeping that night.

☆　　☆　　☆　　☆　　☆

Company N,
75th Infantry (Ranger),
173d Airborne Brigade

The Vietnam War, at least for U.S. forces in country, was winding down in early 1971. President Nixon's Vietnamization program was in its second year, and for once seemed to be working. More and more of the burden of war was being taken over by ARVN forces. In the northern part of South Vietnam, the buildup for Lam Son 719, the ARVN invasion of Laos, was gaining momentum. In the Central Highlands of II Corps Tactical Zone, the 173d Airborne Brigade seemed to be holding its own, but it wasn't enough to prevent NVA forces from pouring into South Vietnam from points all along the Ho Chi Minh Trail. Something big was in the offing, and Company N, 75th Infantry (Ranger), the brigade's long-range patrol element, was running itself ragged trying to locate and keep track of the invading NVA columns.

The official U.S. policy at that point in the war was to avoid major-unit contact and the resulting heavy casualties in favor of "force multipliers." Force multipliers meant using small U.S. units to tackle bigger enemy units, then utilizing the massed firepower of artillery and tactical air to maximize enemy casualties while minimizing friendly casualties. The resulting battle statistics gave the totally false impression that the South Vietnamese forces were much better than they actually

were, and that U.S. forces were making a safe, con-
trolled withdrawal of major elements from combat.
Unfortunately the small, elite units engaging the enemy
saw their heaviest casualties of the war during this
period.

It was into that very volatile situation that Ranger
teams Kilo and Hotel, stationed at LZ English near
Bong Son, found themselves thrust early on the morning of 15 April 1971. For brevity the teams would operate under the callsign Kilo. The warning order stated
simply that the heavy (fourteen-man) team was to conduct an extended seven-day reconnaissance patrol into
the mountainous area just west of the coastal plains
along the South China Sea, twenty-five miles south of
Bong Son. Intel reports indicated a heavy volume of enemy traffic moving from Phu My into the mountains
around Nui Mieu. The traffic consisted mainly of local
Viet Cong forces supplying NVA units staging in that
area.

Phu My was a series of villages and hamlets situated
in a fertile rice bowl at the base of the foothills that extended into the mountainous Central Highlands. It was
a major supply area for new NVA units moving into the
rugged mountains located around the highest peak in
the area, Nui Mieu.

Although the heavy team's primary mission was to
gather intelligence, S.Sgt. Tom Roubideaux and his
teammates decided that it should not keep them from
getting a body count or capturing enemy documents for
intelligence purposes.

Tom Roubideaux had taken over the reins of Kilo
Team just a month earlier. Kilo's previous team leader
had been killed on a patrol after tripping a "friendly"
booby trap while the team was moving through an area
previously designated as "cleared." The loss of their

leader came as a hammer blow to the remaining members of the team. It was apparent to Roubideaux as soon as he was given command of Kilo that he would have to prove himself to the rest of the team. After three patrols and a radio relay mission, the veteran team leader felt that he had finally won their trust.

Roubideaux was back in Vietnam on his fourth combat tour. A Sicangu Lakota from the Rosebud Reservation in South Dakota, he first arrived in country in 1965 as part of the famed 1st Brigade, 101st Airborne Division. Roubideaux was a conscientious objector at the time and assigned as a medic to Charlie Company, 2/502d. He later served as a medic with the Recondos, the battalion recon element. Then he went to Tiger Force, the recon element of the Oh Deuce's sister battalion, the 2/327th. Sometime during that period Roubideaux gave up his status as a conscientious objector and went on to serve briefly with the brigade's LRRP detachment before being wounded in a mortar attack at the unit's compound at Phan Thiet.

As he was recovering from his wounds at the 6th Convalescent Center in Cam Ranh Bay, he heard rumors that the rest of the division was preparing to come over and that it might be losing its "airborne" status. Not wanting to serve in a "leg" division, Roubideaux decided to reenlist with a guarantee of assignment to the 173d Airborne Brigade. After a short stay at Cam Ranh Bay he was transferred to Japan to complete his recovery, then sent home on reenlistment leave.

He spent sixty days out of country before reporting for duty with Alpha Company, 2/503d, 173d Airborne Brigade. He wasn't there long before he volunteered for the 74th LRRP Detachment, the brigade's long range reconnaissance patrol element. While attached to that unit he graduated from MACV Recondo School at Nha Trang.

After completing a year with the "Herd," the young NCO returned to the States and was assigned to the 82d Airborne Division at Fort Bragg. Four months later he once again volunteered to return to Vietnam, this time with Advisory Team 162, serving as a Co Van (adviser) with the 104th Company, 11th Battalion, South Vietnamese Airborne Division.

Early in his military career he had married, had a son, then lost his wife during a tonsillectomy. Soon after, he remarried, leaving his young son in the capable hands of his former in-laws when he returned to Vietnam.

Now, on his fourth tour in Vietnam, Roubideaux was back with the 173d Airborne Brigade as a team leader in Company N, 75th Infantry (Ranger). Like many veteran LRRP team leaders, Roubideaux carried his own radio while on patrol and led his team from the number three slot. An excellent tracker with well-honed jungle senses and excellent night movement skills in the field, he carried a CAR-15 and a .45-caliber automatic pistol. On this patrol he would carry an AK-47.

Kilo's assistant team leader, Specialist Four Campbell, was another veteran long-range patroller. With twelve missions under his belt he had already earned a reputation for being outstanding in the bush, but when orders came down for Campbell to attend MACV Recondo School, the quiet prankster refused, saying that he didn't want to break up the team and would rather be out in the field. Campbell walked near the rear of the patrol, providing half its "heavy" punch with the M-203 grenade launcher mounted on his M-16.

The team's point man was Sp4. Bobby Cantu. A Chicano from San Antonio, Texas, Cantu had six months in country. He was one of those fortunate people who possessed excellent night vision, and he seemed to have a special sense for nearby danger that had saved his life and the lives of his teammates on more than one occasion. Cantu was quiet and reserved, that is until he had too much to drink. Then he became a good-natured, spirited chest beater who excelled at telling outlandish stories to the cherries who gathered around him.

Specialist Four Jowers, a short, baby-faced Ranger from New Mexico, walked the number six slot. Despite five months of very tough experience in the field, Jowers still looked too young to have a driver's license. But he wasn't too young to be very good at his job. Armed with an M-203 grenade launcher mounted under the barrel of his M-16, Jowers was both ruthless and deadly in combat. His fixation with grenades extended to the hand-tossed variety, as the young Ranger carried more than twice the standard combat load, including both the M-33 baseball grenades and the newer minifrags.

The team's rear security was in the very capable hands of Specialist Four Whitlock, a black soldier who called the island of Aruba home. He had seven months' experience in country. Well educated with a pronounced British accent, Whitlock had enlisted in the Army in order to qualify for U.S. citizenship. At five-foot-eleven Whitlock was the tallest man on Kilo team, which might also explain why he elected to carry an M-60 machine gun on patrol. An unusual choice of weapons on a reconnaissance mission, its devastating firepower often meant the difference between life and death in a firefight. Perhaps that was the reason why no one on the team ever questioned Whitlock's decision to carry it. Despite the extra weight of the M-60 and its ammunition, Whitlock still managed to perform yeoman service sterilizing the team's backtrail. And like Cantu, Whitlock also possessed excellent night vision. He also had the ability to move silently in the jungle in total darkness.

The team's junior RTO was a Ranger remembered only as "Tennessee." Quiet, reliable, and comfortable in the field, Tennessee walked in the center of the patrol and carried an M-16 and a .45 automatic. He was a big man, roughly the same height as Whitlock, but rawboned and gangly.

Team Kilo also had a *chieu hoi* named Cam on the team. As an NVA soldier Cam had been wounded in the mouth during a firefight. He was very self-conscious about the resulting slight speech impediment. He spoke fluent French and understood some English. Since Roubideaux also spoke French and had a working knowledge of Vietnamese, there were few communication problems between the two men. Cam had gone out on patrol with other teams, but it would be his first time out with Roubideaux. So Roubideaux sat down for an intense conversation with Cam prior to the patrol to satisfy himself that the tiny soldier was receptive to Roubideaux's style of leadership. Cam appreciated the fact that his team leader had been a Co Van, an adviser to the South Vietnamese military. Cam, carrying an M-16, would walk Cantu's slack on the patrol, a position where Roubideaux could keep an eye on him.

There was also a last minute addition to the team, Sergeant Costello, a Rhode Island native and a Ranger-tabbed "instant NCO" just arrived from the States. It would be Costello's first mission, a shakedown patrol to see if he would be capable of handling his own team in the near future. However, Costello immediately succeeded in offending his new teammates with his arrogance and know-it-all attitude. Chest-thumping was not condoned among Rangers. It was considered bad form, especially when the thumper had no experience to back it up. Roubideaux knew that Costello would also bear watching, so he loaded the new man down with extra radio batteries and assigned him to the number four spot, right behind Roubideaux toward the center of the patrol, where he couldn't cause any damage.

Unlike Kilo Team, Hotel Team consisted of six very experienced Rangers. The team leader was Sgt. Kent Farrand from Oklahoma City, Oklahoma. Married, Farrand was nearing the end of his tour. With only two months left in country he was just beginning to feel the first nag of short-timers' syndrome. The tall, athletic, outgoing NCO had an excellent reputation and had earned the respect of his teammates.

Specialist Four Charles Lyons, from Troy, Idaho, was the team's assistant team leader and point man. A veteran of eight months in country, Lyons was outgoing, likable, and great in the field.

Specialist Four Dave Walker was a unique case study of the type of men who served in the LRP/Rangers. Walker, from Manteca, California, originally arrived in Vietnam as a member of Company F, 58th Infantry (LRP), 101st Airborne Division. He had been badly wounded in the left eye during a mortar attack at Phuoc Vinh in January 1968, just three months into his tour. Eventually he returned to the States, where the Army first put him on TDRL (Temporary Disability Retirement List), then changed it to PDRL (Permanent Disability Retirement List) in September 1969 after they had to remove his damaged left eye. Walker immediately went to an Army recruiter in Stockton,

California, and convinced him to get him back on active duty with a medical waiver. In January 1970, Walker reentered the active-duty Army, got a waiver to return to jump status, then was assigned to Fort Ord, California, as a temporary assistant drill instructor in a basic combat training brigade. A month later he shipped out to Special Forces Training Group at Fort Bragg, North Carolina, where he made it through most of Phase II before he washed himself out and 1049'd to Vietnam. He paid a medic forty-five dollars to pass him on the eye exam, then typed out his own limited physical profile, making sure that there was no mention of a missing eye. Soon he had orders to return to the combat zone assigned to the 173d Airborne Brigade. From the very beginning of his attempt to reenter the service, Walker had been trying to manipulate his way back to Vietnam.

Walker arrived back in country in October 1970, thirty-three months after being wounded. He reported to the replacement center at the 173d Brigade headquarters in Cha Rang Valley, where a recruiter from the brigade's Ranger company spotted the 101st LRP crest on his right shoulder and asked him if he wanted to do some more long range reconning. He didn't have to ask Walker twice.

Married but separated, Walker had been back in country five months before the current mission. Even with one good eye he was still sharp enough in the bush that he rotated point and slack with Lyons. Besides an M-16, Walker carried a chopped-down M-79.

The team RTO was Sp4. David Blow of Dodge City, Kansas. With seven months in the company, Blow was in his prime as a long-range patroller. The tall, lanky Ranger was the team clown and one of the finest RTOs in the company. He carried an M-14E2 because of its weight and size, a very unusual weapon for a radio operator.

Specialist Four Jack Ramsland was a Native American from Alice, Texas. Ramsland had ten months in country and was one of the most experienced Rangers in the company. Tall, dark, and athletically built, he was one of the best long-range patrollers in the bush. An excellent tracker, his weapon for the patrol was an M-60 machine gun, a "pig," the greatest source of firepower on the team.

Specialist Four Joseph Hayes from Weed, California, had nine months in country but only three as a Ranger. He had spent his first six months as a clerk at brigade headquarters before the boredom and routine drove him to join Company N. A natural athlete, the tall, blond Ranger was a natural ladies' man. Even the Doughnut Dollies couldn't help themselves when he showed up.

At the briefing Kilo/Hotel Team was told that their fire support would come from batteries of the 319th Artillery at FSB Hawk's Nest and FSB Uplift. In addition they could count on support from an ARVN 105mm battery stationed at a nearby South Vietnamese Army fire support base. A radio relay team led by Ranger NCO Relando Criado would be set up at Hawk's Nest, a small firebase situated on a high peak not far from Bong Son. The relay team's job would be to handle communications with Kilo/Hotel Team during the patrol. Criado, a Chicano from Sunnydale, California, was getting close to the end of his tour and hoping for a routine patrol without complications.

While most of Kilo/Hotel Team was busy preparing gear for the patrol, Roubideaux, Campbell, and Cantu departed for an overflight of their recon zone. The pilot flew over the coastal plains outside the ascending ridgelines. Roubideaux had instructed him to make a double pass at altitude just outside the actual recon zone, but close enough that they would be able to see down into the valley that comprised most of the team's patrol box.

It didn't take the three men long to get an idea of what they would face on the ground. The terrain was rolling to mountainous, with lots of short scrub and grass along the crests of the hills running into single-canopy forest down in the valleys. Roubideaux decided that because of the limited cover in the area they would go in at last light outside the actual patrol box, then, under cover of darkness, infiltrate into their recon zone. They had practiced night movement on more than one occasion before the mission. However, no one on Hotel Team was comfortable with a night insertion. Costello was the biggest problem, his challenge based on Ranger doctrine. Cantu, the point man, simply lacked confidence in his own ability to locate booby traps in the total darkness. One of Cantu's widowmaker booby traps had killed Kilo's TL a month earlier. Although the accident had not been his fault, the young Ranger still felt responsible. However, Roubideaux was adamant. He felt that their best bet was to enter the recon zone under cover of darkness.

When the three men returned from the overflight at 1430 hours, they informed the rest of their teammates that the insertion was scheduled to go in late that evening. Since both teams had been on stand-down, they were already prepared for a mission when the warning order came down.

At 1730 hours the fourteen-man heavy team arrived at the chopper pad to board Huey slicks. Soon they were airborne, joining up with a pair of Cobra gunships and a third Huey that would serve as the C&C aircraft.

Twenty-five minutes later the two lift ships were

leapfrogging into clearings on a series of secondary ridges outside the team's recon zone. The first two insertions were false, but on the third, four men jumped from each side of the lead ship and three departed each side of the second aircraft as the two helicopters slowed to a hover over a tightly enclosed, grassy clearing. The LZ was on a short finger running down from the dominant ridgeline in the area. The fourteen Rangers dropped eight to ten feet into three-foot-high kunai grass, then faced outward as they waited until the helicopters moved on to the next false insertion. When they were out of sight and sound, the Rangers crawled to their nearby rally point and set up in a tight circle. There they lay dog for thirty minutes as their surroundings slowly returned to normal.

In hushed tones Roubideaux established commo with the relay team on Hawk's Nest, gave them a quick, negative sitrep, then released the choppers. Finally, when darkness had fully descended, he gave the signal to move out, heading up the finger toward the main ridgeline.

The order of patrol beginning from the point man of Team Kilo to the rear security man on Team Hotel was as follows: Cantu, Cam, Roubideaux, Costello, Tennessee, Jowers, Campbell, Whitlock, Lyons, Walker, Farrand, Hayes, Ramsland, and Blow. During the patrol Teams Kilo and Hotel would alternate at the head of the file. When Hotel was at the head of the patrol, Lyons and Walker would alternate point and slack.

As the patrol moved slowly up the finger they hit a number of old, unused game trails and followed them whenever they could. They moved cautiously, patrolling ten minutes, then listening for twenty.

When they finally reached the crest of the main ridgeline they discovered that it connected two separate peaks, one to the north and one to the south. Roubideaux nodded for Cantu to turn right and move along the crest of the ridge. Sticking to old trails, Cantu soon discovered that they were paralleling a major high-speed trail that was covered with fresh sign. They quickly dropped off the main ridge and began moving off the crest of a secondary ridge that sloped downward toward the valley they were to observe. The ridge was covered in knee-high kunai grass and scrub brush, with pockets of triple-canopy jungle covering both flanks. There were no trails anywhere along the crest.

Roubideaux was proud of all his teammates. With the exception of Costello the entire patrol was moving exceptionally well in the darkness, maintaining intervals and observing strict noise discipline. He knew that most of them were uncomfortable with a night infiltration, but he felt that attempting an entry into the valley in broad daylight would only invite detection.

The patrol moved throughout the night, reaching the RZ at first light. Everyone was fully into the mission. As they squatted silently in the faint illumination of the approaching dawn, Roubideaux asked Cam what he thought they should do next. Without hesitation Cam mumbled, "Move no more."

Not far from where they rested was a rocky promontory covered with large boulders. Roubideaux and Campbell agreed that it would make a good laager site. The team leader moved the patrol into the rocks to set up an OP. It was indeed a good spot. From the edge of the promontory they could observe most of their patrol box and the surrounding area, including the village of Phu My nearly four klicks away. Roubideaux assigned security, four men on alert at all times, one man facing each direction at the three, six, nine, and twelve o'clock positions. Watch would begin at 0600 hours. He also had them set out claymores in a fan from three o'clock to nine o'clock. There was a steep, thirty-foot cliff at twelve o'clock, so no claymores were necessary to cover that approach. As half the team grabbed some much needed sleep, those on guard watched in silence as the morning fog lifted out of the jungles. So far there had been no sign of enemy activity.

Roubideaux called in a sitrep to report their position and let the relay team know that they had reached the RZ. The team leader felt smugly satisfied that they would be able to carry out part of their mission from their current location.

They were still in the OP at 1600 hours. It was just past the afternoon siesta when Costello started to get on everyone's nerves. Besides continually breaking noise discipline, he seemed to be functioning poorly under stress. When Roubideaux tried to talk him down, the man threatened to report to Captain Tanaka, the November Company commanding officer, about how Roubideaux had endangered the team by moving at night. By this time everyone else on the team but Costello had come down off the stress high that the night infiltration had brought on. But Costello was still wired.

Soon he was attempting to destroy team integrity, bragging that he could run the patrol better than Roubideaux. None of the other Rangers bought into his phony bravado, choosing generally to ignore him. Their obvious lack of interest seemed only to incite him. Finally tiring of this game, he switched his radio to Armed Forces Vietnam (AFVN), turned up the volume, and began listening to the broadcast. Roubideaux slid over to where Costello sat in the grass and turned the radio off, ordering him to leave it that way.

For the first time the veteran Ranger team leader saw that Costello was not only emotionally immature, he was also a danger to the team. Over the next four hours he found himself continually telling Costello to sit still, be quiet, and stop moving around. Everyone on the team was growing nervous because of the man's conduct.

When Costello finally muttered to no one in particular, "Roubideaux only wants all the glory for himself," it was more than Campbell could take. Whispering between clenched teeth, the angry ATL hissed, "This is a team! Be quiet. Be still."

Cantu quickly added, "Costello, this is Kilo Team, we don't behave that way. Don't get me pissed."

Realizing for the first time that he was the only active member in his newfound fan club, Costello wisely backed off. However, for the rest of the day he sat glumly in the grass, pouting.

Roubideaux planned to move the team down into the valley later that afternoon. He wanted to establish a patrol base closer to the valley floor, then set up an ambush in the late afternoon or evening of the second day. Tennessee had reported spotting movement down in the valley outside the patrol box at 0830 hours that morning. He had observed two people carrying grain bags and what appeared to be weapons, moving parallel to the recon box eighteen hundred to two thousand meters away. One was dressed in blue, the other in black. Both wore flop hats and appeared to have come from the village of Phu My four klicks away.

Nearly all the Rangers kept their fingers crossed that the two men would move into their patrol box, but when they continued walking in the same direction and eventually disappeared from sight the excitement waned quickly. Roubideaux merely called in to report the sighting, not wanting to call in a fire mission on the target since it would only alert the enemy to the presence of a recon team in the area.

At 0900 hours Cantu spotted three more people coming down the same trail. The first man was carrying an AK-47 while the second and third were humping large bags of what appeared to be rice. Using binoculars, Roubideaux observed the men until they disappeared from sight, then called in a second SALUTE (*S*ize, *A*rms, *L*ocation, *U*niform, *T*ime, *E*quipment) report to the relay team at Hawk's Nest.

No more movement was seen down in the valley until 1500 hours, when the team observed what appeared to be the first two men again, in the same general area as before, but closer and without the grain bags. They were moving back toward the village of Phu My. The Rangers saw that both men were wearing pistol belts and carrying M-16s.

Once again Roubideaux called in a SALUTE report. The Rangers watched in silence as the enemy soldiers moved through the valley until they dropped out of sight, disappearing into a thick grove of mature banana trees.

At 1600 hours Roubideaux decided it was time to move out to their second laager site, zigzagging through the patrol box in order to pick up some water on the way.

Although Costello was still pouting, everyone else seemed to be performing exceptionally well. Moving slowly and cautiously downhill through the six-foot-high scrub brush, the team worked closer and closer toward their secondary laager site atop a nearby hill. Dave Walker of Hotel Team, at point, worried about running into one of the dreaded forest cobras moving through the dense cover. It was the kind of terrain they loved.

The hill across the valley had been an important point of reference during their patrol briefing. They had received an intel report stating that over the years a number of pitched battles had been fought on and around it.

A number of caves were also hidden in the sides of the ridgelines coming off the higher elevations, so Roubideaux knew the team had to be very careful as it moved through the area. The new laager site was in the southeastern part of the RZ, directly across from a small secondary valley separating it from the first laager site.

Zigzagging through the patrol box, they crossed no trails as they moved ahead. When they finally neared a small, intermittent stream about twelve inches wide, Roubideaux sent Hotel Team, with Lyons at point, to cloverleaf ahead of the patrol to check out the "blue line." They returned a short time later to report no enemy activity out to a hundred meters to their front.

While they waited in silence, Roubideaux and Cantu determined that the wildlife sounds around them seemed correct, a good indicator that they were alone. Finally Roubideaux gave the signal for the patrol to move down to the stream. They quickly discovered that the water was clear, but there were tens of thousands of hungry land leeches scattered throughout the area. Roubideaux knew that the NVA didn't like these kinds of areas so he set up security, called in his Delta Tangos (defensive targets), and told his comrades to take a thirty-minute break.

A half hour later, refreshed and with full canteens, the patrol moved out again. Just as darkness approached, they got to within sight of the promontory they wanted to reach. While the remainder of the team set up in a tight defensive perimeter, Roubideaux, Cantu, Tennessee, and Cam went up to the hilltop to check it out. The four Rangers soon discovered a main high-speed trail running off the south side of the peak. It dropped off downhill until it tied into with the main trail running up the valley. The higher trail was hard-packed and well maintained. In the thin layer of dust covering the trail were dozens of fresh tracks made by batta boots and sandals. The trail ran east to west and approached to within a hundred meters of the promontory where the Rangers were headed.

It was 1830 hours when the four men returned to the rest of the team hidden down below. Roubideaux wasted no time bringing them up to the promontory. In the fading light they found an extensive area of level limestone, covered by a gigantic stone slab supported by three large boulders. The natural rock formation created a sheltered area large enough to house a full platoon.

Whitlock couldn't help but whisper, "Hey, we're in Fred Flintstone's house."

Tennessee answered, "Yeah, the only thing missing is Wilma."

The patrol carefully checked out the entire area across the face of the promontory. Roubideaux and Campbell agreed that it was a good place to set up an OP. They established their perimeter along the outer edge of the rock house and set out claymores. Their options were slim, but at least from that location they could observe the trail.

Roubideaux decided to call in artillery concentrations for H&I fire, bringing the closest to within a hundred meters of their position. He did that to give the impression to any nearby enemy forces that there were no Americans in the immediate area. H&I fire was usually called in at locations remote from U.S. and SVN perimeters. It was designed to hinder the enemy's free movement and discourage him from remaining too long in one spot.

Roubideaux was not too worried about the close proximity of the concentrations. The team had adequate cover among the rocks, and they could always move under the protection of the slab if the artillery or mortar fire came too close. However, he did not want to set up his perimeter directly under the slab in case the enemy mounted a surprise attack using B-40 rockets and frags.

Everything was quiet until sometime between 2100 and 2200 hours, when Cantu tapped Roubideaux on the leg and whispered that he could hear voices out on the trail.

The team was set up in a tight wagon-wheel perimeter. Clouds had rolled in, making everything so black that even their starlight scopes were useless. Roubideaux wasn't worried about his team being nervous over their inability to see beyond their perimeter; he knew that the night infiltration had given them a lot of confidence in their ability to operate in the dark.

As they sat silently listening to the sounds in the night, they could hear what appeared to be people moving from east to west out on the trail a hundred meters to their front. Roubideaux and Campbell concluded that there were at least four to six enemy soldiers moving down the trail. However, because of the lay of the land, they couldn't tell if the enemy soldiers were using lights to move in the darkness. They were talking loudly, slapping bushes as they passed, and clinking equipment together. Roubideaux smiled to himself; these enemy soldiers had no noise discipline at all. That went on for at least five minutes until they passed out of the area.

Roubideaux immediately called in a SALUTE report, informing the relay team that the enemy was on the move.

About this time, Costello began acting paranoid. He was having visions of Viet Cong soldiers sneaking up on their perimeter. His irrational behavior soon began to spook the rest of the patrol.

Roubideaux had to do something quickly to get their minds off the problem, so he decided to let Costello call in a single-gun fire mission from the ARVN artillery battery. Roubideaux, Cantu, and Tennessee would act as Costello's eyes while he directed the artillery fire.

The fourteen Rangers moved inside the rocks as Costello called in four rounds of artillery on each of the four points outside their laager site. When he had completed this, he adjusted fire down on the trail. During the time Costello played with the artillery, his teammates felt terribly vulnerable. Surprisingly, Costello managed to do a pretty good job directing the artillery fire. Roubideaux let him call in fire once again during the night, just to keep his mind off the danger. He doubted that the two fire missions had resulted in enemy casualties, but they did manage to keep Costello occupied and quieted down for the evening. The remainder of the night proved uneventful.

Roubideaux and Whitlock shared their thoughts during the night, both men expressing bad feelings about the coming day. Roubideaux had a premonition that he was going to hit a booby trap or walk into an ambush, and Whitlock just had a bad feeling in general.

The next day the patrol was preparing to move out at 0700 hours to find a suitable spot for an ambush. Roubideaux, Cantu, and Cam went out to conduct an area reconnaissance before moving down from the hill. Roubideaux left Campbell in charge of the eleven men still at the harbor site, telling Campbell to make sure Costello was facing the rear.

The three Rangers moved cautiously down to the trail and continued along it for about a hundred meters before splitting up to look for a likely ambush site. They were just coming back together again when Roubideaux stopped behind a rock and looked up to see Cam trying to get down among some boulders along the trail. He then spotted Tennessee, who was giving the hand signal for "enemy." Roubideaux turned around quickly, just in time to see a soldier standing three feet away on the trail below him, wearing a black PJ top, olive drab military trousers, jungle boots, and an OD flop hat on a drawstring. The man had an indigenous rucksack on his back and wore a cotton web belt with two nylon ammo pouches around his waist. He was carrying an M-16 rifle, the stock over his right shoulder, holding it by the barrel.

Roubideaux's first thought was that the man was an ARVN soldier or a point man for a Ruff Puff recon patrol. The Vietnamese appeared to have a surprised look on his face when he spotted the Ranger.

Roubideaux was also confused. When he looked back again at Cantu, he noticed that his point man was bringing up his rifle as if to fire. Swinging back around once again, he saw the Vietnamese soldier was also bringing his weapon down into a firing position, using his left thumb to adjust the selector switch. Roubideaux realized at that moment that the soldier facing him was indeed the enemy. The Ranger opened fire, emptying his entire eighteen-round magazine at the Viet Cong, hitting him in the arm and in the lower chest. The VC dropped his weapon and went down hard. Roubideaux could see that the man's left arm was broken.

By this time Roubideaux's AK-47 locked open on an empty magazine. He realized that he was out of ammo just as another enemy soldier stepped up and opened fire on him at point-blank range. As the Ranger jumped backwards to get out of the line of fire, Cantu opened up on the VC slack man, killing him instantly.

Roubideaux, down alongside the trail, could feel something warm running down his back. Tennessee reached him and, kneeling down at his side, asked if he had been hit. Roubideaux said he thought so. It was then that Tennessee discovered what had actually happened. Apparently, Roubideaux's canteen had been hit by an enemy round, and what the team leader thought was blood was only lukewarm water running down his back.

Relieved that he was still alive, Roubideaux went back into action, shouting for Tennessee to get the rest of the team back down to the trail.

High up in the rocks the remainder of the patrol was busy engaging the surviving enemy troops still coming up the trail. But Cam was nowhere to be seen. Cantu had remained where he was and was still returning fire down the trail. Roubideaux had seen only the first two VC in the column, but he was now acutely aware that return fire was still coming from somewhere down the trail.

Suddenly, Roubideaux saw Costello charging down from the rocks, firing as he ran. The VC down on the trail focused their fire on him and Costello immediately dropped his weapon and began screaming in pain, crying out that he had been hit. Whitlock jumped up out of the cover of the rocks and worked his way down to Costello to bandage his wound and shut him up.

Tennessee tossed out a smoke grenade in an effort to mark the enemy positions, only to have it come to rest about thirty or forty feet from where Roubideaux lay behind the boulder. This was not good, because it happened just as a pair of Cobra gunships arrived on the scene. The billowing smoke was too close to the team's position and, especially too close to Roubideaux.

Campbell quickly shouted for Tennessee to throw out another smoke grenade. This time he managed to toss the canister about a hundred feet from where the team lay firing among the boulders. The two gunships then moved in and opened fire on the second smoke, reporting moments later that they were getting kills.

Gunfire was now coming from just behind the large rock in front of Roubideaux. It had to be the enemy slack man who, somehow, had recovered enough from his wounds to get back into the battle. Cantu saw him, too, and yelled out to warn Roubideaux of the danger. Roubideaux pulled out one of the new baseball grenades with the thumb safety and tossed it over the top of the boulder. When there was no resulting explosion, Roubideaux figured that he had simply forgotten to arm it.

Seconds later the team leader spotted a grenade coming right back at him, landing among the rocks across the trail from his position. It looked like the one he had just thrown. The wounded VC must have figured out how to arm the damn thing then tossed it back.

At that point in the battle Roubideaux was still not 100 percent certain if they were fighting enemies or friendlies. Up in the rocks, the rest of the patrol knew only that they were in a firefight, and at the moment they seemed to have the upper hand.

Campbell was on the radio busily working the gunships while the remainder of the Rangers were scattered out in the rocks within a hundred meters of each other in an oblong perimeter. Campbell and Tennessee were down close to the trail, heaving grenades twenty meters to Roubideaux's front, so he knew enemy soldiers were still hidden nearby.

The firefight lasted an hour and a half, the gunships

arriving twenty to twenty-five minutes after the initial contact. The Cobras were busy making rocket and gun runs up and down the trail below the Rangers' positions, trying to force the VC out in the open.

While the gunships were working out, Golf Team, another Ranger patrol from November Company, inserted in the valley below the enemy patrol and began to move up the trail to reinforce Team Kilo/Hotel.

With the reaction force on the ground, Roubideaux moved over to check on Costello. The man had suffered only a couple of ricochet-type flesh wounds in his neck and back, probably caused by rock chips, not bullets. But Costello was acting like he was dying. Anxious to get the wounded man out of the field and away from his patrol, Roubideaux called for a medevac.

While waiting for the medevac, Roubideaux was becoming more and more convinced that they had whacked a friendly ARVN unit. Taking Cantu and Tennessee with him, the three men moved down the trail until they reached the dead bodies of the first two men they had shot. A single unexploded grenade was lying next to the bodies, the thumb safety still on. Either someone else had forgotten to engage the safety on one of the new fragmentation grenades, or the frag that had landed across the trail from Roubideaux had not been his. The three Rangers recovered two M-16s, a pair of rucksacks containing two brand-new claymores, twenty-two fragmentation grenades, sixteen M-16 magazines, a supply of precooked rice, and a bottle of dried minnows. They also recovered U.S. Air Force survival knives from each body. The slack man had a Makarov 9mm pistol in his possession, and both men wore NVA belt buckles.

When Roubideaux checked the pockets of the first man he found a paybook and a diary wrapped in plastic, secured around a wallet by a rubber band. The second man also had a paybook wrapped in plastic tied around a billfold with a piece of string. Their pay records indicated that both men were NVA soldiers. For the first time since the battle began, Roubideaux knew for certain that the men they had killed were indeed the enemy.

When the medevac finally arrived on the scene, Roubideaux sent out the captured weapons and rucks on the penetrator along with the wounded Costello.

Free of their baggage, Kilo Team members moved down the trail to search for more NVA bodies. They soon found two more, killed by the Rangers up in the rocks. They recovered more M-16s, rucks, mixed uniforms, and more U.S. Air Force survival knives. Fortunately they also discovered more paybooks and photographs of the dead men wearing NVA uniforms. However, not one of the enemy soldiers lying dead along the trail was wearing an article of North Vietnamese Army clothing except for NVA belt buckles. All were wearing ARVN-issue trousers and relatively new jungle boots, and all were dressed in black pajama tops. One was even humping a green canvas chest pack custom tailored to hold M-16 magazines (four pockets, each holding two magazines). All wore boonie caps. The men appeared young, well groomed, and healthy except for the slack man, who seemed to be a little older than the rest. Examination of his paybook showed that he had been born in 1942, making him twenty-nine years old at the time of his death. None of the dead had sores or insect bites on their bodies, and their feet and teeth were in exceptionally good condition. They had none of the usual musky smells that went with long periods in the bush.

While his teammates were going through the enemy

gear, Roubideaux wondered what had happened to Cam. The tiny Vietnamese suddenly reappeared a few minutes after the medevac departed as Roubideaux was busy establishing contact with the approaching reaction force. When Roubideaux asked him where he'd been, Cam said only that he had been scared. The team leader didn't pursue the subject any further at that time.

By then the gunships had expended their armament and had to return to base to rearm and refuel. With the air cover gone, Roubideaux got on the radio and told the reaction force to move up the hill to link up with Kilo/Hotel Team. Golf Team reached the top of the hill just before the gunships returned. Right after they had inserted Roubideaux had contacted them to tell them to hold up downhill in the rocks until the Cobras had finished with the VC. He didn't want to risk having them mistaken for the enemy as they moved uphill. It had happened before.

Kilo/Hotel Team was quickly resupplied with ammo and frags by the newly arrived Rangers. Golf Team reported that they had made no contact coming up the trail to Kilo/Hotel's position.

It was 1300 hours. Contact had been made around 0800 hours that morning. At the moment there were nineteen people lined up out on the trail—seven men remaining from Kilo Team, six from Hotel, and six from Golf. Roubideaux figured that all three teams would most likely be extracted after the firefight, or at the very most one team might be left behind to set up an ambush along the trail. Instead, Captain Tanaka ordered Roubideaux to move his heavy team openly down the trail and out into the rice paddy, where they were to set up an OP facing east. Golf Team was to remain behind, booby-trap the four bodies out on the trail, then set up an ambush. An additional six-man Ranger team would be inserted before dark to reinforce Golf Team.

That night Kilo/Hotel Team reported movement across the paddies to their front. Nothing developed from the sighting. At approximately 0300 hours there were a series of "willie peter" (white phosphorous) detonations up on the hill near where the two stay-behind teams were lying in ambush. They had reported hearing movement around them and had moved back to call in a fire mission. When it was over, the teams reported that they had no indication one way or another if they had gotten a body count.

Kilo/Hotel Team was extracted at 0800 hours the next morning. Staff Sergeant Tom Roubideaux was on his way home immediately after the patrol returned to LZ English. The two stay-behind teams were extracted later that afternoon without making further contact with the enemy.

When Kilo/Hotel Team returned to the compound they were not debriefed about the patrol. They discovered to their surprise that Captain Tanaka was giving the entire patrol the cold shoulder. They soon got the word that Costello had returned to the company area before the patrol had come in and had been immediately debriefed by Tanaka and the company operations officer. Costello had quickly painted the false picture that he was the real "hero" of the mission, calling in artillery on the enemy. He had stated that they had been totally surrounded during the night when he had called in the fire mission to save the day. He had also accused Roubideaux of endangering the team by moving at night. To make matters worse, Captain Tanaka had written in the debriefing notes that Costello had saved the team from being overrun, and that he was formally admonishing Roubideaux for endangering the team during the night infiltration. After the dressing-down, Tanaka had handed Roubideaux his PCS (permanent change in station) orders effective in forty-eight hours. Roubideaux accepted them immediately, saying only, "I'm outta here."

There had been a major rift between the Rangers of November Company since Tanaka had taken over, especially between the six "tab" Rangers in the unit and the few old-timers who still remained. Although no one could substantiate it, a number of instances had occurred proving that the "tabbers" were playing favorites within the company. They had their followers from the rank and file, but they were insignificant in number. However, it was an uncomfortable situation for everyone involved.

Two months later Hotel Team was set up on a night laager on a hilltop in that same area. Just before dark they counted 425 NVA soldiers walking away from them down in the valley below. The next morning, while waiting for the arrival of their extraction ships, one of the Rangers who had been on the Kilo/Hotel patrol, Specialist Four Hayes, was killed by an NVA stay-behind force when he wandered too far from the team while making a one-man cloverleaf reconnaissance of the terrain outside the team's NDP. The NVA then took the rest of the team under fire, pinning them down. Lyons, the ATL and point man, slipped out of the perimeter and went after Hayes. When neither man returned, the team leader, Sp4. Robert Joley, went after both of them.

Specialists Four Jake Dymond and Dave Walker, back in the NDP with the radio, were still pinned down by enemy fire coming from the opposite hilltop.

Dymond was calling relay for gunships while Walker was busy dropping M-79 rounds into the enemy positions. Suddenly they heard Lyons whispering to them from a point somewhere down the hill from their perimeter that he had been hit. When the enemy fire finally began to slacken, Walker ran down to the wounded point man and dragged him back into the perimeter. Lyons told them that he had found Hayes dead on the opposite hilltop, and had spotted a number of NVA further back on the crest. When he turned to run, the enemy opened fire and hit him in the knee as he was turning. Lyons managed to crawl back to within thirty meters of the team's perimeter before calling for help. He reported that he had not seen Joley on the way back and could only assume that he had been killed.

Without realizing it, Lyons had passed Joley while crawling back from the enemy positions. The team leader had been lying pinned down in the low grass off the side of the saddle. Five minutes later Joley sprinted back up the hill and dived inside the perimeter. He was breathing hard but had not been hit.

A reaction force landed twenty-five minutes later. Walker led them over to the hilltop where the enemy had opened fire on the team. They soon discovered Hayes's body lying face-up on the trail. He had been shot in the back of the head at close range. The NVA had taken his weapon but left the body untouched.

Staff Sergeant Tom Roubideaux recommended everyone on the team except Costello for Bronze Stars with "V." He did put Costello in for a Purple Heart, which he felt was all that the man deserved. Cam, the ex-NVA who had disappeared at the beginning of the battle, Roubideaux wanted only to shoot. Tom Roubideaux received nothing for his actions during the patrol, however he was richly rewarded by just being able to see his teammates regain their confidence before he departed.

Roubideaux knew immediately after the mission ended that he was finished as a combat warrior. He sensed that he had burned out and was susceptible to making the kinds of mistakes that could get people killed. Fifty-seven months in combat was enough time for anyone. Having transitioned through LRRPs, LRPs, and Rangers, he also realized that some not so subtle changes in professionalism and attitudes had occurred that did not bode well for a career in the military. It was time to leave the service. However, in January 1972 he returned to Vietnam once more to serve a six-month TDY with MACV Advisory Teams 162 and 81. Then, when that tour was over, Tom Roubideaux went home for good.

F Company,
75th Infantry (Ranger),
25th Infantry Division

In early March 1970, 25th Infantry Division G-2 received intelligence indicating that enemy Main Force units were moving into the Renegade Woods to establish base areas for the purpose of running offensive operations in the division's AO. On 30 March, elements of the NVA 271st and 272d Regiments combined to conduct a night assault on Fire Support Base Jay, occupied by units of the 1st Cavalry Division. The determined enemy was thrown back by the Cav troopers, leaving seventy of their comrades dead on the battlefield. Moving under cover of darkness, the mauled NVA headed back to their sanctuary in the Renegade Woods to rebuild and refit for future operations.

The Renegade Woods was a large, level area covered with a dense growth of double-canopy forest. Its few clearings were choked by dense stands of kunai grass bisected by thick hedgerows and dotted here and there with small, isolated pockets of brush and an occasional dead tree or two. The open areas offered some concealment but little or no cover. The enemy had prepared the area well, however, and numerous bunkers and fighting positions had been constructed amid the hedgerows and just inside the edge of the jungle facing the clearings. The NVA/VC had planned ahead to counter U.S. air assaults into the Renegade Woods.

At 0700 hours on the morning of 2 April 1970, Capt.
Paul Schierholz, the commanding officer of Company
F (Ranger), 75th Infantry, was alerted by 3d Brigade,
25th Infantry Division, to send a reconnaissance team
into the Renegade Woods to determine the presence of
the NVA/VC units that had attacked FSB Jay three days
earlier.

At the same time a light aerial scout team from Troop
D, 3/4 Cav, flew out to the area to conduct a visual reconnaissance of the AO. The LOH helicopter drew no
fire nor did it observe enemy activity near the Ranger
team's proposed LZ. However, the crew aboard the
LOH did observe fresh enemy signs in and around
a large clearing approximately twelve hundred meters southwest of the LZ. They also spotted a well-
camouflaged enemy structure just west of the clearing
and marked it for their escorting Cobra gunship. Rocket
and grenade runs on the area soon revealed eight to ten
additional structures. There was no longer any doubt of
an NVA/VC presence in the area. Low on fuel and ordnance, the two aircraft left the area and returned to Cu
Chi to refuel and rearm.

At 0800 hours a thirteen-man Ranger element made
up of Teams Three-Eight and Three-Nine climbed
aboard two slicks from D Troop, 3/4 Cav and, escorted
by a LOH C&C aircraft and a Cobra gunship, they departed for the Renegade Woods. The heavy Ranger patrol was led by 1st Lt. Philip J. Norton. Sergeants First
Class Alvin W. Floyd and Colin K. Hall were the assistant team leaders. Other team members included
Sergeants Fred B. Stuckey, Michael F. Thomas, Samuel
P. Seay, and Charles P. Avery; Spec Fours Donald W.
Tinney, Donald E. Purdy, and Richard F. Guth; and
PFCs Raymond L. Allmon, Steven Perez, and Kenneth
J. Langland.

When the aircraft arrived over the area there was still no sign of enemy activity near the proposed LZ. But an aerial search of the other large clearing by the Cobra gunship revealed additional footprints and a lister bag (a large canvas water bag holding twenty gallons) lying in the open near a well. Warrant Officer Kenneth Strand, the aircraft commander of the escort Cobra, radioed this information to Ranger team leader Norton aboard the lead slick. Lieutenant Norton immediately decided to insert his team at the new location. The insertion was completed by 0835 hours.

As the Rangers deployed from the two helicopters and took up positions in heavy cover on the edge of the LZ, they immediately found signs of recent enemy activity. Spreading out in patrol formation, the Rangers began moving west toward the structures located earlier that morning.

Within minutes of their setting out, an enemy light machine gun opened fire on the point element of the patrol from a range of ten to fifteen meters. Sergeant Fred Stuckey, at point, was wounded in the initial burst of fire. Lieutenant Norton's PRC-25 radio was rendered inoperable when a bullet severed the mike cord. Spec Four Donald Purdy, walking Stuckey's slack, had another round shatter the extractor mechanism on his M-16. Stuckey and Purdy responded immediately by tossing grenades at the enemy machine gun position, killing its crew. Within seconds the Rangers began taking fire from all directions, indicating the presence of at least an NVA platoon, too large a force for thirteen Rangers to take on. Norton decided to withdraw to the east and attempt to work their way around the enemy positions west of the LZ.

While the team was moving, SFC Alvin Floyd, the assistant team leader, contacted the Cobra gunship over the backup radio and asked the pilot to put suppressive fire on the tree line where the enemy was located. He also requested that a reaction force be brought in to develop the situation on the LZ.

The team then split into two elements, with Team Three-Nine moving east under the command of Lieutenant Norton. Team Three-Eight, led by Sergeant Floyd, provided covering fire during Three-Nine's withdrawal. After several minutes of intense small-arms fire the firefight degenerated to occasional sniping. Team Three-Nine took advantage of the lull, maneuvering across the clearing until they reached the cover of the woods one hundred meters to the east. Their withdrawal was covered by the Cobra gunship, which made numerous minigun and rocket runs on the tree line along the western edge of the LZ. On its last pass its 40mm automatic grenade launcher jammed after firing only one of the 250 rounds it carried.

During this time the LOH aerial scout helicopter moved in and made several passes with its M-60 machine gun. With the Rangers moving into the woods on the east side of the perimeter, the two slicks were dispatched to Cu Chi to pick up a reaction force. Before it departed, the pilot of one of the slicks requested permission to land and medevac Sergeant Stuckey, the wounded Ranger, but the aircraft commander of the escorting Cobra refused because a medevac had not been requested and the ground fire at the time was too intense.

As Team Three-Nine reached the woods on the eastern edge of the clearing, it began to receive a heavy volume of small-arms fire from a number of automatic weapons and light machine guns. The team returned fire and turned back toward a bomb crater approximately fifteen by thirty feet wide that it had just passed. Team Three-Eight was just approaching the same crater from the west. Suddenly they were caught in the open by a combination of small-arms and rocket-propelled grenade (RPG) fire coming from hidden enemy positions to their north. Sergeant Floyd and Sgt. Michael Thomas were killed instantly, and Sp4. Donald Tinney was badly wounded. The remaining Rangers laid down a base of heavy suppressive fire while they grabbed their dead and wounded and moved into the protection of the nearby crater. There they found that an RPG round had destroyed their remaining radio, leaving them without communications.

While the Rangers struggled to get the situation under control, Sgt. Colin Hall silenced the light machine gun fire still coming from the west with hand grenades and accurate M-16 fire, and Sgt. Charles Avery destroyed the RPG launcher and an enemy M-79 that had been firing on the team from the north.

Inside the crater, Lieutenant Norton dragged the wounded Tinney to safety. Once out of the line of fire, Norton secured the handset from his dead assistant team leader and replaced his damaged mike cord, enabling him to regain commo. He quickly established radio contact with the C&C aircraft, repeated his request for a reaction force and gunship support, and finally requested a medevac for the three men wounded by the RPG round.

By then the Cobra and the LOH had both expended their ammunition. The LOH pilot had also jettisoned all of the extra ammunition aboard in anticipation of an attempt to medevac the wounded while one of his gunners remained on the ground with the Rangers in order to make space available on his aircraft. But by then the two Huey slicks had picked up the radio traffic on their way back to Cu Chi, had returned, and were on station.

By this time the Rangers inside the crater realized

that they were surrounded. They were taking small-arms fire from all directions, and hand grenades were being lobbed at them from a brushy finger jutting from the wood line to their southwest. Fortunately, the Rangers' own suppressive fire had succeeded in silencing all of the enemy's crew-served weapons.

Suddenly an NVA soldier emerged from the tree line south of the crater and, standing in the open, prepared to throw a grenade at the Rangers' position. Before he could complete the act, he was wounded, then killed, by grenades thrown by Sergeant Stuckey.

By this time PFC Raymond Allmon had gone through the seven hundred rounds of M-60 ammo he had carried on the mission and a fifty-round belt he had removed from Sergeant Thomas's body. He was popping away at the enemy with his .45-caliber pistol.

Private First Class Steven Perez had expended all of his M-79 ammunition, and PFC Kenneth Langland had fired 860 rounds through his M-60 before a major malfunction rendered the weapon inoperable. By 0920 hours the Rangers had used up most of their ammunition and were experiencing weapon failures. The Cobra had expended all of its ammo and was making "dry" gun runs on the enemy positions in an attempt to suppress their fire and prevent them from maneuvering against the Rangers.

At 0922 hours Warrant Officer (WO) James Tonelli, the aircraft commander of one of the two insertion slicks, and his "peter pilot" (copilot), Capt. Philip Tocco, approached the clearing at low level and landed fifteen feet from the lip of the crater in an attempt to medevac the wounded. The aircraft began taking fire immediately from a large number of enemy weapons surrounding the clearing, receiving four hits that miraculously failed to prevent the aircraft from lifting back out.

On the ground, Lieutenant Norton realized that his Rangers were in an untenable position and ordered his men to get aboard the waiting aircraft. While the Rangers scampered out of the crater and climbed into the Huey, Crew Chief Charles Lowe kept a steady stream of M-60 fire churning up the tree line ten meters away. On the other side of the helicopter, the door gunner, PFC Richard Adams—a former member of Team Three-Eight—jumped down to help the Rangers move the badly wounded Tinney on board.

After spending a long thirty seconds trying to achieve lift, the overloaded Huey finally rose from the ground under maximum torque experiencing severe vertical vibration. As the aircraft went through transitional lift and began to move forward, one of its two M-60s jammed. Immediately the Rangers took up covering fire with their individual weapons. With fifteen men aboard, the helicopter limped out of the danger zone and headed back to Cu Chi escorted by the remaining three aircraft. Finally, low on fuel, Centaur Two-Three set down near Trang Bang so first aid could be administered to Tinney and to redistribute the passengers, some of whom were literally hanging from the outside of the aircraft. The helicopter finally reached the 12th Evacuation Hospital at Cu Chi at 1000 hours.

During the battle back at the clearing, 1st Lt. David Parson, a forward air controller, arrived on station at approximately 0900 hours. Piloting an OV-10, he expended fifteen hundred rounds of minigun ammunition strafing the contact area after the Rangers were extracted. During his strafing runs he received heavy small-arms and automatic weapons fire from the ground.

Also at 0900 hours Companies B and C, 2d Battalion, 27th Infantry, were alerted to stand by to be inserted into the area of the battle as a reaction force. Company B had been conducting ambush patrols nine klicks to the south. Company C had been serving as a blocking force for an ARVN infantry unit in contact four klicks to the southwest. In addition, Company A, which had just come in from the field and was on stand-down back at Cu Chi, was also placed on alert.

At 0925 hours Lt. Col. George Custer III, commanding officer, 2d Battalion, 27th Infantry, arrived on station over the contact area in his C&C aircraft.

Company C was the first U.S. infantry unit to reach the battleground. They combat assaulted into the area while artillery fire from Fire Support Bases Hull and Hampton provided blocking fire behind the suspected enemy positions. By 1100 hours Company C's 1st and 3d Platoons had assembled and immediately began moving west toward the area of the Ranger contact. Part of 2d Platoon moved out along a parallel course three hundred meters to the north as a flanking element.

At 1140 hours the 1st and 3d Platoons were in heavy contact, both losing their point men to enemy fire. While an emergency medevac was called in to take out the wounded, the 2d Platoon also began taking enemy fire and, under the cover of gunships, fell back on the rest of the company. For the next six hours Company C was effectively pinned down by highly accurate enemy small-arms fire. During the battle the company lost a platoon leader and platoon sergeant killed in action, and was unable to recover the body of the 1st Platoon point man.

At 1145 hours a light fire team made up of a pair of UH-1C gunships and another FAC aircraft circled the area, trying to locate the source of the enemy ground fire. Suddenly one of the gunships was shot down by small-arms fire. Fortunately the pilot was able to set the aircraft down in a small clearing eight hundred meters west of the contact site. Uninjured, the crew E&E'd to the west, where they were quickly picked up by the second gunship. Within minutes other gunships arrived on the scene to assist the FAC in supporting the rescue operation.

At 1200 hours another FAC pilot arrived on station over the contact area and directed air strikes on suspected enemy positions forward and west of Company C. Between 1315 and 1420 hours resupply ships brought in extra ammo to Company C and evacuated seven wounded soldiers and five heat casualties.

By 1423 hours half of Company B had air assaulted into the action. The B Company element advanced three hundred meters until it reached Company C's perimeter. Company B soon began taking small-arms fire as it linked up with Company C. The B Company element immediately assaulted forward and overran the enemy strongpoint that was keeping Company C pinned down. While the two B Company platoons advanced by fire and maneuver, a squad of enemy soldiers attempted to flank them on the right. However, it was spotted by B Company soldiers, who killed two and chased the others out of the hedgerows, where gunships killed two more.

Company B's 2d Platoon attempted to move forward but ran into some highly accurate NVA sniper fire which killed an RTO, the unit's FO, and pinned down the rest of the platoon. Company B was then forced to pull back, leaving two bodies behind plus the body of the C Company point man it had been trying to recover.

By 1815 hours, A Company had also combat assaulted into an LZ one klick southwest of Companies B and C. Companies B and C drew back and set up a night defensive position under artillery cover and air strikes placed directly on suspected enemy positions. During the air and artillery strikes a large group of enemy soldiers was spotted maneuvering to attack the two-company NDP. A Cobra gunship was called in to break up the enemy element.

By 1820 hours the rest of B Company was on the ground and immediately secured an NDP for the engaged troops to withdraw to. During the next hour the enemy broke contact, a four-ship resupply brought water, food, and ammo into the NDP, and Company C was reinforced with troops from the battalion rear.

During the night, helicopter gunships and flare ships remained on station, but the enemy forces around the American positions avoided contact.

The next day Company B, 2d Battalion (Mechanized), 22d Infantry, joined up with the three companies from the 27th Infantry and prepared to advance into the contact area to recover the five bodies that had been left behind. FAC-controlled air strikes killed numerous enemy soldiers as the infantry companies advanced and recovered the three bodies left behind the day before by Company C.

The rest of the day was marked by frequent enemy contacts between B Company elements and supporting aircraft, with several more enemy soldiers reported killed and a number of individual weapons captured. In addition, much of the equipment abandoned by Company C during the initial contact the day before was recovered.

Later that afternoon the bodies of the two Rangers were recovered by Company A, which then moved further west and secured the downed Huey slick, guarding it until it could be recovered by a CH-47 Chinook helicopter.

After the aircraft had been recovered, all four infantry companies returned to the clearing where the initial Ranger contact had occurred and established a night defensive position. B Company, 2d Battalion, 22d Infantry's APCs (armored personnel carriers) were moved in and positioned strategically around the perimeter, where the American forces spent an uneventful night.

The next morning the four companies resumed operations in the area with the exception of Charlie Company, 2d Battalion, 27th Infantry, which returned to Cu Chi base camp to conduct a twenty-four-hour maintenance stand-down. Company C was replaced in the field by Company A, 2d Battalion (Mechanized), 22d Infantry. The day's operations were marked by frequent discoveries of enemy KIAs and miscellaneous equipment left behind by fleeing NVA.

That night Companies A and B, 2d Battalion, 27th Infantry, established platoon ambushes in the contact area. At approximately 2010 hours the 1st Platoon leader, B/2/27th, called for a clearance before engaging an estimated two squads of soldiers observed approaching from the southwest. Before he could verify whether friendlies were in the area, a large force of 200 to 250 heavily equipped NVA moved into view heading right into the American ambush. The lieutenant in command ordered his men to lie prone in the sparse cover and let the NVA pass. Fortunately for the Americans, the enemy column had out no point or flank security and was observing very lax route discipline. The unit was obviously unaware of the presence of four U.S. infantry companies operating in the area. The NVA passed so close to the hidden B Company soldiers that many of them walked directly over the detonator wires running back from their claymore antipersonnel mines.

Near the platoon's positions the NVA column paused for nearly a minute to allow stragglers to close up. The ambushers at that time saw that the enemy soldiers were heavily laden with light machine guns, mortars, and large quantities of ammunition they were transporting on stretchers. The enemy column was nearly three hundred meters long, and the nervous Americans were beginning to think that the end would never pass. But as the two-man rear security element entered the kill zone, the platoon leader told his men to open fire on them and the rest of the NVA column just disappearing from view into a large wooded area to the east. The American platoon opened fire with M-60s and M-79s, followed immediately by a general engagement with small arms. Within seconds the enemy forces were returning fire with small arms and RPGs.

While the battle raged, B Company's two other platoons consolidated forces at 3d Platoon's location and set up a well-prepared crossfire. Company A, 2d Battalion (Mechanized), 22d Infantry, was recalled to the scene along with a number of helicopter gunships and flare ships. While they were moving into position, U.S. artillery was brought into play. Amazingly, the enemy force avoided further contact with the units brought in to engage them and disappeared into the night.

On 5 April, Companies A and B, 2/22d, and Companies B and C, 2/27th, were ordered to continue their ground reconnaissance of the area of the battlefield, concentrating on the area of 1/B/2/27th's ambush the previous night. The remainder of the day saw the discovery of numerous enemy bodies and abandoned enemy weapons and equipment, and frequent contacts with scattered enemy units which resulted in several more enemy KIA.

The final day of the operation, 6 April, resulted in a *hoi chanh* (prisoner who surrenders) who was flown immediately to Cu Chi for interrogation. A few additional NVA weapons were discovered and a number of enemy booby traps was uncovered.

The operation resulted in 101 enemy KIAs confirmed by actual body count, one enemy POW, and two *hoi chanh*s. Large amounts of enemy equipment and weapons were captured or destroyed. Intelligence reported that the 271st VC/NVA Regiment was badly mauled during the five-day operation. Besides suffering heavy losses in material and manpower, the base areas of the regiment's 2d and 3d Battalions were destroyed. The enemy's offensive capability in the Hieu Thien District of Tay Ninh Province was severely impaired for months to come.

U.S. losses included twelve KIA and thirty-five WIA, of whom eighteen were treated and immediately returned to duty. Three F Company Rangers were killed in the initial ambush that precipitated the successful operation. Sergeant First Class Alvin W. Floyd, Sgt. Michael F. Thomas, and Sp4. Donald W. Tinney lost their lives. The Rangers were awarded a total of seven Silver Stars and six Bronze Stars with "V" device for their heroics that fateful day.

Long Range Reconnaissance Patrol Platoon, 3/506th Infantry, 101st Airborne Division

By late summer of 1968, the 3/506's LRRP platoon had been taken from Headquarters Company and incorporated into Echo Company along with the 4.2-inch mortar platoon and the 81mm mortar platoon. After pulling operations in Da Lat earlier in the year, the battalion had finally returned home to Phan Thiet, where the LRRPs were soon pulling missions in a fan extending from the southwest to the north of the battalion base camp. There were no villages in the areas where the LRRPs patrolled so anyone they encountered was to be considered the enemy, mostly Main Force VC in the jungles with a smattering of local VC in close.

Late on the morning of 15 August 1968 a warning order came down from the battalion S-2 operations officer. It arrived at the LRRP compound, where the platoon sergeant delivered it to Sgt. Sam Jacobs. The four-day mission was being given to Jacobs's Team Romeo-Four. He immediately notified his teammates to get their gear ready, telling them that they had a patrol scheduled for the next morning, 16 August.

Ten minutes later Jacobs caught a flight on an O-1 Bird Dog and flew out over the recon zone to check out the area. The RZ was a large square consisting of nine one-thousand-meter grid squares. It was situated on the northeast end of an area affectionately referred to as

"The Bowl." The lower three grid squares were relatively low; the terrain rose slowly up into the mountains in the middle and northern grid squares.

When Jacobs arrived back at the platoon area just before dark, he called the team together in the platoon tent to brief them on what he had seen. He described the terrain and informed his teammates to pack heavy on ammo and light on water and food. There would be plenty of water in the RZ and food would likely be less valuable a commodity than ammo on the patrol; S-2 had reliable intel indicating that a Main Force VC battalion with NVA advisers was somewhere in the area, building up for a major operation. He said they would not be going on a recon mission this time. Instead, they were going after a body count.

Sergeant Sam Jacobs was a Texas native. Like nearly everyone else on the team, Jacobs had come over with the battalion and had been in country eight months. He was a veteran team leader with several years of college. Although he was quiet, almost shy, in the rear, he was admired by his fellow team leaders and respected by every man on Romeo-Four. Perhaps he sometimes caught a little flak for being a "suck ass" because of his popularity among the officers and the senior NCOs in the company, but those who really knew him understood that this was because Jacobs was a damned fine soldier. He walked slack on patrols because he liked to be up front where he could call the shots in a contact.

His assistant team leader was Specialist Four Michael Lonardi. Lonardi, blond and an inch over six feet tall, hailed from northern California. One of the original LRRPs, he was outgoing and aggressive, which probably contributed to why he liked to walk point. He and Jacobs were the best of friends, and although Lonardi looked up to Jacobs, the two men worked well in harness.

The team radio operator was Specialist Four "Crazy" Borch, a full-blooded Alaskan Inuit. Another original LRRP, the short, stocky veteran was the consummate trickster, only satisfied when he had everyone around him in stitches. Jovial, always the life of the party, he managed to be serious only when he was doing his thing on the radio. He walked right behind Jacobs on patrol.

Specialist Four "Doc" Bussard was the team medic. He had come over on the boat with most of the men in the LRRP platoon. Like Jacobs, he was quiet and reserved in the rear, but more than reliable in a firefight. His white-blond hair posed a camouflage problem, but so far he had managed to hide it. Besides his M-16 and the M-5 medical bag, Doc carried an M-79 grenade launcher.

Specialist Four Burkett was also an original, a full-blooded Cherokee from Oklahoma. He was great in the bush and managed to get along with just about everybody. A six-pack of beer turned Burkett into a raving hothead.

Specialist Four Tim Howard was the only guy on the team who hadn't come over on the boat. A farm boy from the river foothills of southwest Ohio, Howard had only been in country a couple of months. But he hadn't wasted his time sitting in the rear. This would be his ninth mission, his first at rear security. He had carried the radio on previous patrols, but Jacobs put him at drag on this patrol to break him in at another position.

Each man on the team carried a claymore mine, a double basic load of ammo, four frags, a white phosphorous or CS grenade, and a pair of smokes. Since it was a killer mission, no one wanted to risk running out of ammo in the middle of a firefight.

Just before daylight the team was up, packed, and wolfing down a quick breakfast. When they were finished, they grabbed their gear and headed toward the revetments where the choppers had been tied up for the night. The helicopters were already hot and ready to depart when the team arrived. The men climbed quickly aboard and the aircraft went light on its skids, then pulled slowly out of the revetment. Drifting out over the edge of the flight line, the Huey banked over the South China Sea, swung north toward Phan Thiet, then turned west to pass between the base camp and the city. The day promised to be clear and hot as they flew at altitude out toward The Bowl.

Fifteen minutes into the flight the aircraft began to lose altitude. The Cobras went into a high orbit as the slick circled just outside the southwest corner of the team's recon zone. The aircraft commander then flew a false insertion just south of the RZ before swinging north into The Bowl and dropping the team on the second attempt.

After inserting the patrol, the aircraft continued flying north, faking a third insertion into an abandoned rice paddy at the next highest elevation. The helicopter then disappeared in the distance, still heading north.

The team had inserted into a small, oval clearing covered in four-foot-high kunai grass. Exiting both sides of the aircraft, they hit the ground running, merging on the left side of the ship as the chopper lifted out of the LZ. The six LRRPs then sprinted for the tree line twenty-five meters away.

Upon reaching the woods the team dropped into a circular perimeter and lay dog while Borch established commo and gave a quick sitrep. Jacobs decided not to release the choppers at that time because of the hostile nature of the area where they were operating. After waiting fifteen minutes Jacobs gave the signal to move out to the northeast, the team climbing slowly and cautiously toward the distant mountains.

A hundred meters away from the LZ, at a point where the canopy began changing from double to triple, the patrol detected the distinct aroma of Viet Cong and went on alert. The team members looked at one another, then sank slowly to the ground without waiting for a signal from Jacobs. As the six men sniffed the air, trying to determine the direction of the danger, they realized that the thermals climbing up out of the valley behind them were shifting the odors around and confusing their source. The patrol squatted in the underbrush, still strung out in patrol file, herringbone fashion, as they watched the jungle to the right and left of the trail. After a while the prevailing consensus was that the smell seemed to be coming from their east, at or near the same elevation as the team. At that point Jacobs decided to change their route of march to avoid the hidden enemy. He radioed in to release the choppers, then gave the signal for Lonardi to turn 45 degrees to the north and move out again.

The patrol moved north a hundred meters, then began angling back to the northeast, climbing higher all the time. They soon ran across a small trail heading due east. It was definitely not a "high-speed," but appeared to be at least a secondary trail. There were also signs on it that it had been used within the past twenty-four hours. From the depth of the sandal tracks in the middle of the trail, Lonardi could tell that the enemy squad had been carrying heavy loads. The patrol studied the signs for a minute or two, then backed slowly away from the trail to discuss the situation. They set up in a tight wagon-wheel perimeter thirty meters back from the trail, yet close enough so they could still hear anyone passing by or spot their legs moving through the open space under the broadleaf vegetation that began knee-high above the ground. They waited thirty minutes to see if anyone happened by, but when no one came, Jacobs decided to move back up and cross the trail. They would continue heading to the northeast, quartering away from the trail.

Two hours later, approaching midday, the patrol pulled into a dense cluster of underbrush beneath the double-canopy jungle. Quickly setting out their claymores, they sat back to watch and listen while Borch called in a scheduled sitrep. Roughly half the team decided that it was as good a time as any to chow down. While their teammates provided security, three LRRPs prepared and ate dehydrated rations. While the diners were disposing of their trash, the sounds of woodchoppers plying their trade could be heard off in the distance. The LRRPs could not tell for certain the exact direction the sounds were coming from, but it appeared to be either due east or southeast of their location. Borch called in a report, then Jacobs told Lonardi that when they moved out again he wanted the point man to swing to the northwest.

Climbing higher into the mountains, they covered about three hundred meters before running into another secondary trail. Like the first trail they had cut, it, too, ran east-west and showed signs that an enemy squad had recently passed over it. This time, instead of pulling back, the patrol quickly crossed the trail and continued northwestward.

It was nearly 1800 hours and approximately seven hundred meters beyond the second trail when Jacobs called another halt. The team was well up in the high ground just below the crest of a major ridge, but they could see an even higher ridge a hundred meters to their north. Jacobs said he believed a trail probably ran along the crest of the higher ridge, and he didn't want to get any closer to it so late in the day. He signaled the patrol to take a break there in the triple-canopy just off the crest of the secondary ridgeline. There was little cover at ground level, so the patrol crawled in among some large roots before setting up in a circular perimeter. They did not bother putting out claymores since they wouldn't stay there very long. Everyone who was hungry ate a meal while Borch called in another sitrep.

Thirty minutes later Jacobs and Lonardi slipped out to do a cloverleaf recon away from the perimeter and check out a spot about seventy-five meters beyond them that they had noticed on the way in. They were happy to discover that it would make a suitable NDP for the night.

They were gone approximately twenty minutes before returning to the perimeter. Borch called in the coordinates for a series of artillery preplots, including the site where they had just eaten supper.

The team remained in place until dark, then Lonardi led them out to the laager site, a cluster of jagged rock outcroppings surrounded by gigantic trees. It was a perfect place to spend the night, offering both cover and concealment.

They set up in a tight, circular perimeter, then one by one slipped out to place claymores facing the most likely avenues of approach. Jacobs then established a one-man security watch and told his teammates to sit back and relax for the night.

Everyone was up well before false dawn. The sun began peeking over the mountains to the east before some of them had eaten breakfast. Once again Borch called in a sitrep, reporting nothing of any consequence during the night. Twenty minutes later they moved out again, heading due east.

They patrolled approximately six hundred meters, still following the secondary ridgeline, but constantly in the shadow of the main ridgeline one hundred to two hundred meters away. Suddenly they walked into another secondary trail heading downhill to the southeast. It was approximately 1100 hours. Like the trails they had encountered earlier, it also showed signs of recent use by a small enemy unit.

Wasting no more time than they had to, the LRRPs carefully crossed the trail and continued to the east. They had moved another two hundred meters when they crossed what appeared to be a game trail heading due south. Signs of some kind of traffic could be seen on the trail, but the men couldn't tell for certain if they were man-made.

They continued east another four hundred meters, then encountered a well-defined high-speed trail running due south. Here were plenty of fresh signs that someone had used it earlier that morning. The patrol moved thirty meters beyond the trail before stopping to report the discovery.

At 1430 hours and only sixty meters east of the last trail, the patrol set up another OP in a rock formation overlooking the spot where the high-speed dropped off the ridge and ran downhill toward The Bowl. They put out their claymores.

By 1600 hours they had not seen or heard anything on the trail. They pulled in their claymores and Borch called in another negative sitrep, then the patrol moved out once again heading due east.

Four hundred meters east of the last trail they hit another high-speed, this one running to the southwest, back toward the center of their patrol box. By that time Jacobs had gotten the impression that all the trails they had encountered were converging somewhere near the center of their nine-square-klick RZ. The last main trail had also been recently used, just like the other one. All of the tracks were coming in from the northeast and dropping down in the direction of The Bowl.

Once again they moved a hundred meters to the east and set up an OP to watch the trail until dark. They were still in triple-canopy with little or no underbrush to conceal them. It reminded most of the LRRPs of a mature, timbered park back in the States. Again, sensing that they had not yet been spotted, they didn't bother to set out claymores.

As soon as it got dark they moved about fifty meters to the northeast and found a suitable spot for an NDP. They were too far away from the trail to observe foot traffic, but felt that they would still be able to hear anyone coming up or down the steep grade.

In the dark they had to feel their way to set out claymores. Jacobs once again put one man on guard at a time and ordered his teammates to get some rest.

It was close to 2300 hours when Borch heard someone talking out on the trail. When he heard the sounds of equipment banging together, he quietly began to awaken the rest of the team. With everyone on alert and listening, they could tell that someone was passing them out on the trail approximately one hundred meters away. Over the next two hours, twelve groups of enemy soldiers crossed the ridgeline into the steep grade down into The Bowl. From the sounds they made, the team estimated that each group consisted of six to twelve individuals. Twelve such groups indicated the presence of a full company or better.

The traffic died down after 0100 hours and Jacobs again reduced the guard to one-man shifts. Nothing happened during the remainder of the night.

Just after daylight the entire team chowed down, eating in shifts. As they ate they discussed what they had heard during the previous night. They agreed that a large enemy unit had passed. From the sounds of equipment and entrenching tools creaking and banging together, the LRRPs assumed that the enemy unit was moving somewhere to erect a base camp. Also, from the direction of the traffic on all the trails they had crossed, Jacobs had a pretty good idea where he wanted to set up his ambush. He told his teammates that he planned to move them south into the center of the patrol box during the third day, hoping to be in position on the final day to spring a surprise.

The team moved out heading due south, angling away from the trail. Jacobs wanted to see if they could intercept another trail approaching from the east into the grid square to their south.

Quickly and quietly they moved eight hundred meters downhill. They were approaching the vegetation break between triple- and double-canopy when Jacobs stopped the team to have Borch call in a sitrep. It was 1000 hours. Borch had no problems getting good commo. Whiskey Relay was set up on a nearby firebase and was providing excellent communications with Romeo-Four.

The team took a much needed thirty-minute break to catch their breath, then moved out again heading south. They went about 250 meters before they hit another high-speed trail, this time coming in from the east. It showed recent, heavy use. Just like every other trail they had crossed, the traffic was all inbound.

At the exact spot where the team encountered the trail, it broke left to the south/southwest and ran downhill. Jacobs decided to move south another two hundred meters, then cut back to the west again to see if the trail still ran south/southwest. After they turned due west they picked up the trail again only three hundred meters away. Jacobs noticed with satisfaction that it was still heading south/ southwest, directly into the lower center of his patrol box. It was 1300 hours.

The patrol stepped gingerly over the trail and moved another seventy meters before setting up an OP at a spot where they could observe the trail. They watched it until 1500 hours, when Howard whispered to Jacobs, "Is this the trail we're going to ambush in the morning?"

Jacobs grinned back and said, "I've got something even better."

Howard nodded and returned the smile. At that time Jacobs decided to share his plan with his teammates, telling them that he wanted to cut to the west/southwest to parallel the trail a little further. He suspected that the high-speed would eventually cut back to the south again. If it did, he knew just where he wanted to plan their party.

Thirty minutes later they broke cover and moved approximately twelve hundred meters. During that last movement they also recrossed the first two high-speed trails they had encountered the day before.

It was now 1830 hours and Jacobs decided to call a temporary halt. He sent Borch and Lonardi to do a cloverleaf reconnaissance around their halt site and select a spot for an NDP a hundred meters to the south. The patrol had dropped out of the mountains and was back in the foothills and its scattered single-canopy. The recon element returned a short time later, telling Jacobs they had found an excellent location.

An hour later the six LRRPs slipped out of their halt site and moved into the NDP. Quietly they set out claymores and once again established one-man guard shifts.

At 2200 hours the team heard a loud commotion east/northeast of their perimeter. It sounded like someone tossing logs around. The LRRPs realized immediately that on the way in they had skirted an enemy base camp located somewhere north of their NDP. The noise seemed to be emanating from a spot no more than six hundred meters away. Borch called in a sitrep, then quickly established a number of artillery preplots around their perimeter, including three back along their escape route to their original LZ. The sounds continued until 0300 hours, when they suddenly stopped. Jacobs had put the team on 100 percent alert, then, after the noises subsided, he cut it back to two men on at a time. The rest of the night was quiet.

The patrol was scheduled to come out the next day, but no definite time had been established. It would be their final chance to get a body count on the mission, and the attitude of each LRRP was slowly evolving into that mind-set.

When the team awakened the next morning, Jacobs said, "Everyone enjoy a good meal and drink plenty of water, there won't be any time later. I'm going to show you exactly where I'm going to take you."

Then, while everyone was chowing down, Jacobs took out a map and showed his teammates exactly where he figured the enemy base camp was located.

They moved out a short time later heading south/southeast. They had only gone a hundred meters when they encountered another secondary trail. Jacobs figured it was the same trail they had encountered a hundred meters north of their original LZ. It had been used during the previous night.

They continued moving in the same direction another two hundred meters. They could sense they were getting close to something. The hair on the back of everyone's neck was standing straight up.

Without explaining why, Jacobs decided to turn due east once again. They moved approximately two hundred meters, then ran smack into the most beautiful high-speed trail they had ever seen. It came into the recon box from the south/southeast.

Beaming, Jacobs told his teammates that he wanted to set up a line ambush right there along the trail to their front. But the area was so large and open that he was afraid to move them any closer to the trail to set up their claymores.

From their location they could observe the trail for a long way from where it came up out of The Bowl from the south, but to the north the tree line was far too close to give them adequate warning if an enemy patrol came from that direction.

The LRRPs were squatting in the grass parallel to the trail only twenty meters away, getting their magazines and grenades ready for an ambush. None of them liked the idea of not deploying their claymores, but they understood why Jacobs didn't want to get caught out in the open near the trail.

Howard was at the end of the line nearest the woods, quietly pulling the safety tape from a grenade, when someone to his right tossed a twig, hitting him on the side of the head. Immediately Howard turned to his left and looked up toward the trees. What he saw there caused his breath to catch in the back of his throat.

Two Main Force Viet Cong soldiers had just stepped out of the woods and were heading straight down the trail. The enemy soldiers were less than sixty meters away and coming closer with every step.

Fortunately for Howard and the rest of the LRRPs, they were fairly well hidden in the knee-high grass. Seconds later more VC began moving out of the trees right behind the first two. The enemy soldiers were close together, maintaining an interval of less than two meters between each man. Except for the point man, who carried an AK-47 at a relaxed port arms position, the rest of the Viet Cong had their SKSs and AKs slung over their shoulders. When the last man cleared the wood line, Howard and his teammates counted twenty VC out on the trail.

The LRRPs waited breathlessly as they watched the enemy approach. It was already too late to run, and they were not in heavy enough cover to avoid being seen for long. It would only take a nonchalant glance to the right by one of the VC to notice the camouflaged lumps lying out in the low grass. They would have to take their chances by initiating the ambush with small-arms fire and follow it up with grenades.

When the Viet Cong were even with the LRRPs, Jacobs rose up out of the grass and opened fire on "rock 'n' roll." His five teammates followed suit almost simultaneously. Howard took the back end of the enemy column while Jacobs took the point. Everyone else took a portion of everyone in between. The concentrated fire at twenty meters from the recon men dropped fourteen of the closely massed VC in their tracks. The six survivors dropped to one knee at the beginning of the onslaught, then jumped to their feet and ran as the LRRPs changed magazines. Howard noticed that some of them appeared to stumble as they ran. They had either been hit or were tripping over the bodies of their fallen comrades.

The remaining VC weren't even out of the kill zone before the LRRPs had reloaded and were picking off the survivors. The last enemy soldier on his feet dropped right at the edge of the tree line, only a meter from the safety of the woods. When Howard saw him go down, he turned and emptied the rest of his magazine into the tree line.

It was amazing! Six of them had just put down

twenty VC without the enemy getting off a shot. It had been a textbook ambush, the kind stories are written about.

But before they had time to enjoy their success they heard someone shouting in Vietnamese from back in the trees. It was coming from at least a hundred meters away, but it meant that there were more VC back where the dead in the trail had come from.

Borch was already on the radio calling in the contact and requesting gunships and an immediate extraction. There was no time to risk checking out the bodies or gathering up their weapons. On Jacobs's command the team turned and headed southwest, back in the direction of their original LZ. It would probably be only minutes before the enemy came after them.

They were running full tilt and had covered three hundred meters when Jacobs drew up and stopped the team. Gasping for breath, he said that Turret-Six, the battalion commander, had just radioed the relay and told them that he wasn't going to extract the team. Instead of pulling them, the officer had decided to reinforce the team and develop the situation.

Jacobs began screaming at the relay team over the radio, telling them to get them out of there *now*. The relay team told him to head south/southeast approximately eight hundred meters to secure an LZ for the reaction force that was to link up with them. The relay team added that Turret-Six would be on station as soon as possible.

Given the sense of urgency, the team turned to the south/southeast and broke brush as they sprinted the half mile to the LZ. Jacobs realized that by changing directions and cutting back to the southeast, their pursuers would be able to cut off the angle and gain on them.

Five minutes later, panting and gasping for air, they

were at the LZ—alone. While the LRRPs were still trying to catch a second wind, a pair of Cobras arrived on the scene. The two gunships were from the 192d AHC (assault helicopter company) better known as the Tiger Sharks.

The Cobras broke in on the LRRP frequency and told them to hold in place until the reinforcements arrived, then the gunships circled the LZ, covering the team. Down on the LZ, Jacobs got on the radio and tried to reach LRRP Control to find out who was in charge of this clusterfuck.

Ten minutes later, part of a platoon from Bravo Company, 3/506th, arrived at the LZ in four slicks that set down two at a time to discharge their passengers. A green first lieutenant leaped from one of the choppers and ran directly up to Jacobs to introduce himself. He admitted to the LRRP team leader that he was brand-new at this and suggested that the two of them sit down and carefully plan their next move. But he was also quick to point out that it was Jacobs's operation and that he would like to learn from him. The guy was a stud and had been a football player at Iowa State, and his attitude surprised the LRRP team leader.

Jacobs filled in the young officer, then the two of them waited on the LZ for the lift ships to return with the rest of his platoon. In the interim, Jacobs got on the radio with Turret-Six and explained the rules of the game to him, screaming that it was not an LRRP's job to lead an infantry platoon to their graves. He pointed out that LRRPs were supposed to gather intelligence and do hit-and-run stuff. He affirmed that there just weren't enough of them on the ground to handle this kind of an operation. Dissatisfied with the colonel's response, Jacobs threw the handset down and stomped away from the lieutenant. Hands on hips, he looked up at Turret-Six circling overhead and wished that he would come down into rifle range.

It took him a minute or two to cool off, then he walked over and calmly told his teammates that the colonel wanted them to walk point and lead the line doggies back to the ambush site.

Borch looked around at the rest of his teammates and growled, "This fucking guy ain't gonna work."

Everyone complained to Jacobs that they didn't want to do it, but the team leader told them that the colonel had given them a direct order to go back up there so they really didn't have a choice.

The five LRRPs pondered it for a minute or two, then made a pact among themselves that if any of them got killed, whoever was left would get rid of that stupid SOB.

The other half of the reaction force arrived while the LRRPs were discussing the matter of Turret-Six. As soon as the infantrymen were ready to move out, Jacobs told Howard to take point with Lonardi at slack. As the remainder of the LRRPs took their places behind them, Jacobs dropped back to the end of the team to walk with the lieutenant so the two could coordinate the operation.

The infantry officer put a squad out on each flank to protect the main element from walking into an ambush. Although the man was new at the game, Jacobs was relieved to see that he had learned something in ROTC.

Howard led them slowly and cautiously due north on a direct course to where the contact had gone down. When they reached the ambush site twenty minutes later, they discovered blood trails everywhere but no bodies or weapons. Although it had been only an hour and twenty minutes since the team had blown the ambush, the enemy had already policed up the kill zone.

Jacobs knew that if the VC had gotten there that quickly and carried away the bodies of twenty of their comrades along with their weapons, and gear, they were facing more VC than a platoon of infantry and an LRRP team could handle. It also meant that the enemy soldiers were likely close by at that very moment; nobody runs far with twenty bodies and all their gear.

Jacobs quickly communicated his thoughts to the lieutenant, who could only respond that his job was to pursue the enemy. He added that from his perspective it was the LRRPs' job to lead them until they made contact, then he would take over. The LRRPs could then get out of the way—if they were still able.

Jacobs could only shake his head in despair. Frustrated by the stupidity of the situation, he silently gave Howard the sign to lead them into the tree line.

Howard crossed the trail and began moving to the northeast, paralleling the trail on his left. When he finally reached the trees, he was surprised that he was still alive. He had expected the enemy, from the cover of the forest, to open fire on the U.S. soldiers moving out in the open savanna.

Upon entering the woods, Howard immediately encountered a dry creek bed approximately three meters wide running back to the northwest toward the trail. The bank was about four feet high on his side and five to six feet high on the far side. The creek bed itself was level limestone. Intersecting the creek at a point forty feet below where Howard was preparing to cross was a ten-foot-wide, five-foot-deep ravine that extended back away from the creek bed. When Howard first spotted it, his first thought was that it would make an ideal place for an ambush.

Howard quickly worked out a series of signals with Lonardi before crossing the creek. He told him that he would turn to the left when he got up on the opposite bank. If Lonardi saw him curl his right thumb up around the stock of his weapon, that meant the ambush was straight ahead. If he bent the thumb at a 90 degree angle, pointing it toward the barrel of his weapon, that meant that he had only five seconds.

Howard expected an ambush from the time they neared the woods. But if he had been the Viet Cong commanding officer, the ravine would be the spot. He stepped down off the lower embankment and crossed the hard creek bed. The LRRP point man stopped at the opposite bank, slowly scanning the terrain 180 degrees to his front. There was a patch of timber perhaps ten meters wide between him and a large clearing. There were trees on his left toward the high-speed trail, and to his right the deep ravine ran the length of the clearing before hooking to the left into the woods at the end of the open area. The ravine was the perfect spot for a massive L-shaped ambush.

Howard knew that he had flankers coming up on either side of him, but at that moment they were still on the other side of the creek. He climbed up on top of the far bank and passed through the narrow patch of timber until he found himself standing alone at the base of the open clearing extending a hundred meters to his front. Off to his right all the way over to the open ravine there was no cover at all.

Howard knew that he was looking dead ahead at the perfect kill zone. He sensed that there were VC in the ravine looking at him through the sights of their AK-47s at that very moment. Not knowing where the rest of the ambush was going to come from, he raised his hand and clenched his fist to hold up the rest of the element behind him. Slowly he dropped to one knee, trying to give the impression that he didn't suspect anything. But he was desperately trying to buy some time to think of a way to extricate himself from the life-threatening predicament. Howard realized that he was already in the kill zone, but those behind him still had a chance to get out.

Still down on one knee, he shifted his body slowly to his left to where he could just see Lonardi standing behind him at the edge of the creek. He gave him the signal that the ambush was straight ahead, then saw Lonardi motioning with his left hand that there was a low spot in defilade to Howard's immediate front. Howard knew then that Lonardi had also sensed that the ambush was imminent and that the point man was already in the kill zone.

Howard turned slowly back to face the clearing and spotted the slight depression fifteen meters away. His only chance to survive the next few minutes was to somehow make it to that low spot and hope the Good Lord had made it deep enough.

Figuring that the enemy would wait until more of the Americans reached the kill zone before initiating the ambush, Howard decided his best bet was to continue on across the clearing toward the defilade that Lonardi had pointed out. It was only fifteen meters away, but those were the longest fifteen meters that Howard would ever travel. As he stepped out into the open clearing he couldn't help but notice the trails leading out through the knee-high grass where the VC had scattered just before the Americans had entered the woods. He also noticed that most of the trails spidered off toward the ravine to his right.

It was too late to turn back, he was too far into the kill zone. As he stood in the open, his face camouflaged, he had the sensation that his head was at least three feet wide and a hundred gooks were at that moment sizing it up as a suitable trophy to hang in their hunting lodge.

Knowing that Lonardi would stay put outside the kill zone, Howard stood up and motioned for his slack man to follow him. He still had to carry out the subterfuge to convince the watching VC that he suspected nothing.

He edged farther out into the clearing, holding his breath at each step. When he reached the depression he stepped into the center of it with his right foot, letting it collapse under him as he sank into the grass facing the ravine on his right. As soon as he disappeared, the waiting VC opened fire.

Hugging the ground, Howard was instantly aware that the volume of fire cutting through the air above him was as intense as one of the LRRPs' own ambushes. The gully on his right ran parallel to the clearing, then hooked back across his front where the clearing met the trees. It was indeed the perfect L-shaped ambush. And as usual the VC had prepared their battlefield well.

Howard estimated that at least a platoon of VC lined the ravine and were trying very hard to kill him.

Although he was somewhat flattered by the amount of ammo they were expending in the effort, he began to wonder if he was the only recipient of all the attention. All of the small-arms fire from the far end of the clearing was passing directly over him. The enemy fire from the ravine to the right was coming straight at him. Howard could only hope that he was in enough of a defilade to avoid being hit. While lying there motionless he could feel rounds kicking up dirt within inches of his body.

When rounds began ripping down along his right side, he realized that some of the VC must have changed positions. Howard was lying flat on his stomach, arm bent at the elbow, gripping his weapon beside him. With enemy rounds hitting inches from his hand, he was forced to let go of his M-16 to pull his hand in under his right shoulder. It was either move it or lose it. The grass around him was being shredded as bullets searched for him. It would only be a matter of time before he took a hit.

Suddenly the fire coming from the ravine on his right began to slacken, and he heard a heavy volume of fire coming from somewhere back across the creek behind him to his left. He knew then that the rest of the column had gotten hit at the same time the VC had taken him under fire.

With the enemy fire on him finally abating, he knew that the VC were either pulling out or preparing to assault the kill zone. If the latter was the case he had to get his weapon into play before one of them walked right up and put a bullet in his head.

Howard reached out and pulled his M-16 tight into his body, then scooted backwards to take advantage of the full extent of the depression that had so far protected him. At that point the only enemy fire he was still receiving was coming from a tree line at the opposite side of the clearing and to the left of the end of the ravine. The lone VC keeping him pinned down was at least a hundred meters away. Howard figured the ambushers had realized that they had blown their opportunity by firing too early and were now withdrawing from the area. The single VC still engaging him had probably been left behind to discourage pursuit.

Howard slowly raised his head and yelled back for Lonardi to bring up an M-79, the only weapon they had that would drive the VC stay-behind out of his cover.

Lonardi yelled back for Bussard to pass the grenade

launcher up to his position, and minutes later the first HE round burst in the treetops over the VC sniper. The second round hit right where the fire was coming from, causing it to cease immediately. However, Howard stayed put while Lonardi put two more rounds into the same spot. Then, instead of getting up and running for the cover of the creek, Howard spun around and low-crawled the entire thirty-five meters back to where Lonardi sat holding the still smoking M-79.

When the point man reached the cover of the creek bank and linked up with Lonardi, he saw Jacobs, the infantry lieutenant, his RTO, and another line doggie lying in a washout behind a fallen tree a short distance away. Jacobs was on the radio directing gunships and calling for air strikes. When Howard and Lonardi reached them, they literally had to pull fallen limbs off the four soldiers to get them out. The branches had been severed by the intensity of the enemy small-arms fire.

On the other side of the creek the flankers on the right side of the main column were still taking heavy fire from the enemy back in the trees. Jacobs instructed the Cobras to hit the woods across the clearing on the far side of the creek, then circle around and dump everything they had down the right flank where the infantrymen were still engaged. That put an end to the heavier enemy fire, but didn't prevent the Viet Cong from sniping at whoever moved above the knee-high grass.

After the Cobras departed, Jacobs called for an air strike, and soon a flight of U.S. Navy A-6 Intruders came in low and began dropping 250-pound iron bombs into the trees north of where the trail entered the woods, where Jacobs suspected the enemy base camp lay.

All of the enemy fire ceased when the jets began making their bomb runs. Miraculously, none of the Americans had been killed or wounded in the ambush. However, one of the grunts had managed to get a nasty slice over his right eye when he dived for the ground without having his helmet secured.

After the jets expended their loads, Borch and Bussard led a squad from the infantry platoon back to secure the LZ where the reaction force had landed. Soon a full infantry company from the battalion began to combat assault into the same LZ. When the first element arrived they remained at the LZ to secure it for the next flight, and sent the infantry squad, along with Borch and Bussard, back up to rejoin their comrades at the dry creek bed. When the two elements had effected the linkup, Borch told Jacobs that they were supposed to return to the LZ for extraction.

As they prepared to move out, the lieutenant couldn't stop thanking Jacobs for what he had learned that day. He knew that he and his men had survived an ambush that could just as easily have killed them all.

As the LRRPs marched proudly down the dry creek bed on their way back to the LZ, some of the infantrymen still lying prone in the grass above shouted, "You'd better get down, a sniper will get you."

Borch grinned that mischievous grin of his, and said, "They can't shoot us. We're off duty."

The line company remained in The Bowl for a couple of weeks, maintaining sporadic contact with a VC company. They found numerous shallow graves and uncovered a number of enemy base camps in the area. They sustained a number of casualties in the process but killed a large number of VC in two pitched battles.

Company E, 20th Infantry (LRP), I Field Force

Company E, 20th Infantry (LRP), was activated in 1967 to provide a long range reconnaissance asset for I Field Force throughout the II Corps Tactical Zone. The oversize LRP company was made up of four platoons, making it nearly twice as large as any of the divisional and independent-brigade long range reconnaissance units operating in Vietnam. At times during its existence, the company was assigned to support every division, brigade, and regiment operating in the II Corps TAOR. As a result the LRPs of Company E, 20th Inf., managed to see more of the Central Highlands than any other long-range patrol company.

In late January 1969, the company's 2d Platoon was stationed at the Oasis, a brigade-size encampment of the U.S. 4th Infantry Division. They set up shop in a compound at the end of the runway, where they lived in sun-bleached GP Medium tents. The camp was encircled by several layers of concertina wire and sat inside the perimeter of the large compound secured by the 2/8th Infantry, a mechanized infantry battalion, and the 1/14th Infantry, a straight-leg infantry battalion.

Along with a sister platoon, the 2d Platoon had arrived a week earlier from An Khe. Their movement to the Oasis had been by motor convoy—courtesy of the highly suspect E/20th motor pool—consisting of two jeeps and three deuce-and-a-half trucks. As with most long-range patrol company motor pools, the vehicles had been "liberated" from a number of sources unknown. After deploying the two platoons, their gear, and equipment at the Oasis, the convoy did a quick turnaround and returned to the Company E headquarters back at An Khe.

The Oasis had been built by the U.S. 1st Cavalry Division in 1965, prior to conducting operations into the Ia Drang Valley. Subsequently, units from the 101st Airborne Division, 25th Infantry Division, 173d Airborne Brigade, and most recently the 4th Infantry Division had at one time or another called the Oasis home. In addition, a Special Forces mobile strike force was present at the Oasis, conducting its own operations in the area.

On 23 January, S.Sgt. Chuck Vaughn, Team Two-One's team leader, was inside the LRP compound relaxing on stand-down from an earlier mission. At the unit formation that morning he was informed by the officer in charge that a mission assignment for his team had just come down from 4th Division G-2. He was to take a reconnaissance team out on a three-day patrol with a secondary mission of setting up an ambush.

That afternoon, somewhat perturbed by the extremely short stand-down between patrols, Vaughn gathered up his weapon and a couple bandoliers of ammo, then left to conduct an aerial reconnaissance of the patrol's recon zone. Ninety minutes later he was back at the TOC giving a patrol order to the pilots, his teammates, and the unit operations officer. Vaughn immediately complained about the lack of cover and concealment in his recon zone. The RZ was situated on a high plateau in the Chu Pon Massif, southwest of the Oasis and due north of Plei Me. The terrain up on the plateau was level and open. Vast fields of knee-high kunai grass were broken only by small wooded islands and patches of scrub brush. The expansive but sparse thickets would offer little concealment to a recon team trying to remain undetected. The countryside looked a lot like the African veldt.

The 4th Infantry Division's request for reconnaissance patrols on the plateau was due to intelligence reports indicating enemy activity around the village of Chi Khe, in nearby Phu Phon Province. Team Two-One's RZ was less than four klicks from the Nguyen Thi Thi rubber plantation, a suspected enemy sanctuary.

Vaughn was also concerned about an experimental concept that would be used to insert the patrols into the specified target area. The individual who had come up with the idea had named the untried method "hop-scotching." It involved staging teams at strategic locations prior to insertion, then utilizing the assigned aircraft to infiltrate the patrols one after another in an advancing grid pattern in a brief period of time. When Vaughn understood how the plan was to work, he thought that the increased helicopter activity over a relatively small area would only succeed in alerting the enemy that something unusual was occurring.

Staff Sergeant Chuck Vaughn had been in Vietnam only a couple of months. It would be his fourth mission, third as a team leader. The bright young man had enlisted right out of high school, volunteering for airborne infantry training, jump school, the infantry NCO academy, Ranger school, and Vietnam, in that order. His professionalism and dedication more than made up for his lack of field experience. Like everyone else on his team, Vaughn carried an M-16 rifle on patrol. He also carried a URC-10 radio and would occupy the slack position during the mission.

His point man and assistant team leader was Sp4. John Behrs, a Florida native. Behrs, the most experienced LRP on the team, had been in Vietnam just over six months. Quiet, easygoing, but great in the field, he was the natural choice as assistant team leader. At the time of the patrol, Behrs had a medical profile on his feet for a bad case of trench foot, but not wanting to be left behind, he volunteered to go out with the team anyway.

Team Two-One's radio operator and number three man in patrol formation was PFC Larry Hines from San Francisco, California. Somewhat of a pariah as an LRP, Hines was a "flower child" at heart. The newest and shortest man on the team, Hines was given the unenviable job of humping the radio. Always in trouble in the rear, Vaughn had complete confidence that he could do the job in the bush.

The fourth slot was occupied by PFC Robert "Moose" McClure of Abilene, Texas. McClure had attended Texas A&M for a year before dropping out and enlisting in the Marine Corps because he was afraid the war would end before he could get over there. However, an injury during training supposedly ended his hitch. Some said the Marines had kicked him out when they discovered he could spell "helicopter." McClure came from a military family and was "Old South" all the way, the last Confederate warrior. He had served in Germany as an atomic demolitions specialist before volunteering for duty in Vietnam. Upon his arrival in Vietnam he served as a grunt in the 173d Airborne Brigade until someone found out that he could type. Reassigned as a clerk, McClure jumped at the chance to volunteer for the LRPs. Intelligent, caustic, and antiauthoritarian, he was excellent in the bush but in constant trouble in the rear. It was his first mission as an LRP and he was going out prepared. Besides his M-16, Moose was bringing along a chopped-down M-79.

The last man in the patrol was a South Vietnamese Ranger staff sergeant named Nguyen Trinh. The well-educated soldier had been assigned to Echo Company as an interpreter and spoke English very well. The veteran still had family in the North and had served as an officer with the NVA until he made the decision to *chieu hoi*. Now he only wanted to kill his enemies so that his family back home could someday be free. Vaughn had befriended him, and the tough old soldier had returned the favor by volunteering to go out as a member of Vaughn's team. Totally reliable in the bush, it would be Trinh's third mission.

At the end of the briefing, Vaughn informed those present that Team Two-Three had just come in from a mission into the same area. The patrol's RTO, PFC Warner Trei, had reported that throughout the mission their radio transmissions were being jammed by the enemy. That unwelcome bit of news raised the pucker factor among the Team Two-One LRPs at least three notches. But Trinh announced that it only increased their opportunities to kill more enemy.

Team Two-One was ready the next morning when the aircraft arrived at the airstrip to pick up the patrols. They were flown out to the Special Forces encampment at Duc Co, in the low country not far from Plei Me. Team Two-One waited thirty minutes for the C&C aircraft to return to accompany their insertion.

While they were sitting outside the wire under the camp's artillery pieces, a Montagnard soldier came out and saluted Vaughn. Vaughn didn't know what to make of this. When he tried to tell the Montagnard that he wasn't an officer, the soldier replied in his own tongue. As he stood there trying to communicate with the soldier a few 'Yard women came walking down the road toward the encampment. Hines, who was ogling them, made a suggestive comment that embarrassed Vaughn and he chastised the misplaced hippie. That visibly impressed the Montagnard, who then invited Vaughn into the compound. Vaughn followed him inside and raised an eyebrow when the man waved him into the command bunker. It was then that Vaughn realized that the Montagnard was a colonel and the camp commander. Taking a seat behind his desk, he leaned back and put his feet up on it, then offered Vaughn an ice-cold Budweiser from a nearby refrigerator. The colonel must have thought Vaughn was a very important person.

Just then, the LRP team leader heard the sounds of approaching helicopters. Nodding thanks, he ran to the chopper pad outside the compound to board the aircraft with his teammates. Ten minutes later they were approaching the LZ.

The Huey came in low, passing over a thinning tree line as it came to a large expanse of open ground. As they crossed over the last of the woods, McClure and Trinh spotted two Vietnamese standing to one side right at the edge of the trees. The two men were pointing at them as the aircraft approached the LZ. McClure shouted a warning, but the chopper had already passed the spot.

Two hundred meters beyond the two men the Huey slowed four or five feet above the ground. The LRPs were out on the skids by then, and as the chopper began to pick up forward airspeed, the five men dropped to the ground then sprinted for the woods twenty meters away. Looking back to where he had spotted the two men on the way in, McClure could no longer see them.

The five LRPs moved quickly for two hundred meters into the sparse single-canopy. There was no ground cover among the scattered trees. Finally, Vaughn spotted a patch of cover among some low boulders and gave the signal to go to ground there.

The team lay dog for ten minutes while Vaughn made a commo check, reported that they had been compromised on the insertion, and asked to be extracted and reinserted somewhere else. Instead he was told to "Charlie Mike" (continue the mission). Wasting no time, Vaughn gave the order to move out. He wanted to put more distance between his team and the LZ before settling in for the night.

It wasn't long before Trinh, back at rear security, passed the word up the line that they were being followed by one man, approximately one hundred meters back. Unfortunately, the man had spotted Trinh at the same time and had turned and fled. They were approximately five hundred meters from the LZ by then, and if they had picked up a tail already, it was likely to be one of the two men they had spotted on the way in.

Trying to put some distance between themselves and the tracker, the patrol moved off at a faster pace. Vaughn soon found a relatively good spot to set up for a RON (remain overnight) among a cluster of low boulders in the middle of a thicket. In minutes the LRPs had cloverleafed around the area to make sure they were alone, then set out their five claymores. Vaughn called in a sitrep reporting that they had been followed off the LZ.

As darkness approached, Vaughn set up one-man guard shifts and sat back to listen. He suspected that no one would find sleep easy that night. It wasn't long before they heard dogs perhaps four hundred meters away. They sounded as if they were baying on trail. Suddenly the barking stopped about two hundred meters away from the team's perimeter. It grew quiet after that, and the LRPs remained alert and tense the remainder of the night. No one got much sleep.

The next morning the patrol was awake and ready by the arrival of the false dawn. Thirty minutes later they again heard the dogs' baying. It appeared to be coming from the same area as the night before. The sound drew closer and the LRPs prepared to fight. The baying was no more than a hundred meters away when the team spotted a four-man VC patrol walking right in on them. The VC had appeared suddenly, their point man no more than twenty meters away. He was armed with an SKS rifle and carrying it at port arms. All the VC were hatless and wearing khaki shorts and shirts. There was no doubt among the LRPs that the enemy soldiers were looking for them.

When the enemy point man looked up and spotted the LRPs hidden among the rocks, he hesitated momentarily then attempted to turn slowly as if to withdraw. That was when Vaughn gave the command to open fire.

The entire patrol opened up, knocking down the VC point man and wounding the soldier directly behind him. As the survivors turned to run, the LRPs laid down an intense base of fire, trying to establish fire superiority in the event the VC decided to stand and fight. In the middle of the action, Vaughn shouted over his right shoulder for Hines to cover their back door.

Each man fired a couple of magazines before Vaughn finally called for a cease-fire. Out in the kill zone, the VC point man was moaning and trying to sit up. Vaughn ordered Trinh to pitch a frag out near the VC to finish him off.

Vaughn got everyone on his feet and out of the rocks, where the patrol made a quick sweep around the perimeter to make sure that the surviving enemy soldiers were not in the area. Back in the perimeter ten minutes later, Vaughn called in the contact and asked for gunship support and requested an extraction.

The aircraft were at that moment putting in additional teams not far away from Team Two-One's RZ. When the call came in, the gunships and slicks were on station in less than ten minutes. After establishing radio contact, Vaughn tossed out smoke grenades on two sides of the perimeter to mark his position, then radioed the gunships, instructing them to make perpendicular runs from a number of different points of the compass. The Charlie-model gunships came in firing rockets and miniguns into the brush around the patrol.

While the gunships worked out, Vaughn decided to bring back the body of the dead VC when the team was finally extracted because there had been a lot of talk about LRP teams' faking contact on missions to get out of the field early. The young team leader wanted to make sure that no one would accuse him of doing this. So he took McClure out with him to recover the body, making sure the lanky Texan also retrieved the dead man's weapon.

The extraction slick arrived on the scene right after the gunships finished their final gun runs. As the aircraft settled into the thicket, its rotors began chopping the tops out of the slender trees. The team would have to reach up and grab the skids in order to pull themselves into the aircraft. As Vaughn and McClure approached the aircraft carrying the dead VC between them, the port side door gunner suddenly opened fire with his M-60, causing the pilot to jerk the back on the controls and the aircraft to pivot nearly 90 degrees. As the tail boom swung around it missed the heads of the two LRPs by inches.

Vaughn finally managed to struggle aboard, but McClure remained behind on the ground with the dead

VC soldier. Pulling off his rucksack, Vaughn turned around, reached out, and grabbed the body as McClure hoisted it up on the skid. As Vaughn slid the body on board the aircraft, the bowels of the dead man suddenly released, sending a stream of feces directly onto McClure's face and chest. This had to be the origin of the popular Vietnam-era phrase "Shit happens!"

During the flight back to the Oasis, the starboard door gunner got sick from all the blood and gore from the dead enemy soldier blowing back into his "hellhole" and vomited out into the prop wash.

When the aircraft finally set down on the 4th Division VIP pad, the LRPs dumped the VC's body out on the PSP in front of a number of staff officers who were just coming out of the TOC for a photo op. Without waiting for a response from the shocked officers, the aircraft commander quickly lifted off and flew farther down the airstrip, where he set his bird down gently on the helipad next to the LRP compound.

The team was immediately debriefed by the company operations NCO. As soon as the briefing was over, the NCO informed them that they were going to be sent right back out on another mission. When Behrs heard this he left the TOC to return a few minutes later with his profile, saying that he couldn't go back into the bush. And, as there were only four men left on the team, it was decided not to send them back out again.

Company I,
75th Infantry (Ranger),
1st Infantry Division

In February 1969, the 1st Infantry Division was based at Lai Khe, South Vietnam. Lai Khe, nicknamed Rocket City, for good reason, sat amid a large rubber plantation along Highway 13, called Thunder Road, also for very good reason. Major concentrations of VC and NVA forces were arrayed against the 1st Division, especially around Lai Khe. However, that didn't keep troopers of the Big Red One from pursuing the enemy into the Song Be Corridor, the Fishhook, Angel's Wing, the Trapezoid, Hobo Woods, War Zones C and D, and the Michelin Rubber plantation. It was a tremendously large area of operations, abutting all the way up to the 25th Division's AO at Tay Ninh and Cu Chi, and it was a dangerous place to grow careless, even for a brief moment.

The 1st Division's reconnaissance element, Company F, 52d Infantry (LRP), had lost two entire patrols during the final months of 1968. In October, one of them, a six-man team, had been destroyed to the last man during its insertion. Barely a month later, five men from another six-man team had been killed during a reconnaissance mission. The sole survivor had made it out by playing dead. The remaining LRPs of the company had begun to believe that the casualties were a direct result of 1st Infantry Division command structure's flagrant misuse of its long-range patrol assets. The "economy of force" mentality seemed to be the culprit. Sacrificing a "few" to preserve the "many" was seen by some as a noble concept, but rarely by those who happened to be part of the "few."

The Big Red One LRPs had paid a heavy price for finding and fixing the enemy for Division. As a result their numbers were way down. That not only affected the number of teams the unit could put in the field, it also had a major impact on team integrity. When all the LRP companies throughout Vietnam became lettered Ranger companies on 1 February 1969, Company F, 52d Infantry (LRP)—now Company I, 75th Infantry (Ranger)—barely had enough members to stand a platoon formation.

Early on the morning of 26 February 1969, Sp4. Bill Goshen returned from a seven-day leave to Japan. His company commander had offered him the leave ten days earlier as a reward for his performance on a number of tough patrols and also because the officer recognized that Goshen badly needed a break from the action. Upon his return, as Goshen was stepping down from the helicopter that had flown him from Bien Hoa to Lai Khe, he was given the unsettling news that his and another team had been hit hard while he was away. His team had suffered three wounded. On the other patrol, Sp4. Bob Law had been killed diving on an enemy grenade to save his teammates.

Badly shaken, Goshen went directly to the field hospital to visit his wounded teammates and to find out what had gone wrong on the patrol. An hour later, when he returned to the company, he was informed that 1st Lt. Jerry Davis, the acting CO, wanted to see him immediately. Reporting to Davis, Goshen was told that a special mission had just come down from Division

G-2. Davis said he had been ordered to put a scratch team together for the patrol and he wanted Goshen up at point. The company was down to only four teams at Lai Khe, two at Dian and a pair at Quan Loi. The two teams at Lai Khe that were still intact were already out in the field. Davis told him that his patrol would be a patchwork team made up of Goshen, S.Sgt. Enrique Cruz, and four of the survivors from the remaining two teams at Lai Khe. Cruz would be in charge of the patrol, which had been given the unfortunate name Victim Eight.

The team was briefed on the patrol a short time later. No one on the team was happy that Cruz had been put in charge. Although everyone loved the little Guamanian and respected him as a man, he was far too aggressive to run reconnaissance missions. As a member of a long-range patrol he was fine, following orders and doing his job in exemplary fashion, but as a team leader he was just too gung ho. Cruz had come to Vietnam for only one reason—to kill the enemy, and it didn't make him an ounce of difference if he had a thousand men with him or only five. A "tab" Ranger and a Recondo School graduate, Cruz had been in country approximately eight months. On patrol he always carried a CAR-15 with a thirty-round magazine. At the briefing he announced to his teammates that he would walk slack on the outing.

Goshen would serve as the assistant team leader and point man. The Fort Worth, Texas, native had been in country only five months, yet it would be his eighteenth long-range patrol. Airborne-qualified and a Recondo School graduate, Goshen had come to Vietnam right out of Special Forces Training Group at Fort Bragg, North Carolina. An injury had put his jump status on hold and threatened his career in Special Forces, so

Goshen did the next best thing and volunteered for a tour of duty in Vietnam.

The senior RTO was Sp4. James Leibnitz. Leibnitz had been out on a patrol or two, but he had served most of his tour as the company clerk. He was a nice guy, but that couldn't make up for his total lack of experience in the field. Leibnitz had sat around headquarters watching one team after another return from the bush with casualties. Eventually it became more than he could bear, and Leibnitz started volunteering to fill in on teams. His place on the patrol would be directly behind Cruz.

The fourth spot on the patrol would be occupied by Sp4. Larry Wenzel, of Boerne, Texas, the team grenadier. A stocky rodeo cowboy, Wenzel got along with just about everybody. Although he had only been in country for about three months, he had already been out on a number of patrols.

Specialist Four Robert Levine held down the number five slot. A taciturn Midwesterner, Levine was a good-looking, athletic kid who obeyed orders and followed instructions to the letter. He was above average in the field despite the fact that he had only been in country a few days over three months.

The rear security job was in the very capable hands of PFC Gary Johnson. Like Goshen, Johnson was from Fort Worth, Texas. Although the two Rangers had attended different high schools in Fort Worth, they had known each other. Both men had attended college before giving up on the effort and enlisting in the Army. However, unlike Goshen, Johnson had gotten married before leaving for Vietnam. Unfortunately, it didn't take his wife long to find a replacement for her absent husband. Johnson received a "Dear John" letter less than ninety days after arriving in country and barely a week before the mission.

During the premission briefing, a lieutenant colonel from Division staff pointed to a large map overlay of Indochina and began relating to the Rangers how intelligence sources had been tracking a particular NVA regiment all the way from North Vietnam down to a point on the Cambodian border just west of Lai Khe, where they had managed to lose them. The colonel next made it very clear to the six Rangers just what their mission would entail. The patrol was to go into an area just two klicks south of the Fishhook and determine whether or not the NVA regiment had crossed the border into South Vietnam. His estimates put the regiment's strength at more than four thousand men. The Ranger reconnaissance patrol was scheduled to insert at first light the next day, then remain in the field for four days and three nights.

After the briefing ended, the team got together for a final skull session. Cruz outlined each man's duties on the patrol and pointed out the equipment he was to bring along. While the team began putting together its gear, Cruz left to conduct an overflight of the recon zone.

The next morning the six Rangers were cammied up and waiting at the chopper pad just before daylight. Then, cursing the failure of the choppers to arrive on time, they waited around nervously in the darkness for the next sixty minutes. Finally at 0700 hours the birds showed up. As the Rangers were struggling aboard their Huey, the operations sergeant walked up to them and announced, "Men, if you pull off your mission correctly the odds are that at least one of you won't be coming back. But if you can get your hands on some AK-47s, maybe I'll see that you get back in early."

The six members of the team looked at each other in shocked disbelief. There they were, a new team with a tough mission right on the Cambodian border—searching for a four-thousand-man NVA regiment—led by a team leader who wanted nothing more than to make contact with the enemy, and this guy was offering to bring them in early if they could get their hands on an AK or two! Did he think that enemy assault rifles were just lying around unattended in the middle of the jungle? With their pucker factors already at B-52 altitude, the Rangers put an extra cinch in their sphincters and climbed aboard the helicopter.

The team went in at approximately 0730 hours. The Huey slick made a single-ship approach directly into the LZ, using no deception to fool the enemy. It came to a hover eight feet above the ground out over the middle of a rice paddy at least two hundred meters from the nearest tree line. Standing out on the left skid, Goshen looked back at the pilot in disbelief, but jumped when he was given the signal to go. He was followed instantly by the rest of the team. The Rangers hit the ground and found themselves standing in stagnant water two to four feet deep. They had to struggle through the muck and mire of a flooded paddy nearly the length of two football fields before they reached the cover of the wood line. Fortunately, the water grew shallower as they neared the edge of the paddy.

As soon as Goshen reached the forest he discovered a heavily used high-speed trail running just inside the tree line. To make matters worse it was covered with a large number of NVA boot prints less than an hour or two old. Cruz moved up quickly to take a look at the trail, then taking over at point he began to head directly down the trail.

When no one followed, Cruz turned back and demanded to know why. After some whispered discussion with Goshen and the rest of the team about "who" was the team leader and "who" was the point man, an understanding was reached that no one but Enrique Cruz was willing to walk down that trail. Cruz was irate, but had the good sense to know when he had no support from his teammates. So instead of following the trail, he slipped silently into the single-canopy jungle, moving perpendicular to the heavily used high-speed. The rest of the patrol fell into place right behind him as he put some distance between the team and the trail.

A hundred meters from the edge of the woods, the patrol set up in a circular perimeter for fifteen or twenty minutes while Leibnitz contacted the C&C aircraft to release the choppers. He also gave a brief sitrep, reporting the trail they had found and the fresh tracks covering it. When he was done, the team was up again, moving farther away from the LZ and the trail. They moved for three hours over flat to rolling terrain sweltering beneath double- and triple-canopy jungle. Although they found no other signs that enemy troops were in the area, there was still a general feeling of concern among most of the members of the patrol that all was not right.

After three hours of patrolling, Cruz finally decided to call a halt. He signaled the team to rest in an area covered in double- and triple-canopy, setting them up in a tight wagon-wheel perimeter. There was no reason to push them any harder than he had to. They had only three klicks to cover in four days, so they would have the unusual luxury of taking their sweet time covering their patrol box. Besides, every man on the team sensed that he should be extra cautious on this particular mission.

Leibnitz took advantage of the break to call in a sitrep and report their new position.

The Rangers took turns eating, and when they had finished, Cruz decided that they would remain where they were for the rest of the day. No one liked the idea, but Cruz wasn't in a democratic frame of mind.

At 1700 hours the Ranger team leader whispered to his ATL, "Goshen, I want you to go out with me to scout out the area. I want to RON here. You cloverleaf out that way, and I'll cloverleaf out this way."

Goshen, not wanting to spend the night in the same area they had spent most of the day, questioned the wisdom of Cruz's decision, but Cruz was adamant.

Just as the two prepared to move out they heard a sound from the surrounding jungle that neither man could readily identify. Instantly they froze, waiting for the sound to repeat itself, but they never heard it again. Ten minutes passed before Cruz reluctantly gave the signal to move out. He was in a hurry to check out the area before darkness set in.

Twenty minutes later the two Rangers returned to the perimeter, not fully satisfied that they were alone in the jungle. Neither man could put his finger on the source of his anxiety, but their well-developed sixth senses were setting off alarm bells.

Ten minutes later it was beginning to grow dark when Cruz slid over to Goshen and began asking him about their position on the map. For some reason he was questioning the coordinates they had reported to the radio relay team. The two men were sitting side by side, heads not more than twelve inches apart, when the jungle on the southwest side of the perimeter suddenly erupted in a tremendous volume of small-arms fire. A machine gun opened up less than ten meters from the surprised Rangers. The opening burst severed Cruz's head from his body without hitting Goshen at all. The enemy fire was so intense that the Rangers had no time to react. Twelve to fifteen weapons were firing into the Rangers' perimeter from point-blank range. Swarms of bullets from AK-47s and RPDs crisscrossed the kill zone where the patrol sat, unable to escape. Almost immediately hand grenades began sailing in and landing among the Rangers, destroying whatever the bullets had not already harvested.

Every Ranger had been hit in the opening blast, either by small arms fire or shrapnel. Cruz had been killed instantly, but before Goshen could count his blessings, he was hit hard by an AK-47 round in the right shoulder, the impact knocking him forward over Cruz's body. Leibnitz was also killed immediately and his radio was destroyed in the same blast that took his life. Levine was hit so hard by concentrated small-arms fire that his left arm and right leg were nearly severed. He attempted to crawl into nearby cover to get out of the kill zone but was killed by a grenade blast before he had time to bleed to death. Gary Johnson was also hit numerous times as he tried valiantly to return fire. Before being knocked to the ground, he managed to empty a full magazine into the enemy soldiers hidden in the dense vegetation less than ten meters away. His unexpected and intense return fire was likely the only thing that prevented the enemy soldiers from following up their initial ambush with a frontal assault.

Goshen soon recovered enough from the initial shock of being hit to crawl away from the kill zone, but just as he was nearing the point of safety an enemy machine gun found him. A single bullet from the RPD slammed into his side, shattering his hip. Feeling like he had been kicked by a mule, the stocky Texan looked down and saw blood spurting from the wound. In the middle of the blinding pain from his wounds, he suddenly noticed an enemy fragmentation grenade lying no more than six inches from his wounded hip. There was a tremendous blast. Goshen was momentarily stunned. When the fog began to clear, he discovered that shrapnel from the grenade had further damaged his hip and some of it had lodged in his chest. He knew he was in bad shape, but he also knew that he had to get out of the kill zone. He could do nothing to save his life or anyone else's unless he stopped getting hit.

Rolling over on his side, Goshen crawled twenty-five meters from the firing before managing to prop himself up against a tree, facing back toward the team's perimeter. He looked down slowly and saw that his wounded hip was still spurting bright red blood on the jungle floor. He could sense his life draining away.

At this point in the battle the enemy stopped firing and withdrew from the field. At first Goshen could not understand why they had not moved in to finish the job. It had all happened so quickly, and they had been so damned thorough. With a moment to reflect between bouts of intense pain, it became obvious to him that the NVA must have followed him and Cruz right up to the perimeter when they had returned from their cloverleaf recon. Neither man had seen a thing during the sweep outside the perimeter just ten minutes before the firing began.

Suddenly Wenzel ran up and plopped himself down next to Goshen. Good old Wenzel! Goshen had forgotten about him. Wenzel quickly told Goshen that he had taken some grenade shrapnel in his back and had been hit in the hand by an AK-47 round, but he was okay.

Goshen knew there was no time to waste. He told Wenzel, "Get out and head back to the LZ. When you reach it, try to flag down a chopper and get the word back to the company about what happened out here today."

Wenzel refused, saying that he wouldn't leave Goshen behind. Goshen was getting weaker and didn't want to spend the last of his energy arguing with Wenzel. Instead he told him to go back to the perimeter and see if anyone else had survived. He also asked him to find some weapons and bring them back to him. Wenzel nodded and crawled away toward the perimeter.

Before long the Ranger returned with a number of M-16s, Cruz's CAR-15, and Goshen's rucksack. As soon as he made sure that Goshen was armed, Wenzel returned to the perimeter and came back dragging Gary Johnson. Wenzel laid Johnson down next to Goshen, then lay down himself on the other side of the badly wounded man.

Goshen counted more than thirty entry wounds in Johnson, including a sucking chest wound. Fortunately, the courageous young Ranger was unconscious at the time. Goshen and Wenzel attempted to dress Johnson's wounds, using Wenzel's T-shirt to cover a gaping wound in his stomach. When they were finished doing what they could for Johnson, they got a makeshift tourniquet around Goshen's wound and finally succeeded in stopping the bleeding. That done, Goshen bandaged Wenzel's badly butchered hand.

By then it was pitch black in the jungle around them. With their radio destroyed, they had no communication with the outside world. There was no way to let anyone know what had happened to them.

Goshen knew that helicopters would be out looking for them after they failed to make their next two regularly scheduled hourly sitreps. However, their next sitrep was not due for about forty-five minutes, the following one a full hour later. A lot could happen in an hour and forty-five minutes. Unfortunately, he remembered that he and Cruz had just reached the conclusion that they were nearly a full klick from where they had reported they were. This meant that when the helicopters came out to begin the search for the team, they would be looking a full klick away. The odds were not in favor of their seeing another sunrise.

Ten minutes later Goshen and Wenzel spotted what appeared to be hundreds of flashlights moving through the jungle directly toward their position. The two Rangers thought that the entire NVA regiment they had been sent out to find was at that moment sweeping the jungle, looking for the survivors of the ambush. Goshen and Wenzel quickly agreed that they wouldn't allow themselves to be taken prisoner. While Wenzel silently prepared an M-16 and his M-79 grenade launcher, Goshen straightened the pins on several fragmentation grenades and placed them beside him on the jungle floor. He also put his M-16 and Cruz's CAR-15 within easy reach. That done, the two men sat back to wait for the NVA to find them.

The Rangers watched in silence as group after group of enemy soldiers moved past them through the jungle. Amazingly, the NVA did not appear to be looking for them. Instead they seemed to be infiltrating into South Vietnam from across the Cambodian border. There were no trails around so the NVA were forced to bust brush heading from point A to a point B located somewhere to the east.

The enemy foot traffic went on unabated for nearly two hours. This was when Wenzel and Goshen first heard the helicopters in the distance. As predicted, the Hueys were flying over the jungle a thousand meters away. The distant aircraft seemed to have no effect on the NVA soldiers still swarming through the trees.

After a while the helicopters began expanding their sweep area, coming closer and closer to where Wenzel, Goshen, and Johnson lay hidden in the jungle. Each time they flew within a couple hundred meters of the ambush

site, the NVA soldiers quickly turned out their flashlights and froze until the helicopters passed on. As soon
as the helicopters were out of effective range, the lights
came back on and the infiltration proceeded. On two occasions the NVA approached to within ten meters of the
concealed Rangers. The helicopters finally gave up and
left the area around midnight. Sometime between 0200
and 0300 the NVA movement ceased altogether.

Several times during the night Johnson regained consciousness long enough to squeeze Goshen's hand and
say, "Bill, we've got to make it back to Fort Worth."
Then he would shudder and go back under again.
Goshen couldn't get Johnson off his mind. It was tearing him apart to know that his friend was dying and
there was nothing he could do for him.

Goshen and Wenzel thought that the NVA would return in the morning. They prayed until Wenzel eventually fell asleep from sheer exhaustion. Goshen's intense
pain and the knowledge that it would be his last night
on earth kept him awake.

Just before daylight Goshen woke Wenzel, whispering, "It's time to get ready, Larry. The NVA will be coming soon."

It wasn't five minutes later when they spotted seven
NVA soldiers approaching through the jungle. The enemy troops were dressed just like a U.S. long range reconnaissance team, wearing flop hats and flower-power
camouflage. Even their faces and hands were painted.

The seven men approached the kill zone cautiously in
single file, just as the Rangers would have done had the
roles been reversed. When the NVA got to within ten
meters of Goshen and Wenzel, their point man stopped
and fired a short burst into one of the dead Rangers inside the perimeter.

At that moment Goshen fired a single round from his M-16, hitting the NVA in the neck and killing him instantly. Goshen then attempted to shift his fire to the rest of the enemy soldiers, only to discover that his weapon had jammed after firing the first round. The Ranger ATL had not realized that the M-16 had taken an enemy round in the receiver during the ambush the evening before.

Quickly grabbing up Cruz's CAR-15, Goshen opened fire on the remainder of the NVA, emptying the entire thirty-round magazine at them as they disappeared into the jungle. Instead of reloading when the bolt locked open on an empty chamber, the wounded Ranger began tossing grenades into the heavy cover where the enemy soldiers had fled. Wenzel also engaged the NVA, firing his weapon left-handed.

The enemy unit, taken totally by surprise, had not even been able to return fire. When their point man went down, the NVA scattered. Not knowing for certain what they had walked into, they responded as if caught in a kill zone.

At some point during the brief encounter, one of the grenades that Goshen had tossed into the jungle bounced off a tree and ricocheted over to the original perimeter. The resulting explosion set off a smoke grenade strapped to the side of an abandoned rucksack. As the smoke rolled out of the damaged canister, it slowly drifted up through the trees, where the pilot of a LOH scout helicopter flying a few hundred meters away happened to spot it. He was soon directly over the smoke. As he circled over the three Rangers, Goshen managed to get a signal mirror out of his pocket to flash the pilot. When the wounded ATL saw the pilot wiggle his chopper back and forth, he knew they had been spotted. Seconds later the aircraft left the area.

Twenty minutes later a Cobra gunship showed up on the scene and Goshen managed to signal him with the mirror. The Cobra pilot maneuvered his aircraft over the area where the team had been hit and lowered a PRC-25 radio to the ground by rope. Wenzel ran over to retrieve it and soon had it sitting next to Goshen. The ATL quickly got on the horn and gave a lengthy sitrep reporting their dead and the condition of the survivors. Ranger 1st Sgt. Carl Cook and Lieutenant Davis were both on the other end of the transmission. Both men were shocked to learn of the damage the team had suffered. When Goshen next asked for gunships, an aerorifle platoon, and an Air Force pararescue chopper, Davis responded that it would be done.

At that moment some unnamed colonel broke in and ordered Goshen to use proper radio procedure or suffer the consequences. This was too much for Lieutenant Davis. He immediately cut in and told the colonel to get off the air. Angrily, he pointed out to the unwanted and unappreciated intruder that the man doing the talking was the ground commander. The colonel immediately signed off the air.

Soon an Aussie FAC pilot flying an OV-10 was in the air over the team. He announced that his callsign was Sidewinder. Minutes later an air relay aircraft reached the area and went on station. Help was finally on the way.

To let the enemy know that they were still alive and to discourage any of them from crawling up within range, Goshen began firing M-79 rounds into the jungle in a tight circle around their position, trying to cause some of the rounds to burst in the trees.

When the gunships arrived on station a short time later, Goshen used the "clock" method to help them locate the survivors. When they had finally marked the Ranger position, Goshen instructed them to fire up the jungle all around them, keeping the fire at least twenty meters away from the Rangers.

As the gunships shredded the jungle around the team, the ARPs (aero-rifle platoon) inserted into a clearing no more than three hundred meters away. Soon after they were on the ground, an Air Force H-54 rescue helicopter was hovering over the survivors. It attempted to lower a jungle penetrator to the team, but the penetrator was only one-third of the way to the ground when the chopper began taking sniper fire and had to pull out.

At that moment Goshen asked Wenzel to go over and retrieve the AK-47 from the dead NVA point man. Goshen told him that he needed it in case they managed to get out alive. Without asking, Wenzel knew exactly what he meant.

By approximately 1300 hours, Goshen knew that he was not going to be able to remain on the radio much longer. Pain and blood loss had him teetering on the brink of unconsciousness. Even so, he radioed C&C to ask what uniform the ARPs were wearing. When he was told "helmets," he responded weakly that the NVA unit that had come back that morning was wearing soft caps and camouflage fatigues. He cautioned the C&C aircraft to alert the ARPs to shoot anything that moved. It wouldn't be a Ranger because he was passing out.

Before losing consciousness he spotted a helmet bobbing through the trees eight or ten meters away. Goshen managed to alert the approaching soldier by hand signal. Within minutes fifteen members of the aero-rifle platoon had reached the wounded Rangers. Quickly securing the perimeter, they began giving serum albumin to the three wounded recon men. They then called for pararescue to come back in to attempt the pickup. The chopper was soon hovering over the jungle, lowering the penetrator to recover the wounded, but Goshen refused to leave unless the dead were taken out first in a Stokes basket. The ARP commander tried to argue the point, but Goshen refused to listen.

After the Ranger dead were safely aboard the aircraft, the basket was lowered for Johnson, then Wenzel and Goshen were finally pulled out. Goshen made certain that he brought the captured AK-47 out with him.

The dustoff helicopter flew back to Lai Khe and set down at the 1st Division surgical hospital. Many of the Company I Rangers were waiting there when the medevac set down on the heated tarmac. Lieutenant Davis and First Sergeant Cook unloaded Goshen, while other Rangers grabbed the remaining two litters and lifted them out of the helicopter. On his way into triage Goshen looked up at Davis and Cook and asked, "Where's the ops sergeant?"

When Top Cook responded, "He's not here," Goshen handed him the AK-47 and mumbled, "Give it to him and ask him if it's okay if we come in now."

When the litters were placed side by side in triage and a horde of medical personnel descended upon them, Goshen looked at Wenzel and asked, "Are you okay?"

Wenzel grimaced and answered, "Yeah."

But when Goshen looked over at Johnson, he saw that his friend was unconscious and ghostly white.

Goshen woke up the next day to find himself encased in a full body cast. A doctor making his rounds told him that he had been given eighteen units of blood since he arrived and was lucky to be alive. From the pain surging through Goshen's badly tattered body, he was not so sure he had been lucky.

Wenzel was in the next bed. Once again, Goshen asked him if he was okay. Wenzel assured him that he was fine. But when he asked where Johnson was, Wenzel could only shake his head and mutter that he didn't know. Goshen began screaming, and when the doctor came rushing in to find out what was wrong, the young Ranger asked him about Gary Johnson.

The major looked at Goshen with a sad expression and said, "I'm sorry, son, he died in surgery. He'd simply lost too much blood internally."

So that was it? That's all there was? That was the goddamned end of Gary Johnson? Goshen could not accept that. He had gotten close to Johnson in the previous few months, partly because he was a hometown boy and partly because he had been there to help Johnson through the Dear John letter and the anguish it had caused. At that moment Goshen knew that someday he would have to face Johnson's family and explain to them how he died. But just then he didn't need the extra pain in his chest.

Over the next two days most of the Ranger company, along with the Air Force air relay pilot and Sidewinder, the Australian FAC, came by to visit Goshen and Wenzel before they were medevacked to Long Binh. This move was only the beginning of their odyssey. They were soon flown to Camp Zama, Japan, then on to the States, ending up at Brooke Army Medical Center in San Antonio, Texas. The two men were there over a year recovering from their wounds.

Goshen and Wenzel were to discover much later that the ARPs had suffered six KIAs fighting their way to reach them. Less than a month after the devastating mission, renowned LRRP/SOG noncommissioned officer, S.Sgt. Jerry "Mad Dog" Shriver led his Hatchet force into the very same area of the Fishhook looking for the suspected site of COSVN (Central Office-South Vietnam) headquarters. The Hatchet force was quickly ambushed and "Mad Dog" Shriver disappeared covering their extraction. Intel reports later indicated that the NVA unit that had ambushed the Rangers was very likely one of the NVAs' counterrecon teams formed specifically to deal with U.S. long-range patrols both inside and outside South Vietnam.

Cruz and Goshen were awarded Silver Stars for their actions that day. Wenzel, Johnson, Levine, and Leibnitz received Bronze Stars with "V." All were awarded Purple Hearts. Goshen and Wenzel would never forget that eight of the twelve medals awarded their team were posthumous.

Company L,
75th Infantry (Ranger),
101st Airborne Division

Since January 1970, Company L, 75th Infantry (Ranger), the long range reconnaissance element of the 101st Airborne Division, had been running patrols in the northern part of I Corps Tactical Zone. Based at Camp Eagle, between Hue and Phu Bai, the company had moved a number of its personnel to Quang Tri to establish a forward operational base and launch site. With the 3d Marine Division and a full brigade from the 5th Infantry Division (Mechanized) already operating in the area, no one in the Screaming Eagle Ranger company knew why they were being tasked to pull missions in that particular part of South Vietnam. Not privy to the long-range planning of the policy makers at MACV or XXIV Corps headquarters, the Rangers had not yet learned of the planned invasion of Laos by South Vietnamese military forces set for the following year. They were told only that their mission was to provide ongoing intelligence concerning enemy forces and encampments along the north and south flanks of Highway 19, concentrating on the areas around the abandoned U.S. base camps at Lang Vei and Khe Sanh. One year later, Lam Son 719 would witness the ARVN's finest troops being seriously mauled by enemy forces waiting in the hills along the invasion route.

There was little doubt among the Lima Company

Rangers that the area they had been sent to patrol was hot. Nearly every team infiltrated into the area had made contact or sighted enemy troops. Two Screaming Eagle Rangers had already been killed operating there, and fifteen more would die before the invasion began the following year. Even more had been wounded, but that didn't keep them from going right back in to search out the NVA forces pouring across the borders into South Vietnam. Several branches of the Ho Chi Minh Trail entered the country from Laos and North Vietnam, especially in the vicinity of Lang Vei and Khe Sanh, the same area where the Screaming Eagle long-range patrols were encountering the enemy on nearly every mission.

By the end of March, Company L was keeping from two to four teams out on patrol along QR 19 at all times. Their success at finding the enemy and getting out again was a tribute to their professionalism and dedication. In nearly every instance where the Rangers made contact with larger NVA forces, the enemy had paid a heavy price for their indiscretion. Unfortunately, the Rangers were also paying a heavy price.

Back at Camp Eagle on 31 March, Ranger Team Two-Five, led by S.Sgt. Jim Bates, and two other teams had just returned from a relaxing day at Eagle Beach, a secured area on the South China Sea just east of the imperial city of Hue where stressed out Screaming Eagles from the 101st Airborne Division were occasionally allowed to rest and recreate. The three Ranger teams had earned in-country R&R after pulling a number of successful patrols west of Quang Tri.

Early the next morning, SFC Troy Rocha, platoon sergeant of 2nd Platoon, approached Bates and told him that he had another reconnaissance mission coming up. Bates quickly gathered the other five members of his team and took them down to the Ranger TOC for a premission briefing.

The briefing turned out to be a disappointment. Other than learning the location and the date of the impending patrol, Operations had little to offer in the way of intelligence. Most of Bates's questions went unanswered. Unsatisfied with the lack of intel on the patrol's AO, Bates announced that he would be back after lunch to see if anything new about the mission had come in.

When he returned a couple of hours later, he was told only that "sniffer" reports (electronic sensors that pick up the smell of human urine) had recently picked up positive readings over an area located in the northwest corner of South Vietnam, directly above the abandoned Special Forces camp at Lang Vei. Bates had to smile at this bit of news. Every Ranger in the company knew that the area around Lang Vei and Khe Sanh was teeming with NVA. After all, it was dead in the middle of a major infiltration route from both Laos and North Vietnam into the Quang Tri, Con Tien, and Dong Ha areas. Team Two-Five's mission was to sneak in there and find out who or what was generating the "hot" sniffer readings. It would be a six-day reconnaissance mission—outside the artillery fan! Just the thing to create fond memories.

Team Two-Five was one of the finest teams in the company. Although every Ranger believed he was on the best team in the world, Bates was quite certain that that was more than just a boast with Two-Five. He had been out with every man on the team on several occasions and had no reservations about any of them. Each man performed to the best of his ability. It was a veteran team, led by a veteran team leader.

At the time, S.Sgt. Jim "Lobo" Bates had been in Vietnam nine months. The muscular Texan had spent

his high school years in a little town called McCloud
deep in the shadow of northern California's Mount
Shasta. Special Forces-qualified, he was an immediate
success both as a Ranger and team leader.

Bates's point man was Sp4. Mark "Heime" Morrow.
The native New Yorker, in the Rangers nearly seven
months, had been out with Bates on a number of missions. Bates liked him because he was trustworthy, totally open about everything, and just a lot of fun to be
around. His skill in the jungle had earned him his spot
at point.

The team's junior radio operator was Sp4. Richard
"The Kid" Butler. Butler, an Indiana Hoosier, had been
a vital part of Team Two-Five on several earlier missions, and Bates knew without a doubt that the stocky
radio operator could always be counted on to perform
in a tight spot.

Specialist Four Paul "Blinky" Morgucz, one of the
team's scouts, was a suburban Chicago kid who blinked
repeatedly when speaking. But Morgucz never allowed
his affliction to affect his shooting eye or cause him to
miss anything on patrol.

Specialist Four Calvin Dunkle was a native of
Maryland. Like Morgucz, he was a crack shot and totally reliable in a firefight. No one on the team ever had
to look back over his shoulder with Dunkle bringing up
the rear.

The final member of Team Two-Five was S.Sgt. Ned
"Piggy" Norton, from Minnesota. He had earned his
moniker not because of the way he ate, but because of
the great amount of food he humped—and consumed—on patrol. Norton was a graduate of the
Army's NCO academy, not in itself an automatic cause
for acclaim, but the fact that he also wore the Ranger
tab over his Ranger scroll earned him the respect of

every man in the company. As the newest member of the team, he had done so well on the few patrols he had gone out on that Bates had designated him assistant team leader and was grooming him to take out his own team. According to Bates, he wasn't far from assuming that role.

Team Two-Five's performance in the field was second to none, and was probably the reason that it seemed to get the tougher missions.

After the second briefing session, Bates and Norton sat down with their teammates and laid out the rules. There would be absolutely no smoking or cooking on the mission. Each man would carry more than his normal basic load of ammo. They would also carry frags, Willy Petes (white phosphorous grenades), CS, and smoke grenades. Each Ranger would pack an extra battery for the radios and a claymore mine. Dunkle and Morgucz would add cut-down M-79s to their basic armament. It was Bates's theory that when you're going into bear country, you load for bear.

Bates ordered his teammates to pack rations for six days. For Norton that meant a case of dehydrated LRRPs and a dozen cans of fruit C rats. Bates also made sure that they understood that any contact initiated by the Rangers would be opened only on his command. The mission was scheduled to be a lengthy one, but Bates doubted they would stay in for the full term.

The next morning Bates and Norton loaded their gear aboard a 2/17th Cav slick and flew north to Quang Tri to conduct an overflight of the team's AO before the rest of the team arrived that night.

It was 1300 hours before they managed to fly out to their recon zone. The overflight was scheduled in conjunction with the extraction of two other Lima Company long-range patrols that had been in the bush a number of days. They had conducted operations in patrol boxes not far from where Two-Five was scheduled to go in. The two teams were to be pulled out right after Bates and Norton finished their overflight.

Escorted by a pair of Cobra gunships, a chase ship, and a C&C aircraft, the slick bearing the two Rangers made a couple of passes at altitude over the designated patrol area, a heavily forested, mountainous region about nine klicks northwest of the abandoned U.S. Marine base at Khe Sanh and about six klicks due north of the old Special Forces camp at Lang Vei. During the 1968 Tet Offensive, Lang Vei had been overrun by NVA using PT-76 Soviet tanks.

The crests of the major ridgelines in the AO were covered with double- and triple-canopy forest. This dropped down to double- and single-canopy on the ridge flanks. Down in the valleys the primary cover was a mixture of single-canopy and waist-high kunai grass. Stands of tall bamboo marked marshy areas and streams. The NVA needed water and could usually be found near the streams that meandered through the valleys. They were good places to avoid, but great spots to set up OPs over.

He began marking up the six-square-kilometer recon zone he had outlined on his map, laying out a six-day patrol route that would take them from the northwest corner of the AO to the south-southeast, then west, before heading back to the north-northwest and ending up directly across the valley from where they started. Most of the route followed the high ground, but there would be times when they would be forced to go low to find water. In the hot, humid weather characteristic of that part of South Vietnam during that time of year, the patrol could not carry enough water to sustain it over a six-day mission.

There were a number of suitable landing zones inside the patrol's area of operations, but they were far too obvious. Playing it safe, Bates decided to select one of the least likely ones—a single bomb crater located on the side of the same ridgeline where the team was to begin its patrol. It wasn't much to look at from above, but the team leader knew from experience that chances would be slim that the NVA would have posted an LZ watcher at every bomb crater in the area.

For their primary extraction point Bates selected a broad, level area halfway down the ridge just a klick south of their insertion LZ. The clearing was covered in waist-high kunai grass and suitable for a touchdown extraction.

Satisfied that they had all the info they needed, Bates signaled the pilot to begin the extraction. While Bates and Norton's aircraft went into a high orbit, the chase ship, the C&C aircraft, and the two Cobras pulled the first team out of the jungle five klicks south of Team Two-Five's AO. They had managed to stay in for four days without being compromised and had gathered some excellent intel.

When they were safely aboard, it was Bates and Norton's turn. Their Huey quickly joined up with the C&C aircraft and the two gunships, then flew four klicks east of the first extraction to a spot just north of the abandoned Khe Sanh base camp. Bates acted as bellyman as the slick dropped down to pick up Sergeant Vodden's team. Vodden, a Canadian citizen, was putting the finishing touches on a very successful mission. His team had also managed to avoid contact with the enemy and had gathered some valuable intelligence. After the extraction, Bates muttered a silent prayer that his patrol would be as successful as the two coming out.

The five aircraft climbed rapidly to forty-five

hundred feet and flew east in a string formation toward Quang Tri. Bates and Norton were anxious to get back; there was still a lot to do before the rest of their team flew up to rejoin them that night. If everything went according to plan, they were scheduled to go in early on the morning of the fourth.

They were to spend the night in a wooden barracks assigned to them by the 5th Mech. U.S. Navy Seabees had thrown up the plywood and corrugated tin structures a few years before for the Marines who had been stationed there. No longer occupied by the 3d Marine Division, the quarters had been turned over to the soldiers of the 5th Mechanized Infantry Division on their arrival in I Corps. The buildings were conveniently located right next to a large helipad which served as the launch point for the long-range patrols working west toward the Laotian border.

That night Bates was told that the insertion would not be going in as early on the fourth as he had been promised. No reason was given for the last minute change in plans, just that the first-light insertion had been delayed. He was not happy with the news. Bates's team was the only one going in that morning so the problem was not a case of another team inserting before them. He was aware that an extraction had been laid on for the morning of the fourth, but it was scheduled to go down after his team had been inserted.

On 3 April, the day before the actual mission, Bates kept his team busy running immediate action drills, checking the communication equipment, and test firing their weapons. The evening was spent writing letters, relaxing, or in any other activity that would keep them from focusing on the mission. Their minds had to be as sharp as their bodies, and too much training and preparing would only overwind them.

The team was up well before daybreak on the day of the mission. Those who wanted wolfed down a quick breakfast, then joined the rest of the men down on the chopper pad. Each Ranger was present, packed, and ready to go at 0645. They found the three Huey slicks and a pair of Cobras from the 2/17th Cav waiting to crank up for the mission.

Bates couldn't understand why the insertion had been moved back. The team and the chopper crews were all ready to go before 0700 hours. It didn't make sense to wait any longer. But it was nearly an hour later, at 0755, that the word came down to crank the birds. The mission was a go.

The five-ship formation lifted off at 0800 hours and headed west. They had a flight time of forty-five minutes to reach the AO. The pilots flew their aircraft in a string formation until they were three klicks from the recon zone. At that point the C&C aircraft and the chase ship went into orbit outside the AO while the two Cobras moved up to flank positions on either side of the insertion aircraft. The gunships escorted the slick as it carried out three false insertions outside the team's recon box, then swung in to parallel the side of a steep ridge before flaring to a hover directly over a bomb crater.

Team Two-Five was ready. Standing out on the uphill skid, Norton and two of the Rangers dropped ten feet to the ground on the side of the crater, then rolled back into it. Bates and the remaining two Rangers dropped from the downhill skid directly into the crater. Seconds later the aircraft dropped its nose to gather airspeed, then climbed up over the ridgeline.

Down in the crater the six rangers listened to the sound of the Huey fade as the helicopter dropped behind the ridge above them to make another false insertion somewhere on the opposite side. Hopefully the

multiple insertions would confuse the enemy long
enough for the patrol to get out of the immediate area
of the landing zone.

Huddled around the edge of the crater, each Ranger
gave a silent thumbs-up to indicate that he was okay.
Bates nodded his head, then looked at Norton and
pointed to the top of the ridge. Bates wanted to get
away from the damp artillery crater as quickly as they
could. Morrow moved up to the lip of the crater to take
point, slipping uphill through the shoulder-high elephant grass. Bates was right on his tail five meters back,
followed by Morgucz, Butler with the backup radio,
Norton, and Dunkle.

Twenty meters away they reached the single-canopy
forest above the crater. Morrow plowed on for another
five meters before a signal from Bates brought him to a
sudden stop. The six Rangers immediately circled up in
the heavy vegetation to lay dog and listen.

While five of the Rangers provided security, Bates established commo with the choppers. He reported that
the team was in safe and gave a negative sitrep. When
the C&C aircraft, manned by 1st Lt. Kevin Henry, radioed back that the x-ray team was able to pick up their
transmissions loud and clear, Bates "roger'd" and released the aircraft. Seconds later the ships were heading
toward a distant patrol box to extract the other Ranger
team. It was 0900 hours.

The jungle noises around Team Two-Five soon began
to pick up as its denizens quickly forgot the recent human intrusion. Bates waited another five minutes. Then,
satisfied that they had gotten in undetected, he motioned for Morrow to lead them straight up to the top
of the ridge.

It was two hundred meters to the crest, and when the
Ranger point man reached it, he stopped as if he had

smacked into an invisible wall; just in front of him lay a four-foot-wide, hard-packed, high-speed trail, hidden from above by the double-canopy forest that grew along the crest of the ridge. Dozens of prints made by batta boots, sandals, and bare feet attested to the heavy traffic moving over the trail. The loose, undisturbed soil forming the edges of some of the tracks indicated that they had been made very recently. Most of the tracks seemed to be coming from the direction of the border. It was exactly what the patrol had been sent out to find.

Morrow backed slowly away from the high-speed trail, then turned to Bates and whispered that he had discovered a main infiltration trail.

Bates nodded, then pulled the team back ten meters into the trees and set up a security perimeter while he called in a sitrep. He had to use the ten-foot-long pole antenna to reach the relay team.

The high-speed trail ran northwest to southeast, in the same direction as the patrol route that Bates had established after the overflight. While the bulk of the team remained inside the perimeter, Bates sent Morrow to the south-southeast and Dunkle to north-northwest to watch both approaches. Safe from the unexpected arrival of enemy troops, Bates quickly moved up to the trail to take photographs with a 35mm Penn EE camera. When he was done, he pulled back into the perimeter and recalled Morrow and Dunkle.

After looking over their maps, the six Rangers rucked up and moved out again, heading south-southeast through the jungle. They paralleled the trail as much as possible, but occasionally had to step out onto it to avoid the inevitable noise that came from breaking brush. Dunkle, at the rear of the team, was kept busy sterilizing the patrol's backtrail.

The trail ran along the high ground, following the

crest of the ridgeline. Every saddle or low spot in the ridge had steps carved into the slope by the NVA to aid in climbing or descending the steeper grades.

They had followed the trail for nearly an hour, covering three hundred to four hundred meters, when they suddenly found the enemy ahead of them on the trail. It was almost 1400 hours when Morrow stopped in mid-stride, then held up a clenched fist to halt the team. Ahead of him, not more than fifty meters away, he had heard Vietnamese voices. Without realizing it, he had nearly walked up on the back end of an enemy column moving slowly in the same direction as the team.

Bates immediately pulled the team off the right side of the trail and circled them up ten meters back in the brush. Scarcely breathing, the team lay dog while waiting to see what the enemy unit was up to.

After forty-five minutes of hearing and seeing nothing, they moved back out on the trail and continued patrolling cautiously in the same direction the enemy voices had come from. Suddenly they began hearing Vietnamese voices both in front and behind them. They were trapped between two enemy units moving on the trail.

The enemy soldiers didn't sound excited or alarmed, but seemed to be shouting back and forth as if engaging in playful banter. Since the voices appeared to be coming from a reasonably safe distance, Bates decided to continue moving in the same direction. Morrow stepped gingerly out on the high-speed trail and began inching forward, alert and scanning the bare ground ahead of him. Back at the tail end of the patrol, Calvin Dunkle was facing the rear, carefully backpedaling up the trail, weapon at the ready.

Between 1530 and 1600 hours the team began spotting individual NVA moving up the trail ahead of them.

The enemy soldiers were only about thirty meters away, plodding along slowly. The Rangers followed them, trying to maintain their distance. By the end of the day, Morrow and Bates had observed six enemy soldiers but still didn't have a clue as to how many others were ahead of them. As slowly as the team was moving, they were still forced to stop from time to time to avoid closing up on the rear of the enemy column. Bates soon concluded that the NVA in front of them had probably been laying up during the hottest part of the day, and were in no big hurry to reach their final destination.

Several times while they were following the enemy patrol, the Rangers had stopped to reapply their cammo. The stifling heat trapped under the jungle canopy made the Rangers perspire more heavily than usual, and the continuous perspiration made the camouflage paint run.

During the brief moments when the NVA were in view, the Rangers saw that they were wearing khaki uniforms, pith helmets, batta boots, rucksacks, web gear, and pistol belts. Canteens hung by straps over their shoulders. The rucks appeared to be full. Each soldier was armed with an AK-47 or an SKS semiautomatic carbine. The weapons seemed to be new and well maintained.

As they followed the enemy column, the Rangers passed a couple of clearings along the trail that appeared to be used as rest areas. They had just moved across a broad saddle and were beginning to climb the opposite ridge when Morrow threw up his arm to stop the team. It was at a point were the Rangers would have to turn east to continue the patrol route. Morrow had detected the faint sounds of people chopping wood and clearing brush fifty meters or so above them, on top of the high ground.

Norton and Bates drew close together to discuss the

situation. They knew they had people coming up behind them because they could still hear the sounds of voices drawing closer. The team had just passed a wide finger fifteen or twenty meters back down the trail. The fingers appeared to run due north, away from the saddle. Bates decided to take the team back to the finger. With enemy troops ahead and behind them, it was the only spot around that offered the possibility of an extraction site should they get hit. With luck the NVA column behind them would pass them by, allowing them to set up an OP on the finger, where they could monitor the trail during the night. They could then resume the patrol early the next morning.

Bates turned the team around and moved the men back into the saddle. When they reached the point where the finger ran back from the trail to the north, they discovered they still had a problem. When they had first crossed the large, open saddle they had skirted it along the south side. In doing so they had failed to notice that the finger on the north side of the trail had been used before. Now, standing there looking across the finger, they could see fresh signs everywhere on it. The level area appeared to be occupied frequently by the enemy as a rest area.

It was growing late so Bates had no choice but to move off into the finger. When they reached a point fifteen meters back from the trail they discovered that the area opened up and offered little in the way of cover and concealment. Looking desperately for someplace to hide, they started to move to the right oblique, onto higher ground, but saw that there was no more cover in that direction. There was also no area nearby that would allow a helicopter extraction.

Bates realized they had to find some cover quickly and set up an NDP before night fell or run the risk of being detected by the NVA coming up the trail. When he turned to lead his team back out on the finger, he discovered that his men were leaving far too much sign moving around under the trees. He stopped the patrol while he and Norton once again conferred about how they should handle the situation. They were in a very sticky predicament. If they moved back up to the high ground, they would surely leave enough sign of their passage that anyone moving in to use the rest area would immediately detect it. If they retraced their steps back out to the trail they could easily find themselves trapped between two enemy elements.

Exercising their only remaining option, the Rangers moved further back into the rest area, where the cover thickened a little. When the team finally set up a hasty perimeter, they were no more than twenty-five meters north of the main trail.

The vegetation off the saddle consisted of single-canopy forest with thicker double-canopy on both flanks. Thick clumps of grass were scattered around under the trees between the Rangers and the trail, but much of it had been beaten down by the activities of the enemy troops who had used it. It wasn't much, but it did offer some concealment for the team without showing signs of their passage. The terrain on both flanks dropped off at a 30 degree slope. The end of the finger dropped off more steeply before descending all the way down to the valley at the base of the ridge.

It was nearly 1700 hours and the shadows were growing long and dark. Morrow silently slipped out of the perimeter and backed out into the clearing. When he returned, he reported that he was unable to spot the team's position from the center of the rest area. Bates nodded, then whispered that they would stay for the night. It they could make it until morning without being discovered they would be able to get back out on the trail and continue the patrol.

The team set up in a circular perimeter, back to back, rucks touching, its six claymores fanned out in a half-moon covering the rest area and the trail beyond. Bates faced the clearing directly to the south while Norton watched to the east. Dunkle took up a position on Bates's right. Morrow set up to the team leader's left. Butler, carrying the backup radio, shifted to Norton's left. Only Morgucz faced the rear.

Just before 1800 hours, the Rangers heard shouting out on the trail to the team's right front. It was coming from somewhere back along their route of march. From the sound of the voices Bates could tell that the enemy soldiers were alarmed about something. He worried that they had found something on the trail alerting them to the presence of the recon team.

The NVA were no more than twenty-five or thirty meters away, just beyond the Rangers' sight. Immediately after the shouting began, two shots were fired from southeast of the team's position. They appeared to have come from the top of the hill to their left, perhaps sixty meters away. It had to be the NVA they had earlier heard clearing brush. With enemy forces alert to something and on both sides of the Rangers, Bates decided it was time to call for help. He got on the radio and contacted the radio relay team, giving them a partial "SALUTE" report. He said that he would get back to them as soon as he could give a more complete report. As he was signing off the shouting on the trail suddenly ceased. Dropping the handset to his side, he listened intently in the growing darkness. They were still out there. He could barely make out the sounds of people moving about on the trail, but they were no longer talking or shouting. The NVA were on to them.

Five minutes later Bates radioed the relay team that he now had a more complete SALUTE report. He estimated the *S*ize of the enemy unit out on the trail to be somewhere between twelve and twenty. Their *A*ctivity, for the moment at least, was milling about making preparations for a frontal assault. *L*ocation was easy— they were out on the trail, approximately twenty-five meters due south of the team. He could not yet describe their *U*niform because he had not yet managed to get a visual on them, but if they were part of the unit on top of the hill to their southeast they would be dressed in khakis, pith helmets, and batta boots. The *T*ime was "right fucking now, baby." And their *E*quipment . . . well, he would just have to call them back after the enemy started using it on them.

The radio relay team got the message; they wished Bates good luck and said they would be standing by if he needed them.

Bates reached up and clipped the handset to the left side of his LBE, then said a secret prayer that the NVA would pass them by in the night. Even if the enemy soldiers had managed to pick up some sign out on the trail that the team was in the area, there was still a chance they might believe that the LRPs had moved on.

Minutes later Bates knew that their one hope had failed. He could hear the muffled sounds of people scrambling about on the other side of the thin screen of vegetation between them and the high-speed. If the enemy commander had concluded that the Rangers were moving on down the trail, he would have already sent his troops in pursuit.

The NVA commander had correctly guessed where the long-range patrol had gone to ground, and he was getting his people on line to make a frontal assault across the rest area north of the trail. In addition, he had sent elements off to the right and the left just forward and to the flanks of the main body. He was almost ready to give the signal.

Bates frowned as suddenly the sounds of movement out on the trail ceased. The prayer had not worked. It was time for action. Slipping silently over to where Norton squatted facing uphill, Bates whispered in his ear, "We need to get everyone but Cal up on line facing the clearing, now."

Figuring that no one would hit them from the rear or either flank, Bates placed everyone on line facing the immediate threat to their front. Only Dunkle would remain behind the other five, so that he would be in a position to lead the team off either side of the finger if they had to E&E.

Bates looked up and down the line of Rangers. Each man had a claymore detonator in one hand and his weapon in the other. Bates had put his own detonator, alongside Dunkle's, on the ground at his feet. The Rangers waited patiently in the growing darkness.

Five or ten minutes later the Rangers once again heard sounds of movement from their front and on both flanks. Then Bates spotted six or eight NVA moving cautiously up through the trees on his front right flank. At the same time Norton spotted six or eight enemy soldiers approaching from the front left flank. Then there were more NVA slipping through the trees to their immediate front, but farther back than the flankers. Bates had been right about the Uniform; the enemy soldiers were dressed exactly like their comrades up on the hill.

The NVA were advancing slowly through the trees, weapons held at the ready, searching. They were less than fifteen meters away, but the cover where the Rangers had concealed themselves, and the cammo paint and clothing they wore, made them all but invisible. At the last moment Bates remembered that his comrades would not fire until he initiated.

The Ranger team leader had not yet stooped to pick up the claymore detonators lying at his feet. He had already decided to initiate contact with the CAR-15. He needed to be ready to grab the radio handset and call in the contact as soon as the firing started.

Bates was holding his weapon finger on the trigger, still watching the enemy approach, when he saw one of them spot him. In the split second it took Bates to realize that he had just been made, he squeezed the trigger on his CAR-15 and killed the man before he could respond. Without hesitating he swept his weapon to the right, firing five more three-round bursts that succeeded in putting another three or four NVA soldiers down for good.

A fraction of a second after he opened fire, from somewhere miles to his left, Bates heard Norton's claymore detonate. A split second later three more claymores blasted in unison. The jungle was still echoing from the multiple explosions, debris raining down all around, when Bates felt something heavy slam into his left hand. There was no pain associated with the impact, and it didn't prevent Bates from emptying the rest of his magazine into the NVA still standing in the trees to his front. When the weapon finally ran dry, Bates reached down to grab the claymore detonators lying at his feet, only to discover that the rifle guard on his weapon had somehow been smashed. For a second he stared at the red film dripping from his shattered hand guard, then down at his left hand. At that moment he discovered he had taken a single round through the back of his hand, just behind the knuckles. The bullet had entered his hand on an angle, exited through his palm, tearing the muscle apart on the way out, then shattered the hand guard on his weapon.

Still not aware of any pain, Bates grabbed a detonator in each hand. But his left hand no longer worked. So he fired the claymore in his right hand, then shifted detonators and blew the second one.

While Bates was struggling to blow his two claymores, the other four Rangers on line brought their weapons into play, opening fire on the remaining NVA. Bates had been aware that his teammates had discharged their claymores a second after he had opened fire, but he had not distinguished the sounds of their open weapons coming into play a moment later.

The two elements were facing each other fifteen meters apart, exchanging fire as fast as they could empty their magazines and reload. Fortunately for the Rangers, their IADs (immediate action drills) were paying off in big dividends. They were scoring against the NVA, killing and wounding several more. And the enemy soldiers were having problems. Despite the extremely close range, they were firing high. Although the enemy troops had put several hundred rounds downrange at less than twenty meters, Bates was the only Ranger hit.

However, one had to admire the raw courage of the remaining NVA soldiers. Even though forty-two hundred steel ball bearings from the claymores had just killed or wounded a large number of their comrades, the carnage did not keep the survivors from returning fire.

After each Ranger had emptied several mags downrange, they slowly withdrew a few meters back into the trees to consolidate their position. Bates shouted a command, and Dunkle charged off the back side of the saddle running downhill to the north. The rest of the Rangers were right on his tail. It wasn't pretty, but it was the fastest way out of a bad gunfight. No one could accuse *them* of "attacking in another direction." What they were doing was pure, unadulterated, balls-to-the-wall *flight*.

Behind them the remaining enemy soldiers continued firing as they came. As the Rangers stampeded down the slope, they made too much noise for them to hear if they were being pursued. Doing their best to stay together while running downhill, it was all they could do just to remain on their feet.

They had covered nearly two hundred meters down the side of the ridge in about thirty seconds and were nearly halfway to the bottom when Bates shouted for them to hold up for a minute or two. As they stood gasping for breath, they could not hear sounds of pursuit. Norton said he had heard people moving around in the saddle as they were coming down the side of the ridge, but never heard anyone actually drop over the side in pursuit. Up the hill behind them, enemy soldiers were firing blindly over the edge.

Bates took advantage of the lull to call in the contact while Morgucz pulled a battle dressing from his web gear and quickly tied a pressure wrap around the team leader's mangled hand. The wound was nasty and still bleeding badly, but it remained numb enough to allow the team leader to focus on the situation. As soon as Bates got the relay team on the air he reported that they had made contact with an estimated twenty-five to thirty NVA and killed at least six to ten. Almost as an afterthought he added that they had suffered one WIA, code name Lobo. Before the relay team could respond to Bates's report, he told them to scramble the birds.

With the sitrep accomplished, the team leader consolidated the patrol, then told Norton to keep Butler with him in case the team got split up. They had to find a suitable LZ for an extraction and they had to find it fast, before the NVA up in the saddle were reinforced and organized a pursuit.

They started moving again in single file, this time at a slower but still ground-eating patrol pace. Dunkle dropped back to assume his usual position at the team's rear. Bates was confident that the tail gunner would shut their back door if the enemy followed behind too closely. As the patrol continued to move down the side of the ridge, the enemy fire sputtered, then finally ceased.

It wasn't long before Morrow broke into a small clearing situated on a short finger two-thirds of the way down the side of the ridge. Even in the dark Bates could tell that the clearing would make a suitable LZ for an emergency extraction. It was covered in ankle-high grass and was just wide enough to allow a single Huey to touch down and pick up a desperate team. And the best news was that it was right there in front of them. They no longer had any reason to continue looking. The only thing that worried Bates at that moment was the NVA reaching them before the extraction slick arrived.

The Rangers remained back in the trees, watching the clearing and the jungle behind them. Bates, with the handset clutched in his good hand, called the relay team to report the patrol's coordinates. He announced that the patrol had located an LZ and was waiting at that location for the arrival of the lift ship. The relay team radio operator told him that the choppers had launched ten minutes earlier but were still thirty-five minutes out.

While the Rangers waited in silence, Morgucz changed Bates's blood-soaked dressing and replaced it with a double dressing, tightly applied. Bates had lost a lot of blood and was steadily growing weaker. The initial shock of the wound had begun to wear off, and Bates shuddered as waves of pain began to reach his brain. But when

Morgucz stepped forward and offered him morphine, Bates refused, stating that he had to stay alert.

Just over a half hour later the helicopters radioed the team that they were five minutes out and closing on short final. Bates asked if they had the "big guns" with them. When Lieutenant Henry, flying C&C, responded in the affirmative, Bates gave him the coordinates of the last known enemy positions, then told him to have the gunships hit the saddle and the high ground on both flanks.

When the birds arrived on station, four Cobras from the 4/77th ARA quickly went into action. The team leader's coordinates were right on the money. To determine if they were taking fire, Bates instructed the extraction slick to remain on station while the gunships completed a couple of rocket runs.

Down the slope from the saddle, Bates was unable to determine if the Cobras were being fired on, but it wasn't long before the lead ship's wingman reported that the first aircraft had taken fire on his first pass. The four gunships made two runs each before the Cobra leader called the C&C and told him to send in the recovery slick. Their time over target was drawing to a close.

Suddenly the slick came in from the east, hugging the ridge. Bates shouted for the team to move into the clearing as soon as he heard the chopper approaching. Splitting the team into two elements, Bates fired a pen gun flare into the night sky to mark their position. The slick was coming in from a quarter mile out with its running lights on. The pilot radioed that he had a visual on the clearing.

The Cobra gunships were still making rocket runs along the crest of the ridge. The flight leader radioed that they were receiving heavy return fire on every pass from all along the trail.

The Huey flared over the narrow finger and dropped down into the scrubby grass. Bates, Dunkle, and Morrow scrambled aboard the aircraft from the downhill side of the ship while Norton, Morgucz, and Butler piled in from the wooded side. The aircraft commander quickly lifted off from the tiny LZ. Dropping the nose, the pilot banked away from the ridge, then circled out over the valley to head back in the direction of Quang Tri.

They had not yet cleared the Khe Sanh Plateau when Norton unexpectedly turned and jabbed a morphine syrette into Bates's right thigh. Norton knew that Bates would never allow himself the powerful drug while he was still in charge of the patrol. Within seconds the Ranger was out of his pain, and temporarily out of the war.

When the Huey sat down at Quang Tri, Bates was taken directly to the field hospital near the airstrip. After he cleared triage, Bates's wound was cleaned and stabilized and he was given a tranquilizer to help him sleep. Two days later he was medevacked to the 85th Evac Hospital at Phu Bai.

The remainder of the team was thoroughly debriefed the same night they returned from the mission. The next morning they were flown back to Camp Eagle for a well-deserved stand-down. The day Bates arrived at the 85th Evac Hospital the team drove down to visit him. The attending physician told them that when Morgucz had applied the double pressure dressing on Bates's hand, he had succeeded in stopping the loss of blood, most likely preventing Bates from bleeding to death.

The next day Sergeant First Class Rocha arrived at the hospital with a truckload of Lima Company Rangers to look in on their wounded comrade. After a short visit, they departed satisfied that Bates would not only live but return to lead more patrols in the future.

Bates remained at Phu Bai for a week and a half. While there he decided to extend his tour to go back to Special Forces. He had spent eleven memorable months in L Company, but enough was enough. He had made up his mind to make the most of his thirty-day extension leave back in California before returning to Nam and switching berets.

Weeks later, G-2 confirmed that Team Two-Five had killed fourteen NVA during the firefight in the saddle and wounded between seven and ten others. The Cobras from 4/77th ARA out of Camp Evans had undoubtedly run that figure much higher.

Staff Sergeant Jim Bates reported to MACV-SOG CCN at Da Nang in June. He finished up his second tour in Vietnam as the "1–0" (one-zero) of RT Hunter, running missions across the border into Laos. Bates left the service in August 1971 but remained in the reserves, assigned to 12th Special Forces Group. He returned to active duty in 1980, recruited by Col. Nick Rowe to help establish the SERE course at Fort Bragg, North Carolina. He then served a tour in Lebanon (1982–83) in an advisory capacity. He was commissioned as a Special Forces warrant officer in 1990, serving in Okinawa, Japan, with C/1/1, the CINC's (in extremis) unit under the command of Special Operations Command Pacific (SOCPAC). He is presently a CW3, serving as the deputy operations officer for 2d Battalion, 1st Special Forces Group at Fort Lewis, Washington. He is married and has three daughters.

Specialist Four Paul "Blinky" Morgucz served with L Company until the 101st Airborne Division returned to CONUS. At that time he transferred to H Company, 75th Infantry (Ranger), 1st Cavalry Division, where he remained until the 1st Cav returned to CONUS in the summer of 1972, the last U.S. infantry division to leave

Vietnam. He returned home to Summit, Illinois, went to work for the railroad as an engineer, married, and raised two daughters. He passed away in February 2000, awaiting a kidney and a liver transplant. He is sorely missed by his family and his comrades.

Specialist Four Richard "The Kid" Butler returned home from the war to the hills of Indiana, where he became a successful bricklayer. He married and was raising a family when he suddenly passed away in 1988, the victim of a massive heart attack.

Staff Sergeant Ned "Piggy" Norton returned home to Minnesota, where he became a state forest ranger and a loving husband. He attained the exalted rank of ninth degree black belt in karate. He died in 1991 after losing a tough battle with Lou Gehrig's disease.

Specialist Four Calvin Dunkle extended his tour in L Company long enough to attain an early out from the service. After returning to the States, he disappeared.

Specialist Four Mark Morrow left Vietnam and returned to New York. No one has heard from him since.

Efforts to locate Dunkle and Morrow have been in vain. Calvin and Mark, if you read this story, call home; your brothers are looking for you.

Company F, 58th Infantry (LRP), 101st Airborne Division

When the 101st Airborne Division took over the U.S. Marine Corps' tactical area of operations in central I Corps after the Tet Offensive in 1968, the area around the imperial city of Hue became its home for the next four years. Extending west into the A Shau Valley to the Laotian border, north to the TAOR of the 3d Marine Division, and south to the operational area of the Americal Division, the Screaming Eagles shared their neighborhood with more than fifty thousand North Vietnamese Army soldiers. Tasked with protecting the imperial city and U.S. facilities at Phu Bai and keeping open Highway 1, the troopers of the 101st Airborne Division would see more than their fair share of combat.

The division's long-range patrol element, Company F, 58th Infantry (LRP), had arrived in Vietnam in late 1967 as the Division long range patrol company. Made up of graduates of the division's Stateside Recondo School at Fort Campbell, Kentucky, and most of the school's cadre, the company was ill-prepared upon its arrival in country to conduct long-range patrols against the experienced NVA forces operating in the area. An infusion of veterans from the division's 1st Brigade LRRP detachment provided a big assist in making the unit combat ready. In addition, a number of the unit's

junior NCOs were rushed off to attend MACV
Recondo School in Nha Trang for further seasoning. By
the summer of 1968, the unit was finally prepared to
meet the enemy on his own turf.

Unfortunately, during a change in command, the
very poor selection of a new company commander resulted in an unpleasant incident that saw the newly arrived captain trigger a toe-popper mine upon entering
his hootch during the evening of his fourth day in the
unit. After a lengthy but unproductive investigation by
U.S. Army CID officers, the culprits escaped apprehension and the company was subsequently marked for dis-
solution. At issue was the total lack of cooperation
demonstrated by all members of the company during
the CID investigation. The CID's evaluation stated that
the unit was composed of malcontents, psychos, and
criminals, and their recommendation that the unit be
immediately deactivated was not only an expression of
their frustration at not being able to turn up the guilty
parties, but also reflected their rage over their own inability to convince even one member of the company to
squeal on his fellow LRPs. Right or wrong, the
Screaming Eagle LRPs had demonstrated total solidar-
ity during and after the CID's inquisition.

When the new company commander, Capt. Kenneth
Eklund, volunteered to take over the infamous LRP
company, the unit's future as part of the 101st Airborne
Division was still very much in doubt. It took Eklund
six weeks to convince division to give the company another chance to prove itself in the field. When the missions finally came down from Division Staff, they came
in great numbers, and soon the LRPs had earned the ti-
tle of "the eyes and ears" of the division.

But disaster was soon to strike. On Tuesday, 19
November 1968, the company infiltrated two twelve-

man heavy reconnaissance teams into the dangerous Ruong Ruong Valley. At the same time, another six-man patrol was inserted on nearby Leech Island, just east of the valley.

One of the heavy teams, led by S.Sgt. Albert Contreros, went in at last light on the nineteenth. Forced to drop fifteen to twenty feet from the insertion chopper into a ravine choked with tall elephant grass, the twelve LRPs took a pounding just getting to the ground. One of the patrol's veterans, Sgt. John Sours, injured both ankles when he landed on a log hidden in the tall grass. Not wanting to abandon his teammates, Sours remained on the ground with the patrol, arguing that his injuries were minor.

As the patrol moved north into the nearby jungle, they immediately discovered a heavily used high-speed trail three meters wide running along the base of a low ridgeline. Contreros held up the patrol and sent two scouts in each direction to check out the trail. Specialists Four Frank Souza and Gary Linderer moved east a hundred meters to a point where the trail turned north and began to climb the face of the ridge. At the point where the trail turned uphill, the two LRPs discovered a well-camouflaged trail watcher's bunker three meters back from the high-speed. The two men moved uphill thirty meters and discovered that the trail made another 90 degree turn to the right along the crest of the ridge, then continued to the east.

With dusk upon them, they were hesitant about continuing on. Contreros had told them to keep their eyes open for a suitable spot to set up an ambush. The two LRPs had already selected an excellent site atop a gentle knoll overlooking the trail where it turned back along the crest of the ridge.

Before they could decide what to do next, a single

rifle shot was fired from a point three hundred meters east of their location. Convinced that it was probably a signal shot from nearby NVA forces meant to warn of the team's presence in the area, the two LRPs quickly retraced their steps to report back to the team.

They informed Contreros of the trail watcher's bunker and the signal shot, then told him about the knoll. The LRP team leader decided to move up to the high ground and set up an ambush at the bend in the trail.

It was completely dark by the time the patrol set up its perimeter and strung a chain of five claymore mines along the edge of the trail. The ambush preparations complete, they settled in for what they hoped would be an uneventful night.

During the hours of darkness a number of enemy patrols moved carefully down the trail carrying flashlights and hooded lanterns. From their noise discipline and cautious demeanor, the LRPs knew they were searching for whomever had arrived in the two helicopters just before dark. Wisely, the LRPs let them pass by.

At daybreak Contreros discovered that Sours's ankles were not merely bruised, they were broken and had swollen to the point that he could no longer walk on his own. Contreros called to request a medevac helicopter then ordered Souza and Sp4. Riley "Bulldozer" Cox to help Sours back down to the LZ and stay with him until he was extracted. The three LRPs were to cut through the jungle, crossing the trail at the same point where the patrol had first encountered it.

Thirty minutes later Souza and Cox were back inside the perimeter. The extraction had taken place without incident, and the patrol was down one man.

Minutes later the eleven remaining LRPs heard two shots fired somewhere down the trail. No one was certain of their significance, but the veteran LRPs on the team reasoned that NVA forces in the area assumed that the departing helicopter had removed the parties that had landed the night before.

Thirty minutes later a single enemy soldier was sent down the trail past the patrol's location. It was obvious he was being used as bait to make sure the trail was now open. The patrol let him pass.

Another hour had elapsed when the LRPs heard voices coming down the trail from the east. Contreros gave the signal for the patrol to prepare to blow the ambush on his command. Minutes later, as a party of ten NVA strolled into the kill zone, the LRP team leader snapped his fingers and the jungle was torn apart by five simultaneous explosions that sent thousands of steel ball bearings into the kill zone.

When the smoke finally cleared, the LRPs could hear the anguished cries coming from one or two wounded NVA lying out on the trail. At that same moment Linderer and Souza spotted the enemy point man sprinting down the trail toward the trail watcher's bunker. The two LRPs fired him up, Souza wounding him just as he broke left off the trail and disappeared into the jungle.

The tally out in the kill zone was nine NVA. Four of the party were nurses carrying rucksacks full of medical supplies. Three of the females were armed with .45-caliber pistols. A fifth body proved to be that of an NVA major. The dead officer had a map case full of documents. The remaining NVA were infantry armed with AK-47s.

The LRPs quickly stripped the bodies and brought the enemy weapons, rucksacks, uniforms, and documents back inside the perimeter. Contreros got on the radio and reported the contact, requesting an immediate reaction force to develop the situation. Informed that one would be sent out as soon as possible, the LRPs sat back to await their arrival.

An hour later the patrol was informed that not only were no helicopters available to ferry a reaction force out to them, there were not even any available to extract the team. That came as a surprise to the LRPs, who were used to having aircraft standing by on pad alert whenever they had teams in the field. Unfortunately, all of the division's helicopter assets had been allocated to a major combat assault, and the LRPs were, for the moment at least, quite on their own. That fact caused a general constriction of already tight sphincters among the eleven men clustered around the tiny knoll.

An hour had gone by since they had initiated the ambush, an hour that should have seen them reinforced or extracted. They would have to escape and evade before the NVA began to react.

Back at Camp Eagle, Captain Eklund had managed to scrounge up a LOH scout helicopter and was at that very moment out over the area attempting to locate the patrol. He wanted to be able to direct the Rangers to a more defensible position. On the ground, the patrol could hear the steady hum of the helicopter crisscrossing the area but the dense double-canopy jungle made it impossible for them to mark their position unless they tossed out a colored smoke grenade that would also betray their location to the enemy.

Contreros ordered Sgt. Jim Venable, the patrol's assistant team leader, to drop off the back side of the hill into a narrow saddle that connected the knoll and an adjoining ridgeline, where the jungle opened up a little over the saddle, providing a small opening to the sky above. But as Venable lifted the signal mirror over his head, a number of AK-47s opened fire from heavy cover downslope, hitting him at least five times in the arm, chest, and neck. As Cox and Souza ran to Venable and began to drag him back into the perimeter, the NVA hidden in the trees below assaulted uphill toward the LRPs' position.

Within seconds several of the LRPs on top of the knoll poured a heavy volume of fire down the slope to stop the enemy assault. Under their covering fire, Cox and Souza managed to pull the badly wounded ATL back into the perimeter, where a short time later he was extracted by a jungle penetrator.

Over the next four hours the remaining ten LRPs succeeded in beating back a number of enemy assaults without taking more casualties. With the help of artillery from FSBs Brick and Normandy they succeeded in keeping the enemy at bay. But their supply of grenades and ammunition was beginning to run low.

Returning from the brigade-size combat assault, the two aircraft commanders assigned to support the LRPs in the field had been listening to the developing situation on the LRP frequency. Without waiting for authority to do so, Capt. William "Wild Bill" Meacham and Warrant Officer Bill "W. T." Grant called in to report that they were leaving the formation to assist the trapped team.

When they reached the area of the battle they circled the site, waiting for a chance to pull the team out. They watched as a Cobra gunship hovered over the top of the team, doing pedal turns as it punched out rockets into the jungle around the LRPs. Suddenly an explosion ripped the jungle apart at the very spot where the LRPs were fighting for their lives. Meacham and Grant looked down in bewilderment, wondering what had happened on the ground below. Minutes later a voice on the other end of the radio cried, "Cease fire! Cease fire! You're hitting us! You're hitting us!"

After a pause, Sp4. Jim Bacon, the senior RTO, came back on the air and reported that everyone had been hit and the team had suffered a number of KIA. The team leader was down and only three LRPs could still fire a weapon.

Meacham and Grant waited just long enough to assure themselves that there was no possibility of extracting the survivors then headed for the LRP compound back at Camp Eagle. On the way in they radioed ahead to request that a volunteer force from among the LRPs be ready at the chopper pad when they arrived. If no one else could get any help to the trapped team, by God, they would do it themselves.

Back at the LRP compound most of the team members still in the company area were sitting in their hootches, listening avidly to the battle develop over PRC-25 radios. When Meacham called for volunteers, the compound suddenly came to life, dozens of LRPs scrambling madly to get their weapons and gear together.

Specialist Four Tim Coleman, Team One-Six's senior RTO, had returned the evening before from a three-day patrol along the Perfume River. He was monitoring the action in the Ruong Ruong when he heard the call for a reaction force. Coleman grabbed his radio, weapon, and LBE and sprinted downhill for the chopper pad. LRPs were pouring out of the hootches around him like someone had kicked the top off an anthill and were streaming down toward the tarmac, many of them not in uniform or carrying a full combat load.

Specialist Four Joe Bielesch was in the TOC listening to the action with Lt. O. D. Williams, the company executive officer, and Lt. Jim Jackson, the operations officer. When he heard the call for volunteers, the banging of the screen door announced Bielesch's departure to the two officers.

Specialist Four Tony Tercero was a short-timer just two days from the rear at Bien Hoa, and then home. He had come over with the division back in November 1967 and had survived a number of harrowing patrols as a division LRP. Just two days before, Tercero had turned in his combat gear, weapon, and equipment, and he was doing his best to enjoy his last two days in the company. He was going home, and nothing else really mattered. He knew that he would miss the guys—they had been his close family for the previous twelve months—but he had paid his dues and it was someone else's turn to do the fighting.

Earlier that morning Tercero had heard that Contreros's team had successfully ambushed an NVA column and gotten nine KIA. That's a righteous kill, he thought to himself, good for Contreros. Then with nothing else to do for the day, he decided to go down to the acid pad to catch a few rays and watch the guys playing volleyball. While he was there someone showed up with a PRC-25 radio to keep track of what was happening with Contreros's team in the field. It wasn't long before concern developed among the LRPs listening in because the team had not been pulled out. Tercero was worried because no one was following LRP standard operating procedure—a mistake that usually cost lives.

Soon more LRPs began filtering down to the bunker to monitor the radio traffic between Contreros's patrol and the radio relay team set up on Firebase Brick. They could hear Contreros requesting a reaction force. When one was promised, the team elected to remain at the kill zone until it arrived. A fatal decision.

Thirty minutes later it was evident that things were going downhill in a bad way. The promised reaction force had not materialized, and there now appeared to be a problem rounding up helicopters to extract the patrol. Tension built as Captain Eklund went over to the 2/17th Cav compound and secured a LOH helicopter to fly out to the team.

As soon as he was airborne and out above the Ruong Ruong, the LRPs back at the compound heard him establish radio contact with the patrol. He was saying that he was having difficulty locating them in the dense jungle below.

Suddenly the LRPs heard the frantic cry, "Contact! Contact! We've got a man down!"

The voice at the other end of the radio announced excitedly that their perimeter was under attack and requested an emergency medevac.

The crowd around the radio grew as the action out in the Ruong Ruong intensified. Soon most of the company was gathered around the bunker listening quietly to the unfolding drama. Many were murmuring prayers.

Contreros calmly reported that his patrol was engaged in heavy contact, but so far had sustained only one casualty, the team's ATL, Jim Venable. Fortunately the beleaguered patrol was able to get the badly wounded LRP medevacked in the middle of the intense firefight.

The LRPs back at the compound listened as the battle rolled back and forth over the next two hours. In spite of being heavily outnumbered, the shorthanded patrol seemed to be holding its own. Then word came down that Cobra gunships, fixed-wing fighter-bombers, and artillery were finally on the way.

Suddenly there was static on the airwaves, then the patrol's RTO was screaming, *"Cease fire! Cease fire! . . . You've hit us! You've hit us! I'm the only one left. Everyone else is down."*

The LRPs listening back at Camp Eagle were stunned. None of them knew what had happened.

There was a long moment of silence. When nothing else came, anxiety spread among the LRPs as they searched for an explanation.

A sense of utter helplessness and total frustration settled over the LRPs milling about the bunker. Their brothers were out there dying in the Ruong Ruong. Each man knew that he had to do something, yet all were totally powerless.

They listened intently as reports continued to come in from aircraft over the area. Staff Sergeant Richard Burnell's heavy team, set up in the jungle five klicks away, radioed for permission to attempt to reach the team overland. Captain Eklund, fearing an NVA ambush, instead ordered them to go to ground. Sergeant Richie Burns, his 101st Pathfinder Team collocated with the LRP radio relay unit on Firebase Brick, requested helicopters to pick them up as a ready reaction force. Once again the request was refused.

Then Jim Bacon, Contreros's RTO, was on the radio stating that everyone had been hit, most of them seriously. He added that they had at least three dead. It was obvious from the pain and anguish in his voice that he had not escaped being wounded.

Suddenly Wild Bill Meacham was on the radio. He and W. T. Grant were headed for the LRP acid pad. They were coming in hell bent for leather to pick up a reaction force—*any* reaction force. And he was calling ahead to save time.

Without a word more than three dozen LRPs scattered from the bunker and sprinted uphill to their hootches. They were being given the opportunity to help their buddies, and that was all that mattered. No thought was given to the danger they were wading into.

Tercero, dressed in cutoffs and a pair of Ho Chi Minh sandals, ran straight to the supply tent. Gone were thoughts about "coasting" until he caught his Freedom Bird. He only knew that he had turned in all his gear and would have to draw a new issue in order to help the trapped patrol.

When he reached the supply tent he found supply sergeant Joe Miller and his clerk, Bill Kirby—men who didn't ever have their own gear for the field—hanging M-16 bandoliers over their shoulders as they struggled to get ready. When Tercero told them he needed a weapon and some ammunition, Miller told him to help himself, they were heading to the acid pad.

Tercero grabbed an M-16 from behind Miller's desk and located a single loaded magazine that the supply sergeant and his clerk had overlooked. Slamming the magazine into the weapon, he looked about frantically for more ammunition. Scrounging up a couple of bandoliers of 5.56 ammo, he discovered to his horror that they were boxed rounds, not loaded magazines. A single magazine and fourteen boxes of loose rounds! It was a hell of a way to go to war. He would just have to keep reloading that single magazine in the field.

There was no time to scrounge clothes and a pair of boots; he could hear the choppers coming in hot. Dressed in shorts, sandals, and a pretty good tan, he ran out of the supply tent and sprinted for the chopper pad. He reached it just as the two Hueys touched down on the pentaprime.

Tercero climbed aboard the first ship and took up a position just to the rear and between the two pilots. When everyone was aboard, Meacham looked back and shouted over the engine noise, "We've got too many people on board, I'll never get it off the ground!" But when no one responded to his plea, he snarled, "Fuck it, let's do it!"

Specialist Four Tim Coleman had grabbed his web gear and weapon and started for the chopper pad when he remembered his radio. Returning to his cot, he slipped into the straps on the pack frame that held his PRC-25. The screen door slammed behind him as he ran downhill toward the chopper pad.

Sergeant Joe Miller and Sp4. Bill Kirby were REMFs, but they were also LRPs. They knew each of the men trapped out there on that hill, and they had the same drive to go to their aid as anybody else in the company. There might have been just a flicker of fear in the back of Miller's mind as he pushed himself back against the firewall in the second aircraft, but it didn't last long enough to force him off the ship.

Joe Bielesch tried to climb aboard the first aircraft, but there was no room on the cabin floor. His best friend in the world, Riley Cox, was out there with Contreros, and Bielesch was unable to get a seat on the goddamned helicopter. As he stood on the skid looking up at the mass of LRPs inside, he thought to himself, Bullshit, let somebody else stay behind. With a herculean effort he put one boot up on the edge of the cabin floor and shoved his bulky body into the melee, forcing two LRPs on the other side of the cabin out onto the helipad. He smiled smugly to himself as he felt the aircraft struggle to go light on its skids and lift off. We're coming, Dozer! Hang on.

Sergeant Richard Fadeley, a shake 'n' bake E-5, had been playing volleyball with a group of LRPs when he heard that Contreros's patrol was in deep trouble and needed help. The game broke up as the LRPs ran uphill to get their gear. No one had taken the time to discuss the matter; it was enough that fellow LRPs needed assistance. Fadeley was waiting with the rest of the company when the two Hueys touched down on the acid pad.

In seconds both aircraft were filled to the brim with LRPs struggling to secure a place on board. Fadeley found a spot on the second aircraft before the door gunners leaned out of their hellholes and tried to stem the tide of scrambling LRPs.

Aboard Grant's aircraft, he was experiencing the same problem plaguing Meacham—too many LRPs fighting for too little cabin space. Grant looked back over his shoulder and saw an LRP with his arm in a cast kneeling on the floor just behind his seat. "Get off my ship!" the veteran aircraft commander shouted above the roar of the engine. But when the LRP stared back and slowly pointed his CAR-15 in the pilot's face, Grant decided the man had pretty well made up his mind on the matter.

Miraculously both Meacham and Grant managed to get their ships airborne. Neither pilot knew it at the time, but they had twenty-one LRPs aboard the two aircraft. Meacham was certain that his aircraft over-torqued coming off the helipad. That was a major aircraft no-no and potentially fatal, but there was no time to turn back.

The two pilots flew directly to where the trapped team lay dying in the jungle. There would be no time to maneuver for an optimum position over the LZ. They would have to go straight in and unload their human cargo as best they could.

When Meacham reached the ravine where he had put in Contreros's team the evening before, he could hardly recognize the site. Artillery shells, air strikes, and gunship runs had changed the face of the jungle around the hill. He realized that the insertion had to work on the first attempt because there would be no chance to come around a second time.

Tercero had been in constant communication with Meacham and his peter pilot on the way out to the valley. Now, as they approached the LZ, he asked Meacham to point the nose of the aircraft in the direction they had to go to reach the team. Meacham nodded, then told him to head straight up the hill when they got on the ground. Meacham also warned him that there would be NVA between the LZ and the patrol so the LRPs should head toward the sounds of battle.

When the aircraft slowed to a labored hover over the grass-choked gully, Meacham fought to keep the ship from sinking right into the ground. Tercero forced his way to the edge of the cabin floor and stepped out onto the skid. He looked down, saw the elephant-grass just below him, and without hesitation stepped off and dropped into it.

It was fifteen feet to solid ground, and the short-timer hit hard. Pushing himself to his feet, he looked around. Two or three others were just recovering from their own tough landings. Without waiting to see if anyone was following, Tercero pushed through the grass, heading into the jungle above the LZ.

Tim Coleman had just moved out on the port side skid next to Clint Guthimiller as Tercero and four others stepped off and disappeared into the grass. Free of their weight, the helicopter shot straight up and Meacham fought to get it back under control. But it was too late for Coleman and Guthimiller. They had already committed. It was a long way to terra firma and both men crashed and burned on arrival. In pain from the rough landing, they struggled to their feet and started off after Tercero and the others. Guthimiller had an M-60 in his hands and had to be up near the front if his "pig" was to do the most good. Coleman was the only member of the reaction force who had had the foresight to pack a radio. He, too, knew that he would be needed up on the hill.

Seven LRPs from the first aircraft charged into the jungle and headed up the shallow slope. The advance party was made up of Tony Tercero, Tim Coleman, Clint Guthimiller, Joe Bielesch, Dave Bennett, Joe Miller, and Bill Kirby. Not ten feet into the trees they stumbled across the enemy high-speed trail and began to follow it up to where the team was supposed to be.

As they moved up through the splintered trees they ran headlong into a large party of NVA soldiers coming down the face of the ridge. They appeared to be fleeing the area and seemed as surprised to run into American soldiers as the American soldiers were to run into them. The NVA immediately did an about face, splitting into two elements as they ran past the flanks of the knoll where the remainder of Contreros's team lay wounded and dying.

A single NVA soldier suddenly stopped and turned back to fire at the LRPs, hitting Kirby in the left arm. The remaining LRPs immediately laid down a heavy base of fire, establishing fire superiority and putting the NVA to flight. The enemy soldiers turned and retreated around the left side of the knoll. Not seeing any more NVA ahead of him except for the enemy dead that littered the hillside, Tercero continued his charge up the hill.

Suddenly a single NVA soldier popped up from behind a large boulder to Tercero's immediate left front. He was aiming his AK-47 directly at Tercero from less than ten meters away. The surprised LRP knew he was going to die before he could react, but the five-round burst he heard a second later came from behind him, not from the AK-47 in the NVA's hands. Tim Coleman had been the first to react.

When Tercero looked back at the NVA the man was down, dead before he could squeeze off a burst. Tim Coleman had saved Tercero's life. Tercero looked back to offer a silent gesture of gratitude, but Coleman shook it off and motioned for him to get going; they still had to reach Contreros's team. While Tercero turned back up the hill, Coleman got on his radio and told Captain Eklund, "There are still a lot of gooks down here. Get us some more help."

It was only a short distance to the top of the hill. In the lead, Tercero and Coleman could see the naked bodies of the nine NVA killed in the patrol's ambush that morning littering the trail along the right side of the knoll. They looked strangely white, ghastly, and completely out of place lying there.

The LRPs were getting close so Tercero shouted, "LRPs! LRPs! We're coming up!"

From somewhere above them on top of the hill they heard Billy Walkabout shouting, "We're up here! We're up here!"

Then Tercero spotted Walkabout's round face framed in an opening in the leaves just ahead. As he reached the crest of the knoll he stumbled across the body of Terry Clifton lying in a pool of blood, then he saw Linderer, Walkabout, and Bacon huddled in the center of the perimeter around the surviving radio. On the left side of the knoll, Riley "Bulldozer" Cox was struggling to work another magazine into his "borrowed" CAR-15. The body of Sgt. Mike Reiff was pinned against a large tree on the back side of the perimeter. A new man, Sgt. Steve Czepurny, was lying on his stomach next to the trail facing out, weapon ready. Next to him lay the body of another new LRP, Sp4. Art Heringhausen. Contreros and Souza were nowhere to be seen.

Tercero took in all that in an instant as he charged

into the center of the perimeter. Blood, empty shell casings, and shredded vegetation were everywhere. The knoll looked like a slaughterhouse.

Coleman, Bielesch, and the others were right behind Tercero. They immediately headed over to the badly wounded Riley Cox. As Guthimiller reached the perimeter he sprinted across the knoll to set up his M-60 facing down the trail to the east. Bennett, Miller, and Kirby, the wounded supply clerk, took up positions at various points around the perimeter to provide security. Tercero, Bielesch, and Coleman then began to perform field triage on the wounded, trying to establish who they would have to medevac first.

While Tercero checked Bacon, Walkabout, and Linderer, Coleman and Bielesch dressed Cox's wounds. With horrible wounds to his stomach, right arm, and neck, Cox should have been unconscious and out of the battle. But the tough young soldier was still trying to wreak havoc on the enemy. Coleman couldn't help but marvel that a man could continue to fight with a compound fracture of his right arm and his intestines piled in his lap. After dressing Cox's wounds the best they could, Coleman left Bielesch with Cox and moved over to the center of the perimeter to join Tercero with his backup radio.

By then Tercero had discovered that Linderer and Walkabout had managed to get Contreros and Souza out by jungle penetrator before the reaction force had arrived. Tercero immediately established contact with Captain Eklund in the C&C aircraft circling overhead and gave him a full report of the situation on the ground. He requested additional medevac aircraft for the five wounded LRPs from Contreros's team.

When Captain Eklund told Tercero that the second lift ship was at that moment approaching the LZ,

Tercero yelled for Coleman to get back down the hill and guide them and the remaining LRPs from the first aircraft back up to the perimeter.

Tercero found himself in control of the rescue effort. It seemed like a natural thing, and no one questioned it when he had stepped forward to fill the role. He was proud as he watched his comrades carry out their tasks routinely. It was as if each of them had trained for this very moment all their lives.

As Coleman reached the LZ he ran into the four remaining LRPs from the first lift. They had gotten turned around in the elephant grass and were unsure of where the rest of their comrades had gone when they charged off into the jungle, so they had decided to secure the LZ until they got a better handle on the situation. When Coleman reached them he jerked a thumb back over his shoulder, yelling for them to follow the trail back up the hill until they found the perimeter. Without waiting for an answer he dashed out into the LZ, where the second Huey was just settling in.

In the second aircraft W. T. Grant hovered as close to the ground as he could. He held the ship steady as ten LRPs dropped the six feet or so to the ground and milled about in the elephant grass, not sure of which way to go. Suddenly Coleman was there, motioning for them to follow him uphill into the tree line.

Satisfied that he had everyone who had been left on the LZ, Coleman turned and headed back uphill toward the sounds of small-arms fire. When they reached the site of the battle, Tercero instructed Coleman to fill in the rest of the perimeter with the latest arrivals.

Soon Tercero had the first medevac helicopter hovering directly overhead. He shouted for Bielesch to get Cox over to the center of the perimeter so he could be extracted. But Cox, the most seriously wounded

survivor still on the ground, stubbornly refused to go.
He calmly announced that he was staying until the rest
of the dead and wounded had been taken out.

Tercero knew that there would be no reasoning with
Cox, so he lied and said that everyone else was gone,
and that he was the only wounded man left on the
ground. Satisfied, Cox allowed himself to be placed on
the jungle penetrator and pulled up through the trees.

Minutes later the second medevac arrived and pulled
Bacon and Czepurny out of the jungle. Then a third
lifted Linderer and Walkabout. Thirty minutes after hitting the ground, Tercero and his teammates had succeeded in extracting the five wounded survivors of
Contreros's team. All that was left was to recover the
bodies of Clifton, Reiff, and Heringhausen, and then
get themselves out.

By this time three more slicks were approaching the
LZ to deposit fifteen members of an aero-rifle platoon
from the 2/17th Cav. When Tercero found out they were
coming in, he once again ordered Coleman to go back
down the hill to bring them up. As Coleman disappeared down the trail, Tercero directed the final medevac overhead. It would depart minutes later with the
bodies of the three slain LRPs. It was 1730 hours when
the last of Contreros's team was flown out of the
Ruong Ruong.

Coleman reached the LZ as the second aircraft was
dropping its six-man cargo. He ran up to the black E-7
who seemed to be in charge and told him to head uphill
until he hit a trail, then turn right and follow it straight
up to the knoll. As the twelve ARPs disappeared into
the jungle, Coleman turned to meet the third aircraft as
it settled into the elephant grass. Only three cavalrymen
were aboard the final lift ship. Coleman signaled for
them to follow him, then turned and retraced his steps

into the jungle. When he reached the trail he turned right and began moving along it, searching the hillside above to make sure the NVA hadn't moved back in between the LZ and the knoll. Stopping on the trail, Coleman attempted to raise Tercero on his radio but couldn't get through. Clipping his handset to the right side of his LBE, he turned to the three ARPs and said, "It'll be okay. They know we're coming."

Up on the edge of the perimeter, Sgt. Richard Fadeley was guarding the side of the perimeter between the knoll and the LZ. As he searched the trees downhill from his position he thought he saw movement thirty meters away. It was down near the trail, not twenty meters from where it broke to the left and ran uphill. A few minutes earlier he had watched happily as a dozen Cav troopers moved up from the LZ and linked up with the twenty-one LRPs holding the knoll. With everyone now inside the perimeter, he knew that the movement he had just spotted had to be NVA soldiers moving back in to cut them off from the LZ. When he looked again he could just make out the form of a man sneaking along the trail. He raised his M-16 and fired three quick rounds at the soldier's head. He was pleased when he saw the man's body drop behind a large log.

Down on the trail, Coleman had just turned to wave the three cavalrymen on when three rounds cracked past his head. Instinctively he dived behind a nearby log and pulled the Cav medic down with him. He knew the shots had come from near the top of the knoll. Realizing that one of his own men had fired him up, he took his hat off, put it on the end of his rifle barrel, and raised it up above the top of the boulder. When nothing happened, he raised up to have a look uphill, yelling, "Don't shoot! It's me!"

Fadeley knew that he had hit the enemy soldier, but

he also knew there had to be more than one. He was still sighting down the barrel of his M-16 when he spotted a camouflage hat moving along the edge of the log. He was just drawing another bead on the hat when he spotted a mop of red hair a foot or two beneath the hat. He then heard someone holler not to shoot. Horrified that he had almost killed a fellow LRP, he pulled off the target.

Realizing that no more fire would be coming from the perimeter, Coleman turned to the three ARPs and announced, "It's clear now, follow me."

Minutes later Coleman and the three cavalrymen entered the perimeter. Nothing was said about the incident that had nearly taken Coleman's life. But, still shaking, Coleman moved into the center of the perimeter, dropped off his radio, reported to Tercero, then moved over and took up a slot on the perimeter.

When the entire Cav reaction force had reached the knoll, the E-7 walked over to Tercero and demanded that he immediately call in a medevac for one of his troopers, who had broken an ankle on the insert. He also appeared to be upset at taking orders from a young LRP Spec Four dressed in shorts and Ho Chi Minh sandals. It was a case of bad timing on his part. Tercero looked up at the man and said, "Get out of my way before I blow your fucking brains out."

Then signaling Coleman, Tercero shouted, "Coleman, go set up his people." The man hesitated a moment, as if to challenge Tercero's authority, then slowly turned and went out to take up a position on the perimeter.

It was fully dark by the time the reaction force got everything under control, the dead and wounded evacuated, and the abandoned equipment arranged in a pile. When they were done, Tercero radioed for an extraction. He was told that the extraction ships would be back out as soon as they had time to refuel. Tercero ordered everyone to prepare to move back down to the LZ. The Cav NCO told him that he wanted to get his men out first, especially since one of them had broken an ankle on the insertion. Tercero said that would be fine. Although the LRPs had come in first and should be going out first, Tercero thought of the mission as theirs; the Cav were not a part of the original cast.

As the thirty-six-man combined reaction force began to slip off the hill with the Cav in the lead, a single RPG round flashed in from the high ground on the northwest side of the perimeter and detonated in the treetops above the perimeter. Five LRPs in the rear of the formation—Coleman, Bielesch, Miller, Bennett, and Fadeley—were hit by shrapnel from the B-40 rocket, but none of their wounds proved serious enough to impede movement to the LZ.

When they reached the ravine at the edge of the jungle, Captain Eklund came up on the air and reported that the lift ships were inbound. When he turned Tercero over to the pilot of the lead ship, the aircraft commander requested that the reaction force provide illumination to mark their postion. That was when Tercero discovered that in their hurry to get out to the trapped patrol, no one had grabbed a strobe light, flashlight, or pen gun flare.

Pondering for a moment what they could do, Tercero reached into the pocket of his shorts and produced his trusty Zippo lighter. In seconds several more Zippos were produced, and on Tercero's signal the owners lit their lighters and held them over their heads.

Ten minutes later the pilot of the lead ship replied, "I've got your position. I'm coming in."

Soon the aircraft had the LZ lit up with his landing light and was settling into the elephant grass for the first lift. Tercero ordered the worst of the wounded and the injured ARP to board the first Huey. The rest of the Cav followed on the next two aircraft. It was 2100 hours before the last of the LRPs were pulled from the jungle.

It had been the company's shining moment. To a man they had answered the call—each LRP in the unit had made the effort to come to the rescue of his trapped comrades. There had been no shirkers. Even the rear echelon LRPs had come forward, like warriors to the bugle's summons. And when they had landed amidst the enemy, without hesitation they fought their way to the crest of the hill. Even those not trained in that sort of operation nevertheless excelled in carrying it out. Tercero recalls that pride and unit integrity were at their peak that day; they had driven off the enemy and saved their buddies. This action would become part of the LRP legend, part of their mystique. It was the glue that would bind the men of the company together forever.

The only award given to any member of the reaction force for heroics that day was a Bronze Star with "V" awarded to Sp4. Tony Tercero. He received it in the mail months later at Fort Huachuca. Purple Hearts were awarded to Sergeants Joe Miller, Joe Bielesch, Richard Fadeley, Specialists Four David Bennett and William Kirby. Years later Sp4. Tim Coleman would receive a long-delayed Silver Star and Purple Heart. At the time of this writing the survivors of Contreros's patrol, along with pilots Bill Meacham and W. T. Grant, and LRP company commander Kenneth Eklund, are attempting to upgrade Tercero's Bronze Star to a Distinguished Service Cross. Six members of the LRP reaction force that day have since died. Ten others have never been identified.

After his tour as an LRP in Vietnam, Tony Tercero was promoted from E-4 to E-6 within six months. The

20 November mission had changed his perspective on being a soldier forever. He returned to Vietnam in November 1970 and was assigned to L Company, 75th Infantry (Ranger), 101st Airborne Division, the successor unit of Company F, 58th Infantry (LRP). But he ended up serving his second tour at the 90th Replacement Battalion as the NCOIC of the Security Battalion at Long Binh. He extended for an additional six months as NCOIC of security for all U.S. installations in Saigon. He then extended once again for another six months, but was shipped home when his company returned to CONUS.

Epilogue
Year of the Dragon

July 2000

A classic Army anecdote tells of a general inspecting Airborne troops. "And do you like to jump out of airplanes, soldiers?" asks the general.

"No, sir," answers the trooper.

"Then why are you here?"

"Because I like to be around men who do," answers the young paratrooper. Thirty-two years ago, this same esprit de corps drew me and a bold handful of other special young men into long-range patrol units in Vietnam.

An army reflects the society from which it springs. We were a young, adventurous, colorful band of volunteers from every section of the nation representing the wonderful cultural diversity of America. When the tocsin sounded, we answered the call to the colors with open hearts, true believers in American democratic ideals. We were imbued with the precepts of our proud military heritage and, as the last true "citizen soldiers" of the twentieth century, were eager to test our mettle against the foes of freedom as our forefathers had. The "extremely hazardous duty" of infantry combat reconnaissance came with the territory, and it was accepted as a daily part of life. The names of Dieppe, Cisterna,

Pont du Hoc, Myitkyina, Cabanatuan, Munsan-Ni, the Ia Drang, and the A Shau are part of our fraternal tradition.

This oral history of LRRPs, LRPs, and Rangers in Vietnam, compiled through the dedicated and diligent efforts of Gary Linderer, details the exploits of our intrepid band of brothers. It is an illustrious story long buried in the debris and deceit of the otherwise sordid events characterizing American intervention in the small, remote area known as Indochina.

Twenty-five years ago this month, American television broadcast the humiliating and panic-stricken exodus from Saigon. Behind us we left a devastated country sliding helplessly into the brutal and repressive clutches of an Asian communist regime. Bitter controversy has beset the subverted political initiatives, obfuscated agendas, and the inept military prosecution of the war. (Recently declassified documents confirm the perfidy of our government, and its criminal waste of young lives and our national treasure.) However, in spite of this adversity and the self-sanctified attitude of popular opinion, we did our duty to our country.

Today, the shadow of Vietnam falls on us still. The long lost remains of our MIAs are finally being accounted for, and LRRP/LRP/Ranger veterans return to the quiet rice paddies and mountainous tropical jungles which years ago were the killing fields. Our survivors are an older group now, an abstruse melange of Brooks Brothers and Polo, olive-drab and tiger stripe, gold earrings and graying ponytails, airborne tattoos and reunion T-shirts. Some of us are socially dysfunctional; some are "still in Vietnam." The crow's feet of age now web the hawklike eyes, and the thousand-yard stares are wrapped in misty memories, but the intensity and fierce pride remain indelible and unmistakable.

Some remain forever young, their names emblazoned in honor on The Wall and other monuments in the great cities and small towns they once called home. More important, they are loved and remembered eternally in the hearts of their comrades-in-arms who served with them.

To have served with these men and be counted among their number is the greatest honor of all. It was the definitive experience of my life. The extraordinary and exclusive bond of camaraderie forged by combat endures today, still as strong and as sacred as ever. "For those who have fought for it, freedom has a flavor the protected shall never know." If the only glory in war is survival, then the dedication of the men who served in the long-range patrols, even to the last full measure of devotion, is the only honor to emerge from the Vietnam War, because the real heroes will never come home.

—Robert L. McClure
    Company C, 75th Infantry (Ranger),
    I Field Force

Honor Roll of Our Fallen Comrades

173D AIRBORNE BRIGADE

1.	SGT Raymond Hoyt Hudson	173d LRRP	06–15–66
2.	SP/4 William Elice Collins Jr.	173d LRRP	01–23–67
3.	CPL James Elliott Dewey	173d LRRP	04–04–67
4.	SP/4 Clifford W. Leathers Jr.	173d LRRP	06–21–67
5.	SFC Charles James Holland	173d LRRP	08–18–67
6.	SSG John Walter Thompson	74th LRP	01–03–68
7.	SGT Wayne Lynn Harland	74th LRP	05–01–68
8.	SGT Michael Anthony Gerome	74th LRP	05–07–68
9.	SSG Donald Giles Waide	74th LRP	05–07–68
10.	SFC Alain Joseph Tremblay	74th LRP	07–07–68
11.	SSG Laszlo Rabel	74th LRP	11–13–68
12.	SGT Raymond Stanley Reeves Jr.	74th LRP	11–19–68
13.	CPL Arthur Frederick Bell	N/75 RGR	05–12–69
14.	PFC Ronald Steven Holeman	N/75 RGR	07–13–69
15.	SSG Theodore Mendez Sr.	N/75 RGR	07–14–69
16.	PFC Ronald Gene Thomas	N/75 RGR	07–14–69
17.	SSG Cameron Trent McAllister	N/75 RGR	09–07–69
18.	SP/4 Steven Thomas Schooler	N/75 RGR	01–13–70
19.	CPL John William S. G. Kelly	N/75 RGR	02–15–70
20.	SGT Victor Del Greco Jr.	N/75 RGR	03–02–70
21.	SGT John Richard Knaus	N/75 RGR	05–07–70
22.	SGT Paul Lajada Ramos Jr.	N/75 RGR	05–13–70
23.	SGT Bruce Charles Candri	N/75 RGR	07–14–70
24.	SGT Roberto Lerma Patino	N/75 RGR	10–22–70
25.	SSG Juan Santos Borja	N/75 RGR	04–28–71
26.	SP/4 Lawrence Ray Peel	N/75 RGR	04–28–71
27.	CPL Joseph Edward Sweeney	N/75 RGR	05–29–71
28.	SP/4 Joseph D. Hayes	N/75 RGR	06–13–71

199TH LIGHT INFANTRY BRIGADE

1.	SSG Robert J. Carmody	71st LRRP	10–27–67
2.	CPL Linden Brook Dixon	71st LRRP	10–27–67
3.	SGT Stephen Perry Jones	71st LRRP	10–27–67
4.	CPL John Peter Turk	71st LRRP	10–27–67
5.	SSG Robert Alton Williams	71st LRRP	10–27–67
6.	SP/4 Ronald Roy Hammerstrom	71st LRRP	12–07–67
7.	SP/4 Neal Arthur Smith	M/75 RGR	09–06–69
8.	SSG Robert Larry Oaks	M/75 RGR	11–11–69

INDIANA NATIONAL GUARD

1.	SP/4 Charles Kenneth Larkins	D/151 RGR	02–11–69
2.	SGT Robert T. Smith	D/151 RGR	04–12–69
3.	SP/4 Peter Frank Fegatelli	D/151 RGR	05–10–69
4.	SP/4 Bishop Skip Baranowski	D/151 RGR	07–08–69
5.	1LT Kenneth Thomas Cummings	D/151 RGR	09–04–69
6.	1LT George L. Kleiber Jr.	D/151 RGR	09–04–69

82D AIRBORNE DIVISION

1.	SSG Jerry Don Beck	0/75 RGR	04–06–69
2.	SGT Daren Lee Koenig	0/75 RGR	04–06–69
3.	SSG John Anthony LaPolla	0/75 RGR	04–15–69
4.	CPL Michael Joseph Kelly Jr.	0/75 RGR	04–25–69
5.	CPL Charles Herman Wright	0/75 RGR	09–19–69

5TH INFANTRY DIVISION (MECHANIZED)

1.	SFC David Edward Carter	P/75 RGR	08–10–69
2.	SGT David Leon Barber	P/75 RGR	12–21–69
3.	SP/4 Roy Jeffrey Burke	P/75 RGR	12–21–69
4.	SP/4 James Howard Dean	P/75 RGR	12–21–69
5.	SSG Thomas Joseph Dowd	P/75 RGR	12–21–69
6.	PFC Gary Phillip Sinclair	P/75 RGR	12–21–69
7.	SP/4 Ronald Lee Biegert	P/75 RGR	03–15–70
8.	SP/4 William Peter Kastendiect	P/75 RGR	04–01–70
9.	SP/4 Vernon Ray Riley	P/75 RGR	04–28–70
10.	SSG Rodney Kenneth Mills	P/75 RGR	05–05–70
11.	SP/4 Raymond Hugh Apellido	P/75 RGR	09–20–70
12.	SP/4 Anthony Joseph Gallina	P/75 RGR	09–20–70
13.	SP/4 Dale Alan Gray	P/75 RGR	09–20–70

14.	PFC Glenn Garland Ritchie Jr.	P/75 RGR	09–20–70
15.	SGT Harold Erwin Sides	P/75 RGR	09–20–70
16.	PFC Stephen Lee Smith	P/75 RGR	03–01–71
17.	SP/4 James Thomas Williams Jr.	P/75 RGR	03–01–71
18.	SGT Michael Edward Koschke	P/75 RGR	03–20–71
19.	SGT James Daniel Schooley	P/75 RGR	03–20–71
20.	SP/4 Steven Charles Wray	P/75 RGR	04–01–71
21.	SSG Johnny Harold Lawrence	P/75 RGR	04–04–71

23D (AMERICAL) INFANTRY DIVISION

1.	PFC Alex James Hernandez	E/51 LRP	01–10–68
2.	SP/4 Jim Daniel Martinez	E/51 LRP	01–10–68
3.	CPL Solomon Kalua Jr.	E/51 LRP	01–20–68
4.	SGT Daniel P. McLaughlin Jr.	E/51 LRP	01–20–68
5.	SP/4 Terry Ernest Allen	E/51 LRP	03–04–68
6.	SGT James Richard Davidson	E/51 LRP	03–04–68
7.	SP/4 Ramon Sanchez Hernandez	E/51 LRP	03–04–68
8.	SGT Ronald Bryniel Johnson	E/51 LRP	03–04–68
9.	SSG Edward Martin Lentz	E/51 LRP	03–04–68
10.	SP/4 Jose Enrique Torres	E/51 LRP	03–04–68
11.	CPL James Edward Kesselhon	E/51 LRP	03–21–68
12.	SGT Raymond Charles Garcia	E/51 LRP	07–03–68
13.	SGT Alan Francis Angell	E/51 LRP	07–20–68
14.	SGT David James Ohm	E/51 LRP	07–20–68
15.	PFC Bradley Keith Watts	E/51 LRP	09–15–68
16.	SP/4 Joseph Jess Gavia	G/75 RGR	04–24–69
17.	SGT Arthur Edward Scott	G/75 RGR	05–12–69
18.	SP/4 Joel Wayne Forrester	G/75 RGR	05–19–69
19.	CPL Larry Joe White	G/75 RGR	06–30–69
20.	CPL John Willie Bennett	G/75 RGR	10–14–69
21.	SSG Robert Joseph Pruden	G/75 RGR	11–20–69
22.	SP/4 George Thomas Olsen	G/75 RGR	03–03–70
23.	1LT Harold Edward Basehore Jr.	G/75 RGR	04–23–70
24.	PFC Edward Gerard Mathem	G/75 RGR	08–03–70
25.	SP/4 Larry Allen Mackey	G/75 RGR	10–13–70
26.	PFC Barry Howard Berger	G/75 RGR	01–10–71
27.	SSG David Lee Meyer	G/75 RGR	01–11–71
28.	SGT Thomas Edward Snowden	G/75 RGR	05–15–71
29.	SGT Danny Gerald Studdard	G/75 RGR	06–16–71

4TH INFANTRY DIVISION

1.	SGT Ronald Joseph Bonert	2/4th LRRP	06–02–67
2.	SP/4 Daniel Lee Harmon	2/4th LRRP	06–02–67
3.	SSG Dickie Waine Finley	2/4th LRRP	10–21–68
4.	SP/4 Luther Anderson Ghahate	2/4th LRRP	10–21–68
5.	SGT Michael Eugene Lawton	E/58 LRP	12–01–68
6.	SGT Kenneth Charles Hess	K/75 RGR	02–08–69
7.	PFC Nathaniel Irving	K/75 RGR	02–08–69
8.	CPL Frank William Humes	K/75 RGR	07–08–69
9.	SSG Wallace Fred Thibodeau	1/4th LRRP	07–18–69
10.	SP/4 Dennis M. Belonger	1/4th LRRP	07–18–69
11.	PFC Lonnie L. Gibson	1/4th LRRP	09–25–69
12.	CPL Eddie Dean Carpenter	K/75 RGR	11–13–69
13.	SGT Luis A. N. Hilerio-Padilla	K/75 RGR	11–13–69
14.	PFC Robert John Silva	K/75 RGR	11–27–69
15.	SP/4 Kenneth James Smolarek	K/75 RGR	11–27–69
16.	SGT Michael William Lyne	K/75 RGR	01–07–70
17.	SP/4 La Roy Frederich Roth	K/75 RGR	01–07–70
18.	SP/4 Charles R. Willard Jr.	K/75 RGR	01–07–70
19.	SSG William H. Bartholomew Jr.	K/75 RGR	01–23–70
20.	SP/4 Dean Allen Borneman	K/75 RGR	01–23–70
21.	SSG Luther James Doss Jr.	K/75 RGR	04–30–70
22.	SP/4 Frank Edward McClellan	K/75 RGR	06–04–70
23.	SP/4 Earl David Broach	K/75 RGR	08–03–70
24.	PFC Evelio Alfred Gomez	K/75 RGR	08–19–70
25.	SP/4 Antonio Ambrosio Grau	K/75 RGR	08–30–70
26.	SSG William Eugene Roller	K/75 RGR	09–07–70
27.	CPL Frank Howard Miller Jr.	K/75 RGR	09–19–70
28.	SP/4 Roy Christopher Olgyay	K/75 RGR	09–19–70
29.	SSG Robert Wilber Toler Jr.	K/75 RGR	12–05–70

1ST INFANTRY DIVISION

1.	SGT Rudolph Algar Nunez	1st Div LRRP	06–13–66
2.	SSG George Frank Knowlton	F/52 LRP	11–19–67
3.	SGT James Patrick Boyle	F/52 LRP	04–17–68
4.	SSG Jackie Glen Leisure	F/52 LRP	05–12–68
5.	PFC Edwin Everett Carson	F/52 LRP	10–21–68
6.	SGT William Paul Cohn Jr.	F/52 LRP	10–21–68
7.	PFC Gerard Coyle	F/52 LRP	10–21–68
8.	SP/4 Lester Allan Doan	F/52 LRP	10–21–68

9.	PFC Michael Allen Randall Sr.	F/52 LRP	10–21–68
10.	PFC Steven Paul Sorick	F/52 LRP	10–21–68
11.	PFC James Allen Boots	F/52 LRP	11–13–68
12.	PFC Gerard James Blume Jr.	F/52 LRP	11–21–68
13.	PFC Arnold Lee Roy Mulholland	F/52 LRP	11–21–68
14.	SSG Anthony Felix Washington	F/52 LRP	11–21–68
15.	SP/4 Reynaldo Arenas	F/52 LRP	12–31–68
16.	SP/4 Robert David Law	I/75 RGR	02–22–69
17.	SP/4 Robert Levine	I/75 RGR	02–27–69
18.	SSG Enrique Salas Cruz	I/75 RGR	02–27–69
19.	SP/4 James Terry Leibnitz	I/75 RGR	02–27–69
20.	PFC Gary L. Johnson	I/75 RGR	02–28–69
21.	SGT Anthony G. Markevitch Jr.	1/75 RGR	04–16–69
22.	SGT Robert Allen Roossien	1/75 RGR	05–12–69
23.	CPT Michael Patrick Reese	1/75 RGR	05–14–69
24.	SP/4 Charles Edward Smith Jr.	1/75 RGR	08–30–69
25.	SGT Bernard Ambrose Propson	1/75 RGR	09–05–69

9TH INFANTRY DIVISION

1.	SSG Kenneth Ray Lancaster	E/50 LRP	01–03–68
2.	PFC Thomas Wayne Hodge	E/50 LRP	01–24–68
3.	PFC George Jonathan House	E/50 LRP	02–11–68
4.	SP/4 William Francis Piaskowski	E/50 LRP	03–14–68
5.	SSG Johnston Dunlop	E/50 LRP	04–16–68
6.	MSG Joseph Melvin Jones	E/50 LRP	04–16–68
7.	SP/4 Herbert Lee Vaughn	E/50 LRP	05–25–68
8.	PFC James L. Dillard III	E/50 LRP	09–13–68
9.	SSG Herbert Pok Dong Cho	E/50 LRP	09–25–68
10.	CPL Robert John Loehlein Jr.	E/50 LRP	09–25–68
11.	PFC Ronald Kelvin Moore	E/50 LRP	11–04–68
12.	SGT Joseph Philip Castagna	E/50 LRP	12–21–68
13.	SP/4 Richard Roy Bellwood	E/50 LRP	01–25–69
14.	SGT Roman Gale Mason	E/50 LRP	01–27–69
15.	SP/4 Leon David Moore	E/50 LRP	01–27–69
16.	1LT Richard Vickers Thompson	E/50 LRP	01–27–69
17.	SP/4 Irwin Leon Edelman	E/75 RGR	02–18–69
18.	SP/4 Warren G. H. Lizotte Jr.	E/75 RGR	02–26–69
19.	SGT Lonnie Dale Evans	E/75 RGR	04–10–69
20.	SSG Curtis Ray Daniels	E/75 RGR	05–29–69
21.	SP/4 Michael Cory Volheim	E/75 RGR	05–29–69
22.	SSG Herbert Cornelius Frost	E/75 RGR	06–21–69

23.	SP/4 Jonathan Lee Lamm	E/75 RGR	02–11–70
24.	SGT Robert Lamaar Bryan	E/75 RGR	07–13–70
25.	1LT Mark Joseph Toschik	E/75 RGR	08–11–70
26.	SGT Ray Michael Gallardo	E/75 RGR	02–08–72

1ST CAVALRY DIVISION

1.	SP/4 David Allen Ives	E/52 LRP	04–23–67
2.	MAJ David Bruce Tucker	E/52 LRP	10–01–67
3.	SGT David Thomas Dickinson	E/52 LRP	12–06–67
4.	MSG Lewis E. McDermott	E/52 LRP	12–06–67
5.	SP/4 William Robert Critchfield	E/52 LRP	02–27–68
6.	PFC Felix Leon Jr.	E/52 LRP	03–17–68
7.	SGT William Glenn Lambert	E/52 LRP	04–20–68
8.	PFC Robert Joseph Noto	E/52 LRP	04–20–68
9.	SP/4 Richard John Turbitt Jr.	E/52 LRP	04–20–68
10.	SGT Robert Eugene Whitten	E/52 LRP	05–08–68
11.	SGT Juan Angel Elias	E/52 LRP	05–29–68
12.	CPL Donald Robert Miller	E/52 LRP	05–31–68
13.	1LT William Brent Bell	H/75 RGR	03–27–69
14.	SGT Dwight Montgomery Durham	H/75 RGR	04–10–69
15.	SGT Loel Floyd Largent	H/75 RGR	04–10–69
16.	SP/4 Daniel Raymond Arnold	H/75 RGR	05–13–69
17.	SP/4 Lon Michael Holupko	H/75 RGR	07–10–69
18.	SP/4 Daniel Moreland Sheehan	H/75 RGR	07–17–69
19.	SGT Stanley John Lento	H/75 RGR	07–24–69
20.	CPL Archie Hugh McDaniel Jr.	H/75 RGR	07–24–69
21.	SGT Paul John Salminen	H/75 RGR	07–24–69
22.	SGT Kenneth Eugene Burch	H/75 RGR	08–11–69
23.	SP/4 John Charles Williams	H/75 RGR	08–11–69
24.	SP/4 David Torres	H/75 RGR	11–17–69
25.	SP/4 Julius Zaporzec	H/75 RGR	11–17–69
26.	SFC Deverton C. Cochrane	H/75 RGR	06–17–70
27.	SP/4 Carl John Laker	H/75 RGR	06–17–70
28.	PFC Michael Dean Banta	H/75 RGR	10–02–70
29.	SGT Omer Price Carson	H/75 RGR	12–07–70
30.	SP/4 Thomas Washington Lipsey III	H/75 RGR	02–06–72
31.	SP/4 Jaime Pacheco	H/75 RGR	05–25–72
32.	SP/4 Jeffrey Alan Maurer	H/75 RGR	06–09–72
33.	SGT Elvis Weldon Osborne Jr.	H/75 RGR	06–09–72

25TH INFANTRY DIVISION

1.	SP/4 Ervin Leonard Laird	F/50 LRP	02–01–67
2.	SP/4 Larry Paul Blackman	F/50 LRP	02–17–67
3.	SSG Joseph Edward Fitzgerald	3/25th LRRP	05–31–67
4.	SP/4 Carl David Flower	3/25th LRRP	05–31–67
5.	SSG John Andrew Jakovac	3/25th LRRP	05–31–67
6.	SSG Brian Kent McGar	3/25th LRRP	05–31–67
7.	CPL Charles Roland Rogerson	3/25th LRRP	05–31–67
8.	SGT Todd R. Jackson	F/50 LRP	01–30–68
9.	SP/4 John Herbert White Jr.	F/50 LRP	03–01–68
10.	SP/4 Gregory Richard Kelly	F/50 LRP	04–06–68
11.	SP/4 Hubert Arthur Meredith	F/50 LRP	08–01–68
12.	SSG Howard Brown Handley	F/50 LRP	09–13–68
13.	SGT Gary Richard McFall	F/50 LRP	09–13–68
14.	SGT Steven Edward Collier	F/50 LRP	10–27–68
15.	PFC Reid Ernest Grayson Jr.	F/50 LRP	12–28–68
16.	SP/4 Raymond Walter Sullivan	F/50 LRP	01–24–69
17.	SGT Duane Alfred DeVega	F/75 RGR	02–11–69
18.	SP/4 Donald Richard Mayberry	F/75 RGR	03–01–69
19.	CPL Frank Wilder	F/75 RGR	03–01–69
20.	PFC Charles Davis Macken	F/75 RGR	03–08–69
21.	SGT Douglas Ray Pollock	F/75 RGR	03–08–69
22.	SGT Fidel Joe Aguirre	F/75 RGR	03–10–69
23.	SGT John Francis Crikelair	F/75 RGR	08–06–69
24.	SP/4 Ernest Heard Jr.	F/75 RGR	08–07–69
25.	SGT Mack Dennard Jr.	F/75 RGR	09–18–69
26.	SSG Lennis Goddard Jones Jr.	F/75 RGR	11–06–69
27.	SP/4 Kenneth DeWayne Harjo	F/75 RGR	11–18–69
28.	SGT Richard Clark Babb Jr.	F/75 RGR	01–01–70
29.	SFC Alvin Winslow Floyd	F/75 RGR	04–02–70
30.	SSG Michael Francis Thomas	F/75 RGR	04–02–70
31.	SGT Donald Warren Tinney Jr.	F/75 RGR	04–14–70
32.	SP/4 Robert Charles Thompson	F/75 RGR	05–12–70
33.	SGT Donald Allen Davis	F/75 RGR	05–24–70
34.	SSG Robert Bruce Pritchard	F/75 RGR	05–24–70
35.	SGT Milan Lavoy Lee	F/75 RGR	09–19–70

101ST AIRBORNE DIVISION

1.	SSG Donovan Jess Pruett	1/101 LRRP	04–03–66
2.	SSG Percy W. McClatchy	1/101 LRRP	08–13–66

3.	SP/4 David Allen Dixon	1/101 LRRP	05–15–67
4.	SP/4 John Lester Hines	1/101 LRRP	09–15–67
5.	PFC George Buster Sullens Jr.	1/101 LRRP	11–01–67
6.	SP/4 John T. McChesney III	1/101 LRRP	01–23–68
7.	SGT Thomas John Sturgal	F/58 LRP	03–22–68
8.	PVT Ashton Hayward Prindle	F/58 LRP	04–23–68
9.	SGT Thomas Eugene Riley	F/58 LRP	06–02–68
10.	SP/4 Terry W. Clifton	F/58 LRP	11–20–68
11.	SGT Albert D. Contreros Jr.	F/58 LRP	11–20–68
12.	SP/4 Arthur J. Heringhausen Jr.	F/58 LRP	11–20–68
13.	SGT Michael Dean Reiff	F/58 LRP	11–20–68
14.	SSG Julian Dean Dedman	L/75 RGR	04–23–69
15.	SGT Keith Tait Hammond	L/75 RGR	05–05–69
16.	SSG Ronald Burns Reynolds	L/75 RGR	05–08–69
17.	SGT William Lincoln Marcy	L/75 RGR	05–20–69
18.	PFC Michael Linn Lytle	L/75 RGR	10–26–69
19.	SGT Ronald Wayne Jones	L/75 RGR	01–11–70
20.	SSG James William Salter	L/75 RGR	01–11–70
21.	SP/4 Rob George McSorley	L/75 RGR	04–08–70
22.	SGT Gary Paul Baker	L/75 RGR	05–11–70
23.	SSG Raymond Dean Ellis	L/75 RGR	05–11–70
24.	CPL George Edward Fogleman	L/75 RGR	05–11–70
25.	PFC Bryan Theotis Knight	L/75 RGR	05–11–70
26.	SGT David Munoz	L/75 RGR	05–11–70
27.	SSG Robert Lee O'Connor	L/75 RGR	05–11–70
28.	SSG Roger Thomas Lagodzinski	L/75 RGR	05–19–70
29.	SSG John Thomas Donahue	L/75 RGR	05–22–70
30.	SP/4 Jack Moss Jr.	L/75 RGR	08–25–70
31.	PFC Harry Thomas Henthorn	L/75 RGR	08–29–70
32.	SP/4 Lawrence Elwood Scheib Jr.	L/75 RGR	08–29–70
33.	SGT Lloyd Harold Grimes II	L/75 RGR	09–25–70
34.	SGT Robert George Drapp	L/75 RGR	11–16–70
35.	SSG Norman R. Stoddard Jr.	L/75 RGR	11–16–70
36.	SGT Steven Glenn England	L/75 RGR	02–15–71
37.	1LT James Leroy Smith	L/75 RGR	02–15–71
38.	SGT Gabriel Trujillo	L/75 RGR	02–15–71
39.	SP/4 Richard Lee Martin	L/75 RGR	02–21–71
40.	SP/4 David Roy Hayward	L/75 RGR	03–22–71
41.	CPL Joel Richard Hankins	L/75 RGR	03–26–71
42.	SSG Leonard James Trumblay	L/75 RGR	04–06–71
43.	SGT James Bruce McLaughlin	L/75 RGR	04–16–71

44.	CPT Paul Coburn Sawtelle	L/75 RGR	04–16–71
45.	SP/4 Johnnie Rae Sly	L/75 RGR	04–24–71
46.	SGT Gary Duane Cochran	L/75 RGR	05–08–71
47.	PFC Steven John Ellis	L/75 RGR	06–13–71
48.	CPL Charles Anthony Sanchez	L/75 RGR	06–13–71
49.	CPL Johnny Howard Chapman	L/75 RGR	08–20–71
50.	SP/4 Hershel Duane Cude Jr.	L/75 RGR	09–18–71
51.	SP/4 Harry Jerome Edwards	L/75 RGR	01–20–72
52.	SSG James Albert Champion	L/75 RGR	04–24–71
	Missing in Action		

I FIELD FORCE

1.	1LT Calvin Arthur Greene	E/20 LRP	12–19–67
2.	SGT Patrick Lee Henshaw	E/20 LRP	12–19–67
3.	SGT John Richard Strohmaier	E/20 LRP	03–12–68
4.	SP/4 Donald Ray Kinton	E/20 LRP	03–25–68
5.	SGT Edward Gilbert Lee	E/20 LRP	05–13–68
6.	SGT Frederick William Weidner	E/20 LRP	05–20–68
7.	SSG Emory Morel Smith	E/20 LRP	06–13–68
8.	SGT Eric Stuart Gold	E/20 LRP	01–05–69
9.	SGT Paul Robert Jordan	E/20 LRP	01–24–69
10.	SGT Elton Ray Venable	C/75 RGR	02–19–69
11.	SSG Ronald William Cardona	C/75 RGR	07–06–69
12.	CPL Frank Daniel Walthers	C/75 RGR	08–01–69
13.	SSG Harold David Williams	C/75 RGR	08–01–69
14.	SSG William Russell Squier Jr.	C/75 RGR	09–13–69
15.	SGT Keith Mason Parr	C/75 RGR	10–26–69
16.	CPL Walter Guy Burkhart	C/75 RGR	11–11–69
17.	CPL Rex Marcel Sherman	C/75 RGR	11–19–69
18.	SP/4 Richard Gary Buccille	C/75 RGR	12–20–69
19.	SGT William Joseph Murphy	C/75 RGR	02–16–70
20.	SSG Steen Bruce Foster	C/75 RGR	05–14–70
21.	CPL James Lee Loisel	C/75 RGR	05–14–70
22.	SSG Michael Edward Kiscaden	C/75 RGR	07–01–70
23.	SGT Hilburn M. Burdette Jr.	C/75 RGR	07–12–70
24.	SGT John William Rucker	C/75 RGR	12–14–70
25.	CPL Edward Earl Scott Jr.	C/75 RGR	02–22–71
26.	SP/4 Kevin Garner Thome	C/75 RGR	02–27–71
27.	SSG Gordon Keith Spearman Jr.	C/75 RGR	03–10–71
28.	SP/4 Lloyd Eugene Robinson	C/75 RGR	06–11–71

II FIELD FORCE

1.	SGT Daniel Hinson Lindsey	F/51 LRP	12–05–67
2.	1LT John H. Lattin Jr.	F/51 LRP	12–15–67
3.	SP/4 Kenneth Ray Blair	F/51 LRP	08–12–68
4.	SGT Jan Victor Henrickson	F/51 LRP	08–12–68
5.	PFC Willie Whitfield Jr.	F/51 LRP	08–12–68
6.	SP/4 Raymond Michael Enczi	F/51 LRP	10–31–68
7.	SGT Richard Walter Diers	F/51 LRP	11–20–68
8.	SSG Larry LaMont Cunningham	F/51 LRP	12–03–68
9.	SP/4 Leslie Donald Rosekrans	F/51 LRP	12–03–68
10.	PFC David Lee Urban	F/51 LRP	12–03–68
11.	SGT Freemon Evans	F/51 LRP	12–04–68
12.	CPL Roy Antonio Aubain	F/51 LRP	01–04–69

Glossary

AA Antiaircraft.

AC Aircraft copilot.

acid pad Helicopter landing pad.

aerial recon Reconning a specific area by helicopter prior to the insertion of a recon patrol.

AFB Air Force base.

air burst Explosive device that detonates aboveground.

air strike Surface attack by fixed-wing fighter-bomber aircraft.

AIT In the U.S. Army, advanced individual training that follows basic combat training.

AK A Soviet bloc assault rifle, 7.62 mm, also known as the Kalashnikov AK-47.

AO Area of operations, specified location established for planned military operations.

ao dai Traditional Vietnamese female dress, split up the sides and worn over pants.

ARA Aerial rocket artillery.

Arc Light A B-52 air strike.

ARTO Assistant radio/telephone operator.

Arty Artillery.

Arty fan An area of operations which can be covered by existing artillery support.

ARVN Army of the Republic of (South) Vietnam.

'A' Team Special Forces operational detachment that normally consists of a single twelve-man team comprised of eleven enlisted men and one officer.

ATL Assistant team leader.

A Troop or Alpha Troop   Letter designation for one of the aero-rifle companies of an air cavalry squadron.

AVN   Aviation unit.

bac si   Vietnamese for doctor.

baseball   Baseball-shaped hand grenade with a five-meter kill range.

BC   Base camp.

BCT   In the U.S. Army, basic combat training every trainee must complete upon entering service.

BDA   Bomb damage assessment.

beat feet   Running from danger.

beaucoup or boo koo   French for "many."

beehive   Artillery round filled with hundreds of small metal darts designed to be used against massed infantry.

berm   Built-up earthen wall used for defensive purposes.

Big Pond   Pacific Ocean.

Bird Dog   A small, fixed-wing observation plane.

black box   Sensor device that detects body heat or movement. They were buried along routes used by the enemy to record their activity in the area.

black PJs   A type of local garb of Vietnamese farmers also worn extensively by Viet Cong guerrillas.

blasting cap   A small device inserted into an explosive substance that can be triggered to cause the detonation of the main charge.

blood trail   Spoor sign left by the passage or removal of enemy wounded or dead.

Blues   Another name for the aero-rifle platoons or troops of an air cavalry squadron.

body bag   A thick black plastic bag used to transport American and allied dead to Graves Registration points.

"break contact"   Disengaging from battle with an enemy unit.

"bring smoke"   Placing intensive fire upon the enemy. Killing the enemy with a vengeance.

B Troop or Bravo Troop   Letter designation for one of the aero-rifle companies of an air cavalry squadron.

bush   The jungle.

"buy the farm"   To die.

C-4   A very stable, pliable plastique explosive.

C's   Combat field rations for American troops.

C&C   Command & control.

CA Combat assault.

cammies Jungle-patterned clothing worn by U.S. troops in the field.

cammo stick Two-colored camouflage applicator.

Capt. Abbreviation for the rank of captain.

CAR-15 Carbine version of the M-16 rifle.

Cav Cavalry.

CCN Command & Control (North), MACV-SOG.

Charlie, Charles, Chuck GI slang for VC/NVA.

cherry New arrival in country.

Chicom Chinese Communist.

chieu hoi Government program that encouraged enemy soldiers to come over to the South Vietnam side.

Chinook CH-47 helicopter used for transporting equipment and troops.

choa ong Vietnamese for "How are you?" or "Good morning."

chopper GI slang for helicopter.

chopper pad Helicopter landing pad.

CIDG Civilian Irregular Defense Group. South Vietnamese or Montagnard civilians trained and armed to defend themselves against enemy attack.

clacker Firing device used to manually detonate a claymore mine.

CO Commanding officer.

Cobra AH-1G attack helicopter.

cockadau GI slang for the Vietnamese word meaning "kill."

Col. Abbreviation for the rank of colonel.

cold An area of operations or a recon zone is cold if it is unoccupied by the enemy.

commo Communication by radio or field telephone.

commo check A radio/telephone operator requesting confirmation of his transmission.

compromise Discovered by the enemy.

contact Engaged by the enemy.

CP Command post.

CS Riot gas.

daisy chain Wiring a number of claymore mines together with det cord to achieve a simultaneous detonation.

debrief The gleaning of information and intelligence after a military operation.

DEROS The date of estimated return from overseas tour of duty.

det cord Timed burn fuse used to detonate an explosive charge.

diddy boppin' Moving foolishly, without caution.

didi Vietnamese for to run or move quickly.

DMZ Demilitarized Zone.

Doc A medic or doctor.

double-canopy Jungle or forest with two layers of overhead vegetation.

Doughnut Dollies Red Cross hostesses.

drag The last man on a long range reconnaissance patrol.

D Troop or Delta Troop Lettered designation for one of the aero-rifle companies of an air cavalry squadron.

dung lai Vietnamese for "don't move."

Dustoff Medical evacuation by helicopter.

DZ Drop zone for airborne parachute operation.

E-1 or E-2 Military pay grades of private.

E-3 Military pay grade of private first class.

E-4 Military pay grade of specialist four or corporal.

E-5 Military pay grade of specialist five or sergeant.

E-6 Military pay grade of specialist six or staff sergeant.

E-7 Military pay grade of sergeant first class or platoon sergeant.

E-8 Military pay grade of master sergeant or first sergeant.

E-9 Military pay grade of sergeant major.

E&E Escape and evasion, on the run to evade pursuit and capture.

ER Enlisted reserve.

ETS Estimated termination of service.

exfil Extraction from a mission or operation.

extension leave A thirty-day furlough given at the end of a full tour of duty, after which the recipient must return for an extended tour of duty.

FAC Forward air controller. Air Force spotter plane that co-ordinated air strikes and artillery for ground units.

fast mover Jet fighter-bomber.

field Anywhere outside "friendly" control.

finger A secondary ridge running out from a primary ridge-line, hill, or mountain.

firebase Forward artillery position, usually located on a prominent terrain feature, used to support ground units during operations.

firefight A battle with an enemy force.

Firefly An LOH observation helicopter fitted with a high-intensity searchlight.

fire mission A request for artillery support.

fix The specific coordinates pertaining to a unit's position or to a target.

flare ship Aircraft used to drop illumination flares in support of ground troops in contact at night.

flash panel A fluorescent orange or yellow cloth used to mark a unit's position for supporting or inbound aircraft.

FNG Fucking new guy. Slang term for a recent arrival in Vietnam.

FO Forward observer. A specially trained soldier, usually an officer, attached to an infantry unit for the purpose of coordinating close artillery support.

foo gas or phou gas A jellied gasoline explosive that is buried in a fifty-five-gallon drum along defensive perimeters and when command-detonated, sends out a wall of highly flammable fuel similar to napalm.

freak or freq Slang term meaning a radio frequency.

G-2 Division or larger intelligence section.

G-3 Division or larger operations section.

ghost or ghost time Taking time off, free time, goofing off.

gook Derogatory term for VC/NVA.

grazing fire Keeping the trajectory of bullets between normal knee-to-waist height.

grease Slang term meaning to kill.

Green Beret A member of the U.S. Army Special Forces.

ground pounder Infantryman.

grunt Infantryman.

gunship An armed attack helicopter.

H&I Harassment and interdiction. Artillery fire upon certain areas of suspected enemy travel or rally points, designed to prevent uncontested use.

HE High explosive.

heavy team In a long-range patrol unit, two five- or six-man teams operating together.

helipad A hardened helicopter landing pad.

Ho Chi Minh Trail An extensive road and trail network

running from North Vietnam, down through Laos and Cambodia into South Vietnam, which enabled the North Vietnamese to supply equipment and personnel to their units in South Vietnam.

hootch Slang for barracks or living quarters.

horn Radio or telephone handset.

hot A landing zone or drop zone under enemy fire.

HQ Headquarters.

Huey The Bell UH helicopter series.

hug To close with the enemy in order to prevent his use of supporting fire.

hump Patrolling or moving during a combat operation.

IAD Immediate Action Drills; they teach immediate response to certain situations.

I Corps The northernmost of the four separate military zones in South Vietnam. The other divisions were II, III, and IV Corps.

immersion foot A skin condition of the feet caused by prolonged exposure to moisture that results in cracking, bleeding, and sloughing of skin.

incoming Receiving enemy indirect fire.

Indian country Territory under enemy control.

indigenous Native peoples.

infil Insertion of a recon team or military unit into a recon zone or area of operation.

intel Information on the enemy gathered by human, electronic, or other means.

jungle penetrator A metal cylinder lowered by cable from a helicopter used to extract personnel from inaccesible terrain.

KCS Kit Carson Scout. Repatriated enemy soldiers working with U.S. combat units.

Khmer Cambodian.

Khmer Rouge Cambodian Communist.

Khmer Serei Free Cambodian.

KIA Killed in action.

Killer team A small LRP/Ranger team with the mission of seeking out and destroying the enemy.

LAW Light antitank weapon.

lay dog Slang meaning to go to cover and remain motionless while listening for the enemy. This is SOP for a recon team immediately after being inserted or infilled.

LBJ Long Binh jail. The in country military stockade for U.S. Army personnel convicted of violations of the U.S. Code of Military Justice.

LDR Leader.

lifer Slang for career soldier.

LMG Light machine gun.

LOH or Loach OH-6A light observation helicopter.

LP Listening post. An outpost established beyond the perimeter wire, manned by one or more personnel with the mission of detecting approaching enemy forces before they can launch an assault.

LRP Long-range patrol.

LRRP Long-range reconnaissance patrol.

LSA Government issue lubricating oil for individual weapons.

Lt. Lieutenant.

Lt. Col. Lieutenant colonel.

LZ Landing zone. A cleared area large enough to accommodate the landing of one or more helicopters.

M-14 The standard issue 7.62 millimeter semiautomatic/automatic rifle used by U.S. military personnel prior to the M-16.

M-16 The standard issue 5.56 millimeter semiautomatic/automatic rifle that became the mainstay of U.S. ground forces in 1967.

M-60 A light 7.62mm machine gun that has been the primary infantry automatic weapon of U.S. forces since the Korean War.

M-79 An individually operated, single-shot, 40mm grenade launcher.

MAAG Military Assistance Advisory Group. The senior U.S. military headquarters during the early American involvement in Vietnam.

MACV Military Assistance Command Vietnam. The senior U.S. military headquarters after full American involvement in the war.

MACV Recondo School A three-week school conducted at Nha Trang, South Vietnam, by a cadre from the 5th Special Forces Group to train U.S. and allied reconnaissance personnel in the art of conducting long-range patrols.

MACV-SOG Studies and Observations Group under command of MACV that ran long-range reconnaissance and other classified missions over the borders of South Vietnam into NVA sanctuaries in Laos and Cambodia.

mag   Short for magazine.

Maguire Rig   A single rope with loops at the end that could be dropped from a helicopter to extract friendly personnel from inaccessible terrain.

Main Force   Full-time Viet Cong military units, as opposed to local, part-time guerrilla units.

Maj.   Major.

Marine Force Recon   U.S. Marine Corps divisional long range reconnaissance units similar in formation and function to U.S. Army LRP/Ranger companies.

MARS   Military/civilian radio/telephone system that enabled U.S. personnel in Vietnam to place calls to friends and family back in the United States.

Medevac (or dustoff)   Medical evacuation by helicopter.

MG   Machine gun.

MIA   Missing in action.

Mike Force   Special Forces mobile strike force used to reinforce or support other Special Forces units or camps under attack.

Montagnard   The tribal hill people of Vietnam.

MOS   Military occupation skill.

MP   Military police.

MPC   Military payment certificates. Paper money issued U.S. military personnel serving overseas in lieu of local or U.S. currency.

NCO   Noncommissioned officer.

NDP   Night defensive position.

net   Radio network.

NG   National Guard.

no sweat   With little effort or with no trouble.

number One   The best or highest possible.

number Ten   The worst or lowest possible.

Nungs   Vietnamese troops of Chinese extraction hired by U.S. Special Forces to serve as personal bodyguards and to man special strike units and recon teams. Arguably the finest indigenous forces in Vietnam.

nuoc mam   Strong, evil-smelling fish sauce used to add flavor to the standard Vietnamese food staple—rice.

NVA   North Vietnamese Army.

O-1 Bird Dog   Light, single-engine, fixed-wing aircraft used for forward air control.

ONH   Overnight halt.

OP   Observation post. An outpost established on a prominent terrain feature for the purpose of visually observing enemy activity.

op   Operation.

op order   Operation order. A plan for a mission or operation to be conducted against enemy forces, covering all facets of such a mission or operation.

overflight   An aerial reconnaissance of an intended recon zone or area of operation prior to the mission or operation, for the purpose of selecting access and egress points, routes of travel, likely enemy concentrations, water, and prominent terrain features.

P-38   Standard manual can opener that comes with government-issued C rations.

pen flare   A small, spring-loaded, cartridge-fed signal flare device that fired a variety of small colored flares used to signal one's position.

peter pilot   Military slang for the assistant or copilot on a helicopter.

PFC   Private first class.

Pink Team   An aviation combat patrol package comprised of an LOH scout helicopter and a Charlie-model Huey gunship or an AH-1G Cobra. The LOH would fly low to draw enemy fire and mark its location for an immediate strike from the gunship circling high overhead.

pith helmet   A light tropical helmet worn by some NVA units.

point   The point man or lead soldier in a patrol.

POW   Prisoner of war.

PRC-10 or "Prick Ten"   Standard-issue platoon/company radio used early in the Vietnam War.

PRC-25 or "Prick Twenty-five"   Standard-issue platoon/company radio that replaced the PRC-10.

PRC-77   Heavier, longer-range radio capable of voice or code communication.

Project Delta   Special Forces special unit tasked to conduct long-range patrols in Southeast Asia.

Project Gamma   Special Forces special unit tasked to conduct long-range patrols in Southeast Asia.

Project Sigma   Special Forces special unit tasked to conduct long-range patrols in Southeast Asia.

PRU   Provincial reconnaissance units. Mercenary soldiers who performed special military tasks throughout South Vietnam. Known for their effective participation in the Phoenix Program, where they used prisoner snatches and assassinations to destroy the VC infrastructure.

P's or piasters   South Vietnamese monetary system. During the height of the Vietnam War, 100P was equal to about eighty-five cents U.S.

PSP   Perforated steel panels used to build airstrips, landing pads, bridge surfaces, and had a number of other functions.

P-training   Preparatory training. A one-week course required for each new U.S. Army soldier arriving in South Vietnam, designed to acclimatize new arrivals to weather conditions and give them a basic introduction to the enemy and his tactics.

Puff the Magic Dragon   AC-47 or AC-119 aircraft armed with computer-controlled miniguns that rendered massive support to fixed friendly camps and infantry units under enemy attack.

pulled   Extracted or exfilled.

punji stakes   Sharpened bamboo stakes imbedded in the ground at an angle designed to penetrate into the foot or leg of anyone walking into one. Often poisoned with human excrement to cause infection.

Purple Heart   A U.S. medal awarded for receiving a wound in combat.

PX   Post exchange.

radio relay   A communications team located in a position to relay radio traffic between two points.

R&R   Rest and recreation. A short furlough given U.S. forces while serving in a combat zone.

Rangers   Designation for U.S. long range reconnaissance patrollers after 31 January 1969.

rappel   Descent from a stationary platform or a hovering helicopter by sliding down a harness-secured rope.

reaction force   Special units designated to relieve a small unit in heavy contact.

rear security   The last man on a long range reconnaissance patrol.

redleg Military slang for artillery.

REMF Rear echelon motherfucker. Military slang for rear echelon personnel.

rock 'n' roll Slang for firing one's weapon on full automatic.

Round-eye Slang for a non-Asian female.

RPD/RPK Soviet bloc light machine gun.

RPG Soviet bloc front-loaded antitank rocket launcher used effectively against U.S. bunkers, armor, and infantry during the Vietnam War.

RT Recon team.

RTO Radio/telephone operator.

ruck Rucksack or backpack.

Ruff-Puff or RF South Vietnamese regional and popular forces recruited to provide security in hamlets, villages, and within districts throughout South Vietnam. A militia-type force that was usually ineffective.

saddle up Preparing to move out on patrol.

same-same The same as.

sappers VC/NVA soldiers trained to penetrate enemy defense perimeters and destroy fighting positions, fuel and ammo dumps, and command and communication centers with demolition charges, usually prior to a ground assault by infantry.

satchel charge Explosive charge usually carried in a canvas bag across the chest and activated by a pull cord. The weapon of the sapper.

SEALs Small U.S. Navy special operations units trained in reconnaissance, ambush, prisoner snatch, and counterguerrilla techniques.

search and destroy Offensive military operation designed to seek out and eradicate the enemy.

SF U.S. Special Forces or Green Berets.

SFC Sergeant first class (E-7).

Sgt. Sergeant.

shake 'n' bake A graduate of a Stateside noncommissioned or commissioned officers' course.

short rounds Artillery rounds that impact short of their target.

short-timer Anyone with less than thirty days left in his combat tour.

single-canopy Jungle or forest with a single layer of overhead tree foliage.

sitrep   Situation report. A radio or telephone transmission, usually to a unit's tactical operations center, to provide information on that unit's current status.

Six   Designated call sign for a commander, such as Alpha-Six.

SKS   Communist bloc semiautomatic rifle.

sky   To run or flee because of enemy contact.

Sky pilot   Chaplain.

slack   Slang for the second man in a patrol formation. The point man's backup.

slick   Slang for a lightly armed Huey helicopter primarily used to transport troops.

smoke   A canister-shaped grenade that dispenses smoke used to conceal a unit from the enemy or to mark a unit's location for aircraft. The smoke comes in a variety of colors.

Snake   Cobra helicopter gunship.

snatch   To capture a prisoner.

Sneaky Pete   A member of an elite military unit who operates behind enemy lines.

snoop and poop   A slang term meaning to gather intelligence in enemy territory and get out again without being detected.

socked in   Unable to be resupplied or extracted due to inclement weather.

SOI   Signal Operations Instructions. The classified codebook that contains radio frequencies and call signs.

Sp4. or Spec Four   Specialist fourth class (E-4).

Spectre   An AC-130 aircraft gunship armed with miniguns, Vulcans, and sometimes a 105mm howitzer with the mission of providing close support for friendly ground troops.

spider hole   A camouflaged one-man fighting position frequently used by the VC/NVA.

Spooky   AC-47 or AC-119 aircraft armed with Gatling guns and capable of flying support over friendly positions for extended periods. Besides serving as an aerial weapons platform, Spooky was capable of dropping illumination flares.

spotter round   An artillery smoke or white-phosphorous round that was fired to mark a position.

S.Sgt.   Staff sergeant (E-6).

staging area   An area in the rear where final last-minute preparations for an impending operation or mission are conducted.

stand-down   A period of rest after completion of a mission or operation in the field.

star cluster   An aerial signal device that produces three individual flares. Comes in red, green, or white.

starlight scope   A night-vision device that utilizes any outside light source for illumination.

Stars and Stripes   U.S. military newspaper.

stay-behind   A technique involving a small unit dropping out or remaining behind when its larger parent unit moves out on an operation. A method of inserting a recon team.

strobe light   A small device employing a highly visible, bright flashing light used to identify one's position at night. Normally used only in emergency situations.

TA   Target area. Another designation for AO or area of operations.

TAC Air   Tactical air support.

tail gunner   Rear security or the last man in a patrol.

TAOR   Tactical area of responsibility. Another designation for a unit's area of operations.

TDY   Temporary duty.

tee tee or *ti ti*   Very small.

ten forty-nine or 1049   Military form 1049 used to request a transfer to another unit.

thumper or thump gun   Slang terms for the M-79 grenade launcher.

Tiger Force   The battalion reconnaissance platoon of the 2/327, 101st Airborne Division.

tigers or tiger fatigues   Camouflage pattern of black-and-green stripes usually worn by reconnaissance teams or elite units.

time pencil   A delayed-fuse detonating device attached to an explosive charge or a claymore antipersonnel mine.

TL   Team leader.

TM   Team.

TOC   Tactical operations center or command center of a military unit.

toe popper   Small, pressure-detonated antipersonnel mine intended to maim, not kill.

Top   Slang term for a first sergeant meaning "top" NCO.

tracker   Soldier specializing in trailing or tracking the enemy.

Tri-Border   The area in Indochina where Laos, Cambodia, and South Vietnam come together.

triple-canopy   Jungle or forest that has three distinct layers of overhead tree foliage.

troop   Slang term for a soldier, or a unit in a cavalry squadron equal to an infantry company in size.

tunnel rat   A small-statured U.S. soldier who is sent into underground enemy tunnel complexes armed only with a flashlight, a knife, and a pistol.

URC-10   A pocket-size, short-range emergency radio.

VC   Viet Cong. South Vietnamese Communist guerrillas.

Viet Minh   Short for Viet Nam Doc Lap Dong Minh, or League for the Independence of Vietnam. Organized by Communist sympathizers who fought against the Japanese and later the French.

VNSF   South Vietnamese Special Forces.

warning order   The notification, prior to an op order, given to a recon team to begin preparation for a mission.

waste   To kill the enemy by any means available.

White Mice   Derogatory slang term for South Vietnamese Army MPs.

WIA   Wounded in action.

World   Slang term for the United States of America or home.

WP or willy pete   White-phosphorous grenade.

XF   Exfil. Extraction from the field, usually by helicopter.

xin loi / sin loi   Vietnamese for sorry or too bad.

XO   Executive officer.

x-ray team   A communication team established at a site between a remote recon patrol and its TOC. Its function is to assist in relaying messages between the two stations.

'Yards   Short for Montagnards.

zap   To kill or wound.

zipperhead   Derogatory name for an Oriental.

Look for Gary Linderer's first book on LRRPs, LRPs and Rangers in gut-chilling, extreme combat far behind enemy lines. When every mission may well have been their last, these brave men went willingly into harm's way with only their skill, sense of duty, personal weapons, and each other between themselves and death.

Phantom Warriors:
LRRPs, LRPs, and Rangers in Vietnam

by Gary A. Linderer

Published by Ballantine Books.
Available at a bookstore near you.

The bloody history of the 101st LRP/Rangers
by one of its own

SIX SILENT MEN
Book Three
by Gary A. Linderer

By 1969, the NVA had grown more experienced at countering the tactics of the long-range patrols, and SIX SILENT MEN: *Book Three* describes some of the fiercest fighting Lurps saw during the war. Based on his own experiences and extensive interviews with other combat vets of the 101st's Lurp companies, Gary Linderer writes this final, heroic chapter in the seven bloody years that Lurps served God and country in Vietnam. These tough young warriors—grossly outnumbered and deep in enemy territory—fought with the guts, tenacity, and courage that have made them legends in the 101st.

SIX SILENT MEN
Book Three
by Gary A. Linderer

Published by Ivy Books.
Available in your local bookstore.